Dictionary of
ASTRONOMY

terms and concepts of space and the universe

Dictionary of ASTRONOMY

terms and concepts of space and the universe

Iain Nicolson

BARNES & NOBLE BOOKS

A DIVISION OF HARPER & ROW, PUBLISHERS

New York, Cambridge, Hagerstown,
Philadelphia, San Francisco, London,
Mexico City, São Paulo, Sydney

This work was first published in Great Britain by Arrow Books Ltd. under the title
Astronomy: A Dictionary of Space and the Universe. It is here reprinted by arrangement.

First BARNES & NOBLE BOOKS edition published 1980.

ISBN: 0-06-463524-4

80 81 82 83 84 10 9 8 7 6 5 4 3 2 1

Using this Dictionary

Not all the terms defined in this dictionary are cross-referenced to one another every time they occur. Only when the understanding of a term used in an entry adds to the student's comprehension of the particular area under discussion will the term be marked in small capitals, thus:

Aerolite. Term used to describe a METEORITE of stony composition.

A single arrow has been used for 'See'; double arrows for 'See also'.

A table showing the Greek alphabet and a guide to further reading may be found at the back of the book.

Photographic acknowledgements

Photographs have been reproduced by courtesy of:

Hale Observatories: PLATES 1, 4, 9, 17, 18, 20, 23
Royal Observatory, Edinburgh: PLATES 2, 21, 24
Royal Greenwich Observatory: PLATE 3
Lick Observatory: PLATES 5, 16, 19
National Aeronautics and
Space Administration (NASA): PLATES 6, 7, 8, 10, 11, 12
M. J. Hendrie: PLATE 13
British Insulated Callenders Cables Ltd: PLATE 14, 15
Science Research Council: PLATE 22

Introduction

Astronomy is concerned with the study of the universe, its constituent bodies and phenomena. Although we tend to regard the subject as relating only to what goes on beyond the atmosphere, it is important to bear in mind that the Earth itself is no more than a small and rather insignificant body in the universe, subject to the same laws as all the other astronomical bodies. In studying astronomy, we are really studying the environment of the Earth in the widest possible sense. In the next few paragraphs I present a very brief outline of the scope of astronomy, in order to give an overview of the subject and to direct the reader to central aspects and topics defined later in the text.

The science of astronomy is by no means an isolated discipline; it draws upon a wide range of subject areas, notably mathematics, physics and chemistry, but also biology, geology and a host of other subjects (⟡ASTROPHYSICS; ASTROCHEMISTRY; EXOBIOLOGY; PLANETOLOGY). With advances in astronomical techniques and instrumentation, particularly in the field of space research, the relationship with engineering disciplines (particularly electronics) and the reliance on electronic computers is steadily growing. The increasing capital costs of new astronomical facilities, and the costs of space missions, are such that there are economic and political aspects too.

Astronomy differs from many other sciences in that it is primarily an *observational* science rather than an *experimental* one. In physics and chemistry, for example, it is possible to set up experiments under (hopefully) controlled conditions, to change these conditions, and observe the results; in astronomy, apart from using space probes in our immediate locality, we cannot experiment with stars, planets or galaxies; we cannot, for example, compress a star and see what happens. Instead, the astronomer must rely on receiving information from astronomical sources and interpret his observations in order to develop and test his theories. This information arrives mostly in the form of ELECTROMAGNETIC RADIATION, such as light, radio waves, and so on. Observation is hampered by the ATMOSPHERE which only transmits to ground level a small proportion of this radiation and, until some three decades ago, virtually all astronomical observations relied upon visible light only. With the development of new techniques, and particularly with the advent of ARTIFICIAL SATELLITES and SPACE PROBES, it is now possible to study the entire ELECTROMAGNETIC SPECTRUM, and many new branches of astronomy have developed (✧GAMMA-RAY ASTRONOMY; X-RAY ASTRONOMY; INFRA-RED ASTRONOMY; RADIO ASTRONOMY; RADAR ASTRONOMY).

The fundamental types of observation which the astronomer can carry out include the measurement of position and motion (ASTROMETRY), the measurement of brightness (✧PHOTOMETRY; MAGNITUDE; LUMINOSITY), and the analysis of the quality of light and radiation received from a source (✧SPECTROSCOPY; COLOUR INDEX; POLARIZATION OF LIGHT; ✧DISTANCE DETERMINATION IN THE UNIVERSE).

The scale and structure of the universe

In very brief outline, our present picture of the universe is as follows. We live upon the EARTH, which is a PLANET, a small solid body travelling in an ORBIT round a typical STAR, the SUN. The Earth is also our observing platform, and its motions affect our observations of the universe (✧CELESTIAL SPHERE; PARALLAX; ABERRATION OF LIGHT. Our nearest celestial neighbour is the Earth's natural satellite, the MOON, a body about one quarter of the Earth's size and moving round the Earth at a mean distance of 384 000 km; light, travelling at some 300 000 km per second (✧VELOCITY OF LIGHT), requires nearly 1·3 seconds to reach us from the Moon. To date, the Moon represents the only other celestial body on which men have set foot (✧APOLLO PROJECT).

The Sun lies at a mean distance of just under 150 million km, this distance being defined to be the ASTRONOMICAL UNIT; light requires about 8·3 minutes to cover this distance. It is a gaseous body, about 100 times the radius of the Earth and nearly 330 000 times as massive. It produces energy by means of internal FUSION reactions and is the fundamental energy source which sustains life on Earth.

The Sun, together with nine planets, their satellites, minor bodies such as COMETS, METEOROIDS and ASTEROIDS, and a tenuous quantity of INTERPLANETARY MATTER, make up the SOLAR SYSTEM. In order of distance from the Sun the planets (which are described individually in the text) are Mercury, Venus, the Earth, Mars, Jupiter, Saturn, Uranus, Neptune and Pluto. The four innermost planets are known as the TERRESTRIAL PLANETS while the next four are often referred to as the JOVIAN PLANETS. The mean distance from the Sun to Pluto is 39·4 astronomical units and light requires some 5·4 hours to cross this distance (compare this with 1·3 seconds for the Earth–Moon distance).

The distances, even to the nearest stars, are many orders of magnitude greater than the scale of the Solar System. The nearest star, PROXIMA CENTAURI, is roughly 250 000 times further from us than the Sun and light requires over 4·2 years to cover this distance. The term LIGHT YEAR (i.e. the distance travelled in one year by a ray of light) is frequently used to describe distances in the universe. If a star is located at a distance, say, of 100 light years, then the light we are now receiving was emitted 100 years ago, and our information concerning that star is 100 years out of date. Stars are essentially self-luminous gaseous bodies, but they differ widely in their individual properties. For example, some stars are smaller than the Earth (◊WHITE DWARF, NEUTRON STAR), while at the opposite extreme others are larger than the radius of the Earth's orbit (or possibly even of Saturn's orbit); ◊GIANT; SUPERGIANT. Other properties which may have widely differing values include temperature (◊EFFECTIVE TEMPERATURE), LUMINOSITY and mean density. The study of the life-cycles of stars forms the subject of STELLAR EVOLUTION (◊HERTZSPRUNG–RUSSELL DIAGRAM).

The Sun and the visible stars are members of a large star system, or galaxy, which we refer to as the GALAXY (2) (◊MILKY WAY). This is a disc-shaped structure, some 100 000 light years in diameter, containing some 100 000 million stars together with gas and dust (◊INTERSTELLAR MATTER; NEBULA: H II REGION). The Sun is located just over 30 000 light years from the galactic centre.

Beyond the confines of our own galaxy lie thousands of millions of galaxies, and these too differ widely in their individual properties (◊GALAXIES, CLASSIFICATION OF). The Galaxy is part of a group of some twenty galaxies, known as the LOCAL GROUP; other CLUSTERS OF GALAXIES contain up to a few thousand members, and it may be that clusters of galaxies are themselves part of a greater hierarchy of 'superclusters'. In addition to what may be termed 'normal' galaxies (although many would question that there are such things), there are galaxies and associated objects with peculiar properties, notably SEYFERT GALAXIES, RADIO GALAXIES and QUASARS.

Observations (◊RED-SHIFT) indicate that all the galaxies beyond the Local Group are moving away from us with speeds proportional to their distances, the relationship between distance and speed being given by HUBBLE'S CONSTANT. This implies that the entire universe is expanding, each galaxy or cluster of galaxies moving away from every other one; it does *not* imply that *we* are at the centre of the universe. Although the whole area of COSMOLOGY is open to debate, the evidence at the moment favours the theory (◊BIG-BANG THEORY) that the universe in its present form originated in an explosive event some time between ten and twenty thousand million years ago; material hurled outwards from the explosion gave rise to the galaxies, which are still moving apart. Whether the expansion will continue forever or will eventually cease (to be followed by a contraction phase; ⊳OSCILLAT-ING UNIVERSE) is still unclear; whether or not the universe is finite or infinite is likewise unresolved.

Astronomy is now in an exciting phase. Discoveries, such as QUASARS, PULSARS and, possibly, BLACK HOLES, together with the spectacular results obtained by planetary probes, have stimulated wide interest and at the same time challenged or overturned some cherished theories, and even persuaded us to question the basis of some of our physical laws. Astronomy encompasses situations which cannot be produced in the terrestrial laboratory and so not only draws on other sciences, but feeds back to these subjects new data which could not be obtained in any other way. Many challenging problems remain to be solved: the origin of the Solar System, the energy sources which power the many unexplained violent events in the universe, the origin and evolution of the universe itself, the origin of life, and the prevalence of life throughout the universe, to name but a few. Within the context of this dictionary I hope it has been possible to capture the flavour of some of the new research as well as summarizing the basic framework of the subject.

Summary of the Scale of the Universe

Distance (mean values)	In commonly used units	In metres	Time taken for light to cover this distance
Radius of Earth	6378 km	$6·378 \times 10^6$	0·022 seconds
Earth–Moon	384 000 km	$3·84 \times 10^8$	1·3 seconds
Radius of Sun	696 000 km	$6·96 \times 10^8$	2·3 seconds
Sun–Earth	149 600 000 km	$1·496 \times 10^{11}$	8·3 minutes
Sun–Pluto	39·4 a.u.	$5·9 \times 10^{12}$	5·5 hours
Sun–nearest star (Proxima Centauri)	4·2 l.y. 1·3 pc	$4·1 \times 10^{16}$	4·2 years
Radius of Galaxy (approximately)	50 000 l.y. 15 000 pc	5×10^{20}	50 000 years
To Andromeda galaxy	2 200 000 l.y.	2×10^{22}	2 200 000 years
*To most distant observed objects	over 10^{10} l.y.	over 10^{26}	over 10^{10} years

*This value is rather uncertain because: (a) new objects are being discovered quite frequently, and (b) the value of distance is dependent on the assumed value of HUBBLE'S CONSTANT, which is revised from time to time.

Units and Terminology Used in this Book

Power notation

If a number, y say, is multiplied by itself, we can express the result of $(y \times y)$ as y^2 (y squared or y raised to the power 2); or again, $y \times y \times y = y^3$ (y cubed or y raised to the power 3). In general terms if we multiply together a number (n) of ys, we denote the result by y^n. For example, $2^6 = 2 \times 2 \times 2 \times 2 \times 2 \times 2$ ($=64$). A negative index ($-n$) is used to denote the reciprocal of y^n (i.e. $y^{-n} = 1/y^n$). For example, $2^{-1} = \frac{1}{2}$; $2^{-2} = \frac{1}{2^2} = \frac{1}{4}$, and so on.

In astronomy we very frequently use very large or very small numbers, and it is convenient to express these in terms of powers of 10, where 10^n represents the number 1 followed by n zeros. Thus, $10^0 = 1$, $10^1 = 10$, $10^2 = 100$, etc.

Commonly encountered multiples of ten may be expressed as follows:

one thousand $= 1000 = 10^3$; one thousandth $= 1/1000 = 10^{-3}$
one million $= 1\,000\,000 = 10^6$; one millionth $= 1/1\,000\,000 = 10^{-6}$
one billion $= 1\,000\,000\,000 = 10^9$; one billionth $= 1/1\,000\,000\,000 = 10^{-9}$

A number such as $365\,500\,000$ would be represented by $3 \cdot 655 \times 10^8$, while $2 \cdot 5 \times 10^{-6}$ would denote $2 \cdot 5/1\,000\,000 = 0 \cdot 000\,002\,5$.

Units of measurement

In general, SI units are used throughout the book, but astronomy has its own particular units, and these are employed where their usage is commonplace. The SI, or International System of Units, consists of six basic units from which other units are derived by multiplication and/or division of suitable combinations of basic units.

The six fundamental SI units are:

Mass: kilogramme (kg); a common multiple is the tonne $= 10^3$ kg
Length: metre (m); a common multiple is the kilometre (km) $= 10^3$ m
common sub-multiples are
centimetre (cm) $= 10^{-2}$ m
millimetre (mm) $= 10^{-3}$ m

micrometre (μm) = 10^{-6} m
nanometre (nm) = 10^{-9} m

Time: second (s);   common sub-multiples are
millisecond (ms) = 10^{-3} s
microsecond (μs) = 10^{-6} s
nanosecond (ns) = 10^{-9} s

Temperature: kelvin (K) often expressed as degree kelvin or K

Electric current: ampere (A)

Luminous intensity: candela (cd)

Of these six, only the first four, kg, m, s and K, are frequently encountered in the text.

In these units, velocity is expressed in terms of metres per second (m/s or m s^{-1}) and acceleration in metres per second per second (m/s^2 or m s^{-2}).

Other units often encountered in the book are:

Energy: joule (J); a derived unit, = kg × m^2/s^2, i.e., kg m^2 s^{-2}; it is equivalent to the kinetic energy of 2 kg moving at 1 m s^{-1}

Power: watt (W); 1 W = 1 J s^{-1}; 1 kilowatt (kW) = 10^3 W

Force: newton (N); kg m s^{-2}; 1 N = the force which will accelerate 1 kg at 1 m s^{-2}

Units of angular measurement are:

degree (°)   1 degree = 1/360 of a circle
minute (′)   1′ = 1/60 of 1 degree; often expressed as minute of arc
second (″)   1″ = 1/60 of 1 minute; often expressed as second of arc
                       or arcsec
radian (rad)   2π rad = 360°; 1 rad = 57·3°. An angle of 1 rad measured from the centre of a circle cuts the circle in two points such that the length of the arc between these points equals the radius of the circle.

A solid angle (i.e. an angle measured in three-dimensional space rather than on a plane surface) is expressed in terms of the steradian (sr); a solid angle of 1 sr measured from the centre of a sphere takes the form of a cone which cuts the surface of the sphere in an area equal to the square of the radius of the sphere. 4π steradians make up an angle equivalent to a complete sphere.

Units and Terminology Used in this Book

Astronomical distance units in common usage are:

astronomical unit (a.u.)	$= 1 \cdot 496 \times 10^{11}$ m
light year (l.y.)	$= 9 \cdot 46 \times 10^{15}$ m $= 63\ 240$ a.u.
parsec (pc)	$= 3 \cdot 09 \times 10^{16}$ m $= 206\ 265$ a.u. $= 3 \cdot 26$ l.y.

Fundamental constants of nature

The four basic constants are as follows:

velocity of light (c)	$= 2 \cdot 998 \times 10^8$ m s^{-1}
gravitational constant (G)	$= 6 \cdot 670 \times 10^{-11}$ N m^2 kg^{-2}
charge on the electron (e)	$= 1 \cdot 602 \times 10^{-19}$ coulomb
Planck's constant (h)	$= 6 \cdot 624 \times 10^{-34}$ J s

A

Aberration of light. The apparent displacement of a star from its mean position on the celestial sphere due to the velocity of the Earth in its orbit round the Sun. The phenomenon was discovered in 1729 by James Bradley who was, in fact, trying to measure stellar PARALLAX. The displacement is caused (see Figure 1) by the combination of the velocity of the Earth and the velocity of light approaching from the source; if the Earth were stationary light from a star would arrive from the true direction of this source, but the motion of the Earth causes the light to appear to be approaching from a point which is slightly displaced in the direction of the Earth's motion. In the course of a year, as the Earth travels round the Sun, a star will trace out a small ellipse in the sky about its mean position. The maximum radius of this ellipse (in radians) is equal to the ratio of the speed of the Earth to the speed of light (30 km s^{-1}:300000 km s^{-1}), i.e. about 20·5 seconds of arc. The eccentricity of the ellipse depends on the CELESTIAL LATITUDE of the star (the figure becomes a circle at the pole of the ECLIPTIC and a straight line on the ecliptic).

The displacement due to aberration is much greater than that due to parallax (the annual parallax of the *nearest* star is 0·76 seconds of arc) and this must be allowed for before the parallax can be determined for a star. A similar, though much smaller, aberration effect occurs due to the speed of rotation of the Earth on its axis; this is known as *diurnal aberration*.

Absolute magnitude. The APPARENT MAGNITUDE which a star would have if it were located at a standard distance from the Earth of 10 PARSECS, i.e. 32·6 light years. Clearly the apparent magnitude of a star depends upon the amount of light it emits ($\Diamond$LUMINOSITY) and on its distance (brightness diminishes as the square of distance); if all stars were at the same distance then their apparent magnitudes would be true indicators of their relative luminosities. By definition, the absolute magnitudes of stars provide a measure of their relative luminosities, by comparing the apparent brightnesses which stars would have if they all lay at the same distance.

Absolute magnitude is usually denoted by M, or M_v to signify absolute visual magnitude (proportional to the amount of visible light

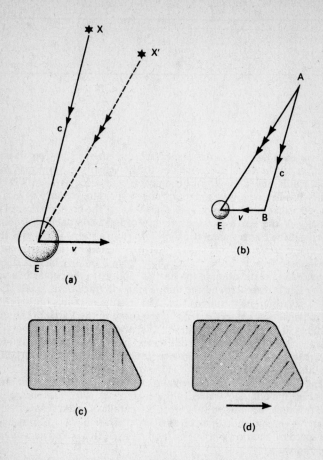

Figure 1. Aberration of light. The direction from which a ray of starlight approaches the Earth depends upon the *relative* velocity of the Earth and the ray of light. Thus in (a) we see a ray of light XE approaching the Earth from the true direction of the star. Because of the Earth's motion (velocity v), the ray of light (velocity c) *appears* to approach along direction X'E. In (b) the ray of light from the star is represented by the vector AB. If we imagine the Earth to be stationary, then the apparent direction AE along which the ray of light approaches is obtained by adding to AB a vector BE (equal and opposite to the velocity of the Earth), and joining the points E and A.

A common analogy is to compare the motion of raindrops down the window of a stationary motor car (c) with their motion down the window of a moving car (d).

emitted). For the Sun, M_v is $+4.8$, i.e. if the Sun were removed to a distance of 10 parsecs, then it would appear as a faint naked-eye star. On the other hand, the star Rigel in the constellation of Orion has $M_v = -7$, compared with an apparent magnitude, $m_v = 0.1$. Rigel is thus inherently 11.8 magnitudes more luminous than the Sun (a factor of almost 60000). By way of contrast, the nearest star, PROXIMA CENTAURI, has $M_v = +15.5$, so that it is nearly 11 magnitudes fainter than the Sun. ($\Diamond$HERTZSPRUNG–RUSSELL DIAGRAM, Figure 24.)

Absolute space. $\Diamond$ETHER.

Absolute zero. The lowest possible temperature; according to the KINETIC THEORY OF GASES, this is the temperature at which all motion of atoms and molecules ceases. This temperature is equivalent to -273 degrees centigrade, and defines the zero of the kelvin, or absolute, temperature scale.

Absorption line. $\Diamond$SPECTRUM.

Acceleration. Rate of change of velocity. This is expressed in units of metres per second per second ($m\,s^{-2}$), or other equivalent units; thus, an acceleration of $10\,m\,s^{-2}$ would imply an increase in velocity of 10 metres per second in one second.

Achromatic lens. A compound lens made up of two or more components (of different types of glass) which minimizes the effects of CHROMATIC ABERRATION (see Figure 10). Such a lens will normally bring two different colours to the same focus with only a small spread in focal length for the other colours; even so, the false colour introduced into the image is not wholly removed.

Active galaxies. Galaxies which are unusual in that they appear to be suffering or have suffered violent release of energy. ($\Diamond$SEYFERT GALAXY; RADIO GALAXY.)

Aerolite. Term sometimes used to describe a METEORITE of stony composition.

Aether. $\Diamond$ETHER.

Age of universe. $\Diamond$COSMOLOGY.

Airlock. A compartment attached to a spacecraft which can be independently depressurized and repressurized, providing a link between the spacecraft interior and the space environment. The interior of the spacecraft can be maintained at pressure while an astronaut enters and leaves by the airlock.

Albedo. The proportion of incident light (or radiation) reflected back in all directions from the surface of a body. For a completely black body – absorbing all incident radiation – the albedo is 0; for a perfect reflector it is 1. For example, the albedo of the Moon is 0·07, implying that only 7 per cent of the Sun's radiation is reflected by the Moon, the remaining 93 per cent being absorbed (and so heating the Moon). Clouds, snow and ice have high albedos. Thus Venus (wholly cloud-covered) has a mean albedo of about 0·76, the Earth (partly cloud-covered) 0·39, and Mercury (no atmosphere) 0·06.

It has been estimated that the albedos of some of the asteroids are so low that their surfaces reflect less light than carbon paper.

Alpha particle. ◇HELIUM; RADIOACTIVITY.

ALSEP – Apollo Lunar Surface Experiments Package. The array of experiments carried on each Apollo mission for deployment on the lunar surface (◇APOLLO PROJECT). The precise content of each package differed, but by way of example, the Apollo 17 ALSEP consisted of a heat flow experiment, a lunar ejecta and impact monitoring device, a seismometer, a lunar atmosphere composition experiment (capable of measuring a gas density as low as 10^{-18}, i.e. one million million millionth, that of the Earth's atmosphere at sea level), and a gravimeter experiment.

Altitude (1). The angle between the horizon and a star, measured in a direction perpendicular to the plane of the horizon. Together with a

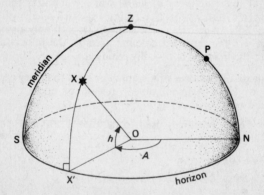

Figure 2. Altitude and azimuth. The figure shows the hemisphere of sky seen by the observer, O. The points on the diagram are: Z = zenith; P = north celestial pole; N = north point of the horizon; S = south point. The star X has altitude h = angle X'OX, where X' is a point vertically below X, and azimuth A = angle NOX' (this is equivalent to the angle measured on the surface of the celestial sphere, the spherical angle PZX). The angle ZOX is the zenith distance, z, of the star X.

value of AZIMUTH, this specifies the position in the sky of a celestial body at a particular instant, as seen by an observer at a particular point on the Earth's surface (see Figure 2).

Due to the rotation of the Earth, the altitude of a star continually changes; for example, an observer in the northern hemisphere will see a star rise in the east, reach its maximum altitude when due south (culmination; ◊TRANSIT), and set in the west. Observers located at the north or south poles, however, will see stars move parallel to the horizon, so maintaining constant altitude.

Altitude (2).   The height of an object (e.g. an artificial satellite) above mean sea level.

Andromeda galaxy, M31.   One of the nearest galaxies, and the first for which the distance was determined. The distance measurement was made in 1923 by E. E. Hubble, his original value being 750000 light years; the current value is 2200000 light years. It is a spiral galaxy (◊GALAXIES, CLASSIFICATION OF) similar to our own, with a diameter of some 100000 light years, and a total mass (stars and interstellar material) of about 3×10^{11} (300000000000) solar masses. It is accompanied by two smaller satellite elliptical galaxies. The Andromeda galaxy may be seen with the naked eye under good conditions. See) Plate 20.)

Angstrom unit.   A unit of length frequently used to describe the wavelengths of light. It is equal to 10^{-10} metres (i.e. one ten thousand millionth of a metre) and is denoted by the symbol Å. Most of the visible spectrum lies in the wavelength range 3900 to 7500 Å.

Angular momentum.   A property of rotating bodies or systems of masses which is dependent upon the distribution and velocities of the masses about the axis of rotation. The angular momentum of a single particle of mass, m, moving in a circular orbit of radius, R, at velocity, v, is given by mvR. Angular momentum is a conserved quantity; i.e. the total angular momentum of a system is constant. Thus if a large slowly rotating gas cloud contracts, its rotational velocity must increase to conserve angular momentum; as it contracts, therefore, it spins more rapidly. The conservation of angular momentum is of central importance to such questions as star formation, the origin of planetary systems, etc.

Annual parallax.   ◊PARALLAX.

Annular eclipse.   ◊ECLIPSE.

Anomalistic year.   ◊YEAR.

Antimatter.   Term applied to atomic particles which have 'mirror image' properties of ordinary particles; i.e. an antiparticle has the same mass but opposite charge and spin to a normal particle. The antiparticle of the electron is the positron. If a particle and its antiparticle meet, they annihilate each other with the release of energy, i.e. they achieve total conversion of mass into energy.

It is generally accepted that antimatter does not exist in bulk in the universe (i.e. we will not find whole stars or galaxies made out of antimatter), but this has been disputed.

Apastron. The point in the orbit of a body round a star at which the distance of that body from the star is a maximum.

Aperture. ⟡TELESCOPE.

Aperture synthesis. A technique in radio astronomy, pioneered at Cambridge, UK, which allows the signals received by a system of small radio telescopes to be combined electronically to give the RESOLVING POWER of a much larger instrument. Essentially the technique involves the use of a number of fixed and movable radio dishes arranged along a railway line; by varying the separation of the dishes and making use of the rotation of the Earth, the dishes are made to sweep out the area of a very large radio dish.

Apex of the Sun's way. The direction of motion of the Sun relative to the stars in the local part of the GALAXY (2). Observations of the PROPER MOTIONS of stars indicate that they show a tendency to diverge from a point in the constellation Hercules, and to converge towards a point in the constellation Columba. These observations indicate that the Sun is moving at a velocity of about 19·5 km per second, towards a point at right ascension (RA) 18 h and declination (dec) $+30°$ in Hercules (the solar apex) and away from a point at RA 6 h and dec $-30°$ in Columba (the solar antapex). (See Figure 3.)

Aphelion. The point at which a body in an elliptical orbit round the Sun is at its greatest distance from the Sun (⟡ORBITAL ELEMENTS, Figure 29a). (⟡PERIHELION.)

Apogee. The point at which a body moving in an elliptical orbit round the Earth is at its greatest distance from the Earth. Strictly speaking, the term apogee refers to distance from the centre of the Earth; in the case of near-Earth satellites, however, the term is sometimes loosely used to indicate the greatest altitude of the satellite above the Earth's surface

---

Figure 3. Apex of the Sun's way. (a) The Sun, S, is moving relative to the neighbouring stars. However, (b) it appears to us as if the Sun were stationary, and the neighbouring stars were drifting past the Sun in a common direction. (c) Projected on the celestial sphere, the apparent motions of the stars are shown, the stars appearing to diverge from the point A, ahead of the Sun (the apex of the Sun's way, or solar apex), and to converge towards the point A' behind the Sun (or solar antapex).

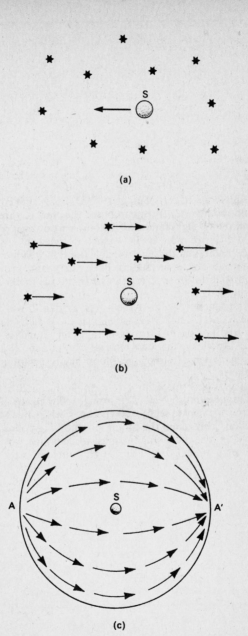

(a)

(b)

(c)

(the term 'apogee altitude' would be better in this context). (◇ PERIGEE.)

Apollo Project. The US manned lunar landing programme. Project Apollo was first publicly proposed by NASA in July 1960, when the original intention was to aim for a manned lunar orbital flight. On 25 May 1961 (a few weeks after the first manned spaceflight by the Soviet cosmonaut Yuri Gagarin) President John F. Kennedy proposed to Congress that the US should establish as a national goal the intent to achieve a manned lunar landing by the end of the decade. To effect a manned landing required the development of the launch vehicle, Saturn V, which had a first-stage THRUST of about 3 400 000 kg.

The Apollo spacecraft consisted of three principal components, the command module (CM) which housed the crew of three for the outward and return flight (and was the only part of the craft to return to Earth), the service module (SM) which included the rocket motor for the return flight, and the lunar module (LM) in which two members of the crew made the lunar landing, and which contained a second propulsion system to lift off from the lunar surface to effect a link-up in lunar orbit with the CM.

The first manned flight of the series, Apollo 7, was launched into Earth orbit on 11 October 1968. This was followed by the lunar orbital flight of Apollo 8 over Christmas of that year; launched on 21 December 1968, Apollo 8, with the crew of F. Borman, J. Lovell and W. Anders, made ten orbits of the Moon before returning to Earth on 27 December.

The first landing was achieved by Apollo 11 on 20 July 1969 in the Mare Tranquillitatis. Neil Armstrong followed by Edwin Aldrin became the first men to set foot on another world, while Michael Collins remained in orbit round the Moon in the CM. Apollos 12, 14, 15, 16 and 17 also made successful landings, while on the Apollo 13 mission the SM oxygen tank exploded on the outward part of the flight; fortunately the crew was able to use the LM oxygen and power and return to Earth after looping round the Moon. Apollos 15 to 17 carried with them the lunar rover, a self-propelled vehicle which greatly extended the range of the astronauts' surface sampling expeditions. The final mission of the series, Apollo 17, took place between 7 and 19 December 1972.

The entire project was a major technological success, with six successful landings, and the successful outcome of the potentially disastrous situation which arose on Apollo 13. Experimental packages, including seismometers, solar wind detectors, laser reflectors, etc., were deployed on the lunar surface, and the results obtained from these devices, together with the analysis (on Earth) of a total of 387 kg of lunar samples, have led to a fuller and deeper understanding of the nature of the Moon and its probable origin. In addition, much has been learned about the conditions under which the planets must have formed. (For fuller details, ⟡MOON (2).)

Apparent magnitude. The apparent brightness of a star, or other celestial body, expressed in terms of the system of stellar magnitudes. The system had its origins in the classification by brightness of some thousand stars carried out by Hipparchus in the second century B.C., and was standardized by Pogson in 1850. The mean of the twenty brightest stars in the sky is defined to be magnitude 1 (or first magnitude), while the faintest stars normally visible to the unaided eye on a clear dark night are said to be of magnitude 6 (or sixth magnitude); stars which are between these extremes take intermediate values of magnitude. Thus, the brighter the star, the lower its magnitude.

Sixth-magnitude stars are defined to be 100 times fainter than first-magnitude stars, i.e. a difference of 5 magnitudes corresponds to a difference in brightness of a factor of 100. The scale is logarithmic: a difference of 1 magnitude corresponds to a difference in brightness of $\sqrt[5]{100} = 2 \cdot 512$. Pogson defined the difference in apparent magnitude between two stars whose magnitudes were m_1 and m_2, and whose apparent brightnesses were b_1 and b_2, by means of the following:

$$m_1 - m_2 = -2 \cdot 5 \log_{10} b_1/b_2$$

Thus stars of magnitude 2 are $2 \cdot 512$ times fainter than magnitude 1, magnitude 3 stars are $2 \cdot 512 \times 2 \cdot 512 = 6 \cdot 31$ times fainter than magnitude 1, and so on. Celestial objects brighter than first magnitude may have zero or negative values of apparent magnitude, while stars fainter than sixth magnitude have higher values. Examples of apparent magnitudes are given below:

Object	Apparent magnitude	Apparent brightness compared to magnitude 1
Sun	$-26 \cdot 7$	$1 \cdot 2 \times 10^{11}$
Full Moon	$-12 \cdot 7$	3×10^5
Venus (at greatest elongation)	$-4 \cdot 4$	$1 \cdot 4 \times 10^2$
Sirius (brightest star)	$-1 \cdot 4$	$9 \cdot 1$
Faintest naked-eye star	$+6$	10^{-2}
Faintest detectable object	$+23$	$1 \cdot 6 \times 10^{-9}$

The difference in apparent brightness between the Sun and the faintest detected objects is nearly 50 magnitudes, or a factor of 10^{20} (one hundred million million million).

Apparent magnitude is usually denoted by m, or by m_v to denote apparent visual magnitude (i.e. a measure of the brightness in visible light only). Where the term 'apparent magnitude' is used without qualification, it may be taken to mean apparent visual magnitude.

Apsis (pl: apsides). The points in the orbit of a celestial body at which it is at its closest to, or greatest distance from, the centre of gravitational attraction, e.g. PERIHELION, APHELION. At these positions the body has zero RADIAL VELOCITY relative to this centre. The line of apsides is the line joining the apsides.

Areography. The study and mapping of the surface of the planet Mars.

Ariel. Series of UK scientific/astronomical satellites launched by NASA as part of a cooperative UK–US programme. Of particular interest is Ariel 5, launched on 15 October 1974 to study X-ray sources.

Artificial satellite. A man-made object placed in orbit round the Earth or some other celestial body. The first artificial satellite to be placed in orbit round the Earth was the Soviet Sputnik 1, launched on 4 October 1957.

Artificial Earth Satellites leave a very wide range of uses at the present time, including the following: astronomical observatories (studying wavelengths of radiation which cannot penetrate the atmosphere); scientific satellites (studying the upper atmosphere, and near-Earth environment); geodesy (studying the shape and structure of the Earth); Earth resources; meteorology; communications (television, telephone, etc); navigational aids; military reconnaissance.

The extent to which satellites are involved in aspects of everyday life is scarcely appreciated by most people.

Ascending node. ⬦NODE.

Ashen light. The phenomenon, occasionally reported by Earth-based observers, of the apparent faint illumination of the unlit hemisphere of the planet Venus, when it is in a crescent phase. Although similar in appearance to the illumination of the dark side of the Moon by Earth-light, no such explanation is possible in the case of Venus since that planet has no moon. The reality of the phenomenon has been questioned.

Asterism. ⬦CONSTELLATION.

Asteroids. Otherwise known as the minor planets, these are small rocky bodies 99·8 per cent of which move in orbits that lie between the orbits of Mars and Jupiter (⬦SOLAR SYSTEM, Figure 38b). The first asteroid, CERES, was discovered in 1801 as a result of renewed interest in the problem of the 'missing planet' which, according to BODE'S LAW, ought to lie at a mean distance from the Sun of 2·8 astronomical units. Since that time many more asteroids have been found; orbits have been calculated for some 2000 of them, but it is estimated that there must be about 100000 asteroids in all.

The composition of these bodies is thought to be similar to that of the terrestrial planets, and mean densities have been estimated at $3 \cdot 5 \times 10^3$ kg m^{-3}. It has often been suggested that they represent the fragments of a planet which once orbited the Sun at a distance of about 2·8 astronomical units, and for some reason broke up. More popular is the view that the asteroids represent material which did not accrete to form a full-scale planet either because of a shortage of material, or as a result of the perturbing effects of Jupiter. The estimated total mass for all the minor planets (which range in diameter from about 800 km to less than 1 km) is less than 0·1 per cent of the Earth's mass.

A small proportion of asteroids move in highly elliptical orbits as a result of which some can make close approaches to the Earth (e.g. EROS and HERMES), and others can make close approaches to the Sun (◊ICARUS).

It is thought likely that METEORITES represent fragments of collisions between asteroids.

Astrochemistry. The study of the chemistry of, and chemical processes operating in, astronomical sources and phenomena. As far as interstellar material is concerned much of the chemistry involved is organic. (◊INTERSTELLAR MOLECULES.)

Astrodynamics. The study of the motion of bodies in gravitational fields, with particular reference to the motions of artificial satellites and space probes. (◊CELESTIAL MECHANICS.)

Astrograph. A telescope system designed specifically for the accurate photographic recording of the positions of astronomical objects. For the measurement of such quantities as stellar PARALLAX and PROPER MOTION instruments of long focal length (often refractors) are employed; these give a large plate scale (i.e. a small area of sky is spread out over a large area of the photographic plate) which facilitates the accurate measurement of position.

Astrology. The study which, it is claimed, can determine the characteristics of individuals and the probable future course of events by reference to the positions of the celestial bodies. In ancient times and in the Middle Ages, astronomy and astrology were closely linked, but there is now no link between the two subjects. There appears to be no scientific basis for astrology, and there is certainly no doubt that the sort of 'pop astrology' which appears in newspaper and magazine horoscopes is nonsense.

Serious students of astrology maintain there is more to the subject than that. It is suggested that there are certain characteristics common to individuals born under the same sign of the ZODIAC (see Figure 49), and while the most elaborate statistical techniques would be required to test such a claim, one can at least suppose that there might be a measure of truth in it. After all, the sign of the Zodiac under which one is born is simply an indication of the time of year that birth took place, and it is not inconceivable that the time of year of birth might have some subtle influence on personality.

Many astrologers maintain that the planets (not the stars) exert the claimed influence on human affairs, and that one's detailed personality traits and likely future development are determined by the relative configuration of the planets at birth. It is difficult to see what form such an 'influence' could take, and most astronomers would completely reject the notion that some sort of causal relationship exists between planets and people; for one thing, it would appear to imply the existence of some influence that is independent of distance. Nevertheless, there have been some curious statistical results obtained which suggest that a correlation has been established between the planet which was rising or at culmination (⟡TRANSIT) at the time of an individual's birth and the subsequent occupation of this individual. Even granting the validity of the conclusion (which is open to considerable dispute), the existence of a correlation between two phenomena does not of itself mean that there is a cause-and-effect relationship between these phenomena. There are many examples of spurious correlation; an extreme example would be the statement, 'All men breathe, and all men die. Therefore breathing is the cause of death'! All that can be said is that while many of the claims of astrology are wholly without foundation, and there appears to be no scientific basis for the subject 'there remain some aspects of astrology which require explanation; it would be unwise to keep a completely closed mind on the subject.

Astrometric binary. ⟡BINARY.

Astrometry. The branch of astronomy dealing with the precise measurement of the position and motion of astronomical bodies.

Astro-navigation (1). Navigation at sea, or on the land surface, by reference to the positions on the CELESTIAL SPHERE of bodies such as the Sun, the Moon and the stars. Since the Earth is (very nearly) spherical, it follows that the altitude of the Sun or a given star at upper TRANSIT depends upon the latitude of the observer on Earth; in principle, the observer's latitude may be obtained by measuring the altitude of the Sun at upper transit (latitude = $90°$ + declination − altitude). In principle, too, provided that the RIGHT ASCENSION of the Sun or star and the Greenwich SIDEREAL TIME are known, the determination of the instant of upper transit of the Sun or star may be used to calculate longitude. Again, if the Greenwich sidereal time is known, simultaneous observations of three stars should pinpoint the position of the observer.

Astro-navigation (2). Navigation in space by reference to celestial bodies. The orientation in space of a spacecraft may be determined from reference to the fixed stars; the determination of position within the Solar System is a three-dimensional problem requiring reference to the positions of the Sun, the Earth and another celestial body.

Astronaut. One who travels in space (in the USSR the term cosmonaut is used). Due to a number of factors, the degree of skill and technical knowledge required, the physical and mental stresses involved in spaceflight, etc., extremely careful selection procedures and long training periods are required for prospective astronauts. In addition, additional training is required for specific missions; for example, each member of the US SKYLAB crew had to complete some 2150 hours of specific training, including simulator time, medical training and EVA mock-ups.

With advances in techniques (for example, the development of the SPACE SHUTTLE) it should become possible for non-trained personnel to participate in spaceflight, travelling in spacecraft piloted by professional astronauts.

Astronomical unit (a.u.). A unit of distance measurement defined to be the semi-major axis of the orbit of the Earth, or the 'mean' distance between the Earth and the Sun. It is equal to $1 \cdot 496 \times 10^{11}$ metres (i.e. 149 600 000 km).

One of the earliest attempts to measure this quantity was made by the Greek observer Aristarchus in about 280 B.C. who estimated that the Sun lay some twenty times further than the Moon (his estimate was too small by a factor of 20). In the eighteenth and nineteenth centuries measurements were made utilizing transits of the planet Venus (✧ TRANSIT), and the 1882 observations yielded a value of $1 \cdot 488 \times 10^{11}$ m. Observations of the close approach to the Earth of the ASTEROID Eros led to a value accurate to about one part in ten thousand. The current value is based on precise radar determinations and is accurate to about one part in a hundred million. (✧ DISTANCE DETERMINATION IN THE UNIVERSE.)

Astrophysics. That branch of astronomy concerned with the physics of, and physical processes operating in, stars and other celestial bodies. It may be argued that the subject of astrophysics really began with the development of SPECTROSCOPY in the nineteenth century.

Atmosphere. The gaseous mantle surrounding a planet or other celestial body; the outer layers of a star. The ability of a planet to retain its atmosphere depends on a number of factors, notably the ESCAPE VELOCITY at its surface, the temperature (the higher the temperature, the faster the atoms and molecules move, and the easier it becomes for them to escape) and the chemical composition of the gas (light gases such as hydrogen escape more readily than heavy gases such as carbon dioxide).

Atmospheric pressure. The pressure (i.e. the force per unit area) exerted on the surface of a planet by the weight of gas contained in a column extending vertically upwards to the limit of the atmosphere. At the surface of the Earth, the average value of atmospheric pressure is 10330 kg per square metre (kg m^{-2}); this value is equivalent to 1013·25 millibars, and may be referred to as 1 atmosphere. By way of comparison, the atmospheric pressures at the surfaces of Venus and Mars are, respectively, 100 and 0·008 atmospheres.

Atmospheric refraction. Rays of light entering the Earth's atmosphere (i.e. passing from the vacuum of space to the medium of air) are bent, or refracted. As a result of this, the apparent positions of stars are displaced by a small amount towards the zenith, i.e. the effect of atmospheric refraction is to increase the apparent altitudes of stars. At relatively small values of zenith distance, the effect is small, and is

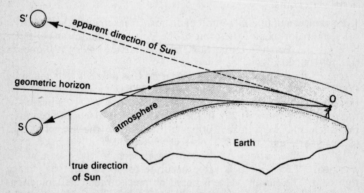

Figure 4. Atmospheric refraction. The effect of atmospheric refraction on the apparent position of the rising or setting Sun as seen by the observer, O, is shown here, greatly exaggerated. A ray of light from the Sun, which is, in fact, below the observer's horizon, travelling in the direction SI enters the atmosphere at point I and is bent in such a way that it reaches O. To the observer it appears as if the ray of light is approaching along direction S'O. Thus, the Sun *appears* to be above the horizon. The maximum displacement in position due to this effect is about 35 minutes of arc.

proportional to the tangent of the zenith distance. However, at large zenith distances, the effects are quite appreciable; at the horizon (zenith distance $= 90°$) refraction increases apparent altitudes by about 35 arc minutes. This means that the disc of the Sun may be seen above the horizon when, geometrically, the Sun is actually below the horizon (see Figure 4).

Atom. The smallest basic unit into which a chemical element may be subdivided, i.e. the basic building block of matter. The idea of the atom dates back to the work of the Greek philosopher Democritus in the fifth century B.C. which suggested that matter could not be subdivided infinitely; instead there must be a basic indivisible particle. The theory of atoms was developed notably by the English chemist Dalton when, in 1803, he introduced the idea of combinations of atoms, or molecules.

In the twentieth century it has become apparent that the atom itself has a complex structure, and that a large (and steadily increasing) number of sub-atomic particles exist. For many purposes, however, we can take a fairly simple view of the atom, based on the model produced by Neils Bohr in 1913. We imagine the hydrogen atom to consist of a nucleus comprising one particle, the positively charged PROTON, around which revolves a single negatively charged particle, the ELECTRON. The electron is permitted to move only in certain orbits; if the electron absorbs energy, it may move to a larger (higher energy) orbit, while if the electron drops down to an orbit of smaller radius (and lower energy), energy is released as a quantum (or packet) of radiation ($\Diamond$SPECTRUM).

More massive atoms contain in their nuclei more protons and an additional type of particle, the NEUTRON, which has zero charge but almost the same mass as the proton. A typical atomic nucleus has a radius of about 10^{-14} metres, the radius of the atom (i.e. of the electron 'orbits') being about ten thousand times larger (10^{-10} metres). The mass of the atom is concentrated in the nucleus.

There are ninety-two naturally occurring elements and each is symbolized by a letter, or pair of letters; thus H is hydrogen, He is helium, and so on. Atoms are characterized by their atomic mass (A), i.e. the number of protons and neutrons in their nuclei, and atomic number (Z), the number of protons in their nuclei (this is equal to the positive charge on the nucleus). Z is usually depicted as a subscript and A as a superscript; for example, hydrogen, with $Z = 1$ and $A = 1$, is denoted $_1H^1$, while helium, with $Z = 2$ and $A = 4$ (two protons and two neutrons in the nucleus), is denoted $_2He^4$. A heavy element like iron (chemical symbol Fe) is $_{26}Fe^{56}$, there being 26 protons and 30 neutrons in its nucleus.

A neutral atom has the same number of electrons as protons (and so is electrically neutral); an atom which has too many or too few electrons is said to be ionized ($\Diamond$ IONIZATION). Atoms with the same number of protons, but different numbers of neutrons, are called isotopes (e.g. two isotopes of Uranium are $_{92}U^{235}$ and $_{92}U^{238}$).

All the matter in the universe appears to be made up of the same basic elements, the same types of atoms. Our understanding of what goes on inside stars, or in the universe at large, is intimately linked to our knowledge of the atom and its structure.

Atomic mass. $\Diamond$ ATOM.

Atomic number. $\Diamond$ ATOM.

Aurora (pl: aurorae). A diffuse glow or a pattern of light patches, streamers or rays seen in the sky at high latitudes. The aurora seen in the northern sky is called the aurora borealis (or Northern Lights) and that seen in the southern hemisphere, the aurora australis.

The zones of maximum auroral activity lie in rings of about 20 degrees radius around the north and south magnetic poles; the aurorae are thought to be due to the effects of charged particles ($\Diamond$ PROTONS) entering the upper atmosphere along lines of magnetic force and inter-acting with the upper atmosphere to cause fluorescence. The particles descend from the VAN ALLEN BELTS as a result of the influx of clouds of particles from the Sun, and the frequency of auroral displays is closely related to the SOLAR CYCLE. Aurorae generally occur at alti-tudes of about 100 km.

Autumnal equinox. $\Diamond$ EQUINOX.

Axial period. The period of time taken for a body to complete one rotation on its axis. The period is usually referred to rotation relative to the stars, i.e. the sidereal rotation period; thus the axial period of the Earth is 23h 56m, although the mean solar day consists of twenty-four hours.

Axis (pl: axes). A reference line in space or drawn through a body. Usually this is a line about which a body has some degree of symmetry, e.g. a line passing through the centre of a sphere or which runs centrally through the length of a cylinder. For an ELLIPSE the major axis is a line passing through the centre and crossing the greatest diameter of the figure.

Axis of rotation. A real or imaginary line passing through a body, around which that body rotates.

Azimuth. The angle, measured parallel to the horizon in a clockwise direction from north, between the MERIDIAN and a celestial body; i.e. this is the angle between the north point of the horizon and a point on the horizon vertically below the celestial body (see Figure 2).

Azimuth may take any value between 0° and 360°. In some textbooks, azimuth is defined as being measured clockwise from north from 0° to 180° if the object is east of the meridian, and anticlockwise from north, 0° to 180° if the object is west of the meridian. Together with a value of ALTITUDE (1), this specifies the position in the sky of a celestial body as seen at a particular instant from a particular point on the Earth's surface.

B

Baily's beads. Brilliant points of light seen at the edge of the Moon's disc during a total eclipse of the Sun, just at the onset and termination of totality. They are due to sunlight passing through valleys and indentations at the edge of the Moon's visible disc.

Ballistic trajectory. The path followed by a projectile, i.e. a body making an unpowered flight under the action of gravity, having been given some initial velocity. For example, neglecting the effects of air resistance, a bullet follows a ballistic trajectory after being fired from a gun. A rocket likewise follows such a path once the motors cease firing: in practice a spacecraft follows a ballistic trajectory apart from brief periods (usually of a few minutes at most) of powered flight during initial acceleration, brief course-correction manoeuvres, and final deceleration.

A ballistic missile follows such a path after the initial launching.

Balmer series. A series of lines in the SPECTRUM of the hydrogen (H) atom, most of which occur in the visible part of the spectrum. These lines correspond to transitions between the second energy level (i.e. the second permitted orbit for an electron in order of distance from the nucleus) and higher levels (upward transitions give rise to absorption lines, downward transitions to emission lines) (see Figure 41b and c).

The line of longest wavelength (656·3 nanometres) corresponds to a transition between levels 2 and 3 (this is the smallest energy transition in the series) and occurs in the red part of the spectrum; this line is usually referred to as Hα (hydrogen alpha). The next line, Hβ, occurs at a wavelength of 486·1 nm, and corresponds to a transition between levels 2 and 4. The next two lines, Hγ and Hδ, occur at wavelengths of 434 nm and 410·2 nm respectively. The wavelengths of lines in the series converge to the series limit at 364·6 nm, in the ultra-violet. This limit corresponds to the maximum possible transition in the series (i.e. to the maximum energy change; if an electron in level 2 absorbs more energy than this limiting value it will be removed from the atom, i.e. the atom will become ionized (◊IONIZATION).

Absorption lines of the Balmer series are conspicuous in the solar spectrum and in the spectra of many stars. (◇LYMAN SERIES; PASCHEN SERIES.)

Barnard's Star. A faint red star, one of the Sun's nearest neighbours, lying at a distance of 6 light years. Its ABSOLUTE MAGNITUDE is 13·25 (corresponding to a luminosity of less than one 2000th that of the Sun) and its spectral type, M5 V (◇SPECTRAL CLASSIFICATION). It is notable for having the largest known value of PROPER MOTION, 10·3 arcsecs per annum; it would thus move across the sky through a distance equal to the apparent diameter of the Moon in about 180 years. It is of particular interest because investigations by P. van de Kamp indicate that it has in orbit round it two planets with masses slightly less than that of Jupiter. Although these findings have been challenged, it is quite widely accepted that this particular star does have a planetary system. (◇PLANETS OF OTHER STARS.)

Barycentre. The centre of mass of the Earth–Moon system. If two bodies move under the influence of their mutual gravitational attractions, they will describe orbits around a point between them, the centre of mass of the two bodies. The relative distances of the two bodies from this point will be inversely proportional to their masses. Thus, for example, if one body is twice the mass of the other, the centre of mass will lie one third of the way from the more massive body to the less massive one (i.e. their distances are in the ratio 1:2) (see Figure 5a).

In the case of the Earth and Moon the ratio of masses is approximately 81:1. The barycentre is therefore located at a distance from the Earth's centre equal to 1/82 of the distance from the Earth to the Moon, and on the line joining the centres of Earth and Moon, i.e. at a distance of about 4700 km from the centre of the Earth. The point is, in fact, located *within* the Earth (see Figure 5b).

Beta particle. ◇ELECTRON; RADIOACTIVITY.

Big-Bang theory. A theory which suggests that the universe originated from an extremely hot, dense fireball which exploded, sending matter outwards; the observed expansion of the universe is considered to be due to this initial explosion.

This is currently the most popular theory of COSMOLOGY and suggests that the evolution of the universe has followed the route described below. At the instant of the big bang (between ten and twenty thousand million years ago), the temperature of the universe was in excess of 10^{10} K, but dropped rapidly, within about 1000 seconds, to 10^9 K. During this period, hydrogen and helium formed in roughly their present abundances (◇HELIUM PROBLEM). The universe was at that stage composed largely of hydrogen, helium and radiation, and as the expansion continued, the matter and radiation cooled down.

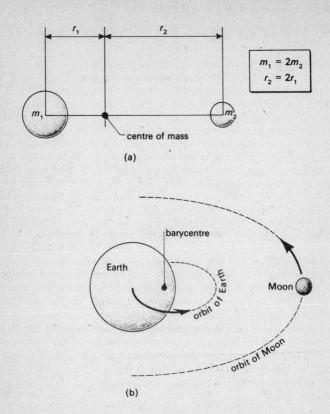

Figure 5. Barycentre and centre of mass. (a) The centre of mass of a pair of bodies, m_1 and m_2, lies on a line between their centres. If, as in the example, $m_1 = 2m_2$, then m_2 will be twice as far from the centre of mass as m_1; i.e. $m_1/m_2 = r_2/r_1$.

(b) The centre of mass of the Earth–Moon system is called the barycentre. Since the ratio of the masses of Earth:Moon is about 81:1, it follows that the Moon lies about 81 times further from the barycentre than does the Earth. In fact the barycentre lies within the globe of the Earth. Earth and Moon complete an orbit of the barycentre in 27·3 days.

After about 10^9 years, the formation of galaxies may have taken place, and these continue to move away from one another as the expansion of the universe continues. The radiation released from the primeval fireball has now cooled to a temperature of the order of 3 K, and it appears that this radiation has been detected in the form of the MICROWAVE BACKGROUND RADIATION.

Current observations suggest the universe will expand without limit (but ◇OSCILLATING UNIVERSE).

Binary. Two stars which travel round each other under their mutual gravitational attraction; the stars may be considered as moving round their common centre of mass. Binaries are more common than is generally realized, and it may be that more than 50 per cent of all stars are contained in binary systems. The mean separation of stars in binary systems is of the order of 10 to 20 astronomical units.

Binaries may be subdivided into: visual binaries, where the two component stars are directly visible; SPECTROSCOPIC BINARIES, where the stars are too close together to be seen as individuals, but analysis of their combined spectrum reveals that two stars are present; and ECLIPSING BINARIES, where each star alternately passes in front of the other, eclipsing it, and causing the combined brightness of the two stars to diminish. Eclipsing binaries are generally also spectroscopic binaries. A further class is made up of astrometric binaries, where the existence of a companion to a star may be deduced from the small perturbations in the motion of the visible star caused by the gravitational attraction of the companion.

With visual binaries, it is generally the case that one star is brighter than the other, and the brighter star is designated the primary. Observations over a period of time reveal the apparent orbit of the companion relative to the primary, and this will be an ellipse. To obtain the true orbit of the secondary, allowance must be made for the angle of inclination of the orbit to the line of sight; the apparent orbit is in general a foreshortened version of the true orbit.

From the true orbit, if the distance is known, it is possible to obtain the period, P, and semi-major axis, a, of the orbit of the companion relative to the primary. Applying Kepler's third law (◇KEPLER'S LAWS), and using the following system of units – mass expressed in solar masses, distance in astronomical units, and time in years – we have the following simple relationship,

$$m_1 + m_2 = a^3/P^2,$$

where m_1 and m_2 are the masses of the stars making up the binary. From this relationship, the combined mass of the two stars may be obtained. If the ratio of distances (r_1, r_2) of the two stars from their centre of mass can also be obtained, then the ratio of the masses can be found; for,

$$m_1/m_2 = r_2/r_1.$$

The study of binaries is of the utmost importance in astronomy, for it offers the only direct method of obtaining stellar masses.

BL Lacertae object. One of a class of objects named after B L Lacertae, a highly variable object. Such objects – also known as Lacertids – emit most strongly in the infra-red and are characterized by rapid brightness variations at radio, infra-red and optical wavelengths. They are extra-galactic objects possible related to QUASARS and SEYFERT GALAXIES.

Black body. An ideal emitter or absorber of radiation. A perfect black body will absorb all radiation which falls on it, and will emit radiation which has a continuous SPECTRUM determined only by the temperature of the black body (see Figure 6). The distribution of energy radiated against wavelength follows a curve known as a black-body (or Planck) spectrum and, for a given temperature, there is a particular wavelength at which the maximum emission takes place (◊ WIEN DISPLACEMENT LAW).

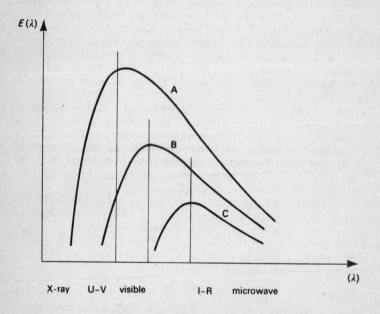

Figure 6. Black-body radiation. The graph shows the amount of energy emitted, $E(\lambda)$, plotted against the wavelength, λ, of that radiation for three black bodies (perfect emitters of radiation), A, B and C. In each case there is one particular wavelength at which the maximum quantity of energy is emitted. A is hotter than B, and B is hotter than C. It may be seen that the hotter the body, the shorter the wavelength at which the maximum radiation is emitted; thus A might appear blue in colour, B yellow and C red. In addition, the hotter the body the greater the *total* amount of energy emitted. Stars behave rather like black bodies in their emission of radiation.

Stars and hot solid bodies are not perfect black bodies, but their radiation can be described in terms of black-body properties.

Black dwarf. ◊STELLAR EVOLUTION.

Black hole. A region of space into which matter has fallen and from which no material object, light, or signal of any known kind can escape. In others words, within this region of space, the gravitational field is too powerful to let anything escape.

The basic concept is not new and – in a sense – dates back to the suggestion made in 1798 by Pierre Laplace that there might exist in the universe massive bodies which would be quite invisible because the force of gravity at their surfaces would be too great to allow light to escape; i.e. at the surface of such a body the ESCAPE VELOCITY would be greater than the speed of light. Current models of black holes are based on the GENERAL THEORY OF RELATIVITY, from which it can be shown that if any given amount of matter is compressed sufficiently, so that it is contained within a critical radius known as the SCHWARZSCHILD RADIUS, no signal can ever escape from it.

A black hole would arise if a quantity of matter were compressed inside its Schwarzschild radius, and the boundary of the black hole (known as the EVENT HORIZON) would be a sphere having this radius. Nothing which falls inside can ever escape again. It is important to note that a black hole is not a solid body; it is a region of space whose radius depends only on the *amount* of matter that has fallen inside. What happens to that matter thereafter has no bearing on the hole's size, and any matter which subsequently falls in only serves to increase the radius of the hole.

The Schwarzschild radius is normally very tiny. For the Sun, it is only 3 km, and if, in some way, the Earth could be compressed within its Schwarzschild radius, the resulting black hole would be only the size of a marble.

If black holes *do* exist, they will most probably have been formed as a result of the collapse of the most massive stars as they run out of fuel at the ends of their life cycles (◊STELLAR EVOLUTION). Most stars collapse to form dense compact objects (◊WHITE DWARF; NEUTRON STAR), but the most massive stars will continue to collapse until, in principle, all their matter is compressed into a point of infinite density known as a singularity. Before this happens, the shrinking star will have passed inside its Schwarzschild radius, giving rise to a black hole, and disappearing forever from view.

Black holes may be important energy sources, as matter falling in towards a black hole, before crossing the event horizon, may release considerable amounts of energy. A rotating black hole (essentially similar to the simple stationary one described above) is even more efficient in this respect. Not surprisingly black holes have been canvassed as possible 'explanations' of hitherto unexplained energy sources in the universe.

The most hopeful way in which black holes may be detected is by looking for their effects on matter in their vicinity. For example, if a black hole is a member of a BINARY system, then the visible star will be seen to follow an orbit round an invisible object; again, if material is falling into a black hole, it will become excessively heated and will emit X-rays. There are a number of possible candidates under investigation, and the best remains CYGNUS X-1 which is an X-ray source containing a massive invisible object.

Black holes remain a subject of controversy. There are those who deny that they could possibly exist, there is debate over whether or not objects such as Cygnus X-1 really contain black holes, and the problem of their central singularities is far from being resolved. In a singularity, gravitational forces become infinite, and matter must literally be crushed out of existence; what happens to it then? New concepts in physics may well be required to answer that question.

Blink comparator. A device which allows two photographic plates of the same region of sky to be compared so as to reveal any changes of brightness or position in objects on the plates. The two plates are viewed alternately in rapid succession through an eyepiece; any object which has changed its appearance or position in the time interval between the taking of the two photographs will show up to the eye as a 'blinking' spot. Such a device was used in the discovery of the planet Pluto.

Bode's law. More properly known as the Titius–Bode law, this is a curious numerical relationship between the mean distances of the planets from the Sun, which was first pointed out by the German astronomer J. Titius, and later popularized by J. Bode in 1772.

The 'law' is obtained in the following way: we take the sequence of numbers, 0, 3, 6, 12, . . ., and so on, where each successive number is double the preceding one (with the exception of the first two), add 4 to each, and divide each number by 10. We now express the mean distances of the planets from the Sun in terms of astronomical units (i.e. we take the Sun–Earth distance to be unity), and compare these values with the sequence, as shown on the table on the facing page.

Out as far as Uranus, which, incidentally, had not been discovered when the 'law' was first pointed out, the agreement between the sequence and the actual distance is remarkably good. The absence of a planet at a distance of 2·8 astronomical units is to some extent covered by the existence of the asteroids. The law does not seem to hold for Neptune and Pluto. Whether or not the Titius–Bode law has any real physical significance is not yet clear; it may be that the sequence represents those distances at which conditions were favourable for the

Planet	Mean distance from Sun	Corresponding value of Bode's law
Mercury	0·39	0·4
Venus	0·72	0·7
Earth	1	1
Mars	1·52	1·6
Asteroids (typical)	2·8	2·8
Jupiter	5·2	5·2
Saturn	9·54	10
Uranus	19·2	19·6
Neptune	30·1	38·8
Pluto	39·5	77·2

(The sequence may be expressed as, distance, $r = 0\cdot4 + 0\cdot3 \times 2^n$, where n is $-\infty$ for Mercury, 0 for Venus, 1 for Earth, and so on.)

formation of planets, but on the other hand the 'law' may simply reflect the distances at which the planets have settled down, long after their formation. The 'law' may be no more than a coincidence, but it is certainly a striking one.

Bolometer. ◊ BOLOMETRIC MAGNITUDE.

Bolometric magnitude. A measure of the total amount of radiation of all wavelengths received from or emitted by a star, and expressed in terms of the stellar magnitude scale. The apparent bolometric magnitude (denoted m_{bol}) is proportional to the logarithm of the quantity of radiation received from a star (◊ APPARENT MAGNITUDE). The absolute bolometric magnitude (denoted M_{tol}) is proportional to the logarithm of the quantity of radiation emitted by a star (its LUMINOSITY), and is equal to the apparent bolometric magnitude which that star would have if it were located at a distance of 10 parsecs (◊ ABSOLUTE MAGNITUDE). Since the total amount of radiation emitted by stars is always greater than the amount of visible light they emit, the value of bolometric magnitude is always *less* than the value of visual magnitude. A device which responds to radiation of all wavelengths is called a bolometer.

Bremsstrahlung. ◊ FREE–FREE RADIATION.

Butterfly diagram. A representation of the numbers and latitudes of sunspots throughout one SOLAR CYCLE or series of cycles. At the beginning of each eleven-year cycle, spots appear at relatively high latitudes (typically 30° north or south of the Sun's equator) in relatively small numbers, while by the middle of the cycle, much larger numbers of spots are visible at mean latitudes of about ±15°; by the end of the cycle, few spots are seen and these tend to occur near the equator. The diagram plots the latitudes of spots against time, and because of the way the numbers and latitudes of spots vary through the cycle, the resulting appearance is not unlike that of butterfly wings (see Figure 7).

A diagram of this type was first plotted by Maunder at the Royal Greenwich Observatory in 1904.

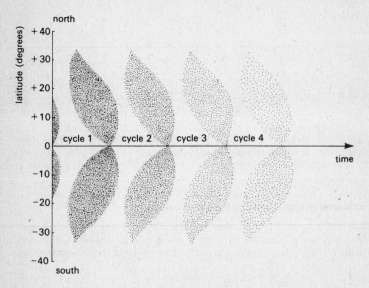

Figure 7. Butterfly diagram. If the position of each sunspot is plotted on a diagram of latitude against time over a series of eleven-year sunspot cycles, the resulting diagram is known as the butterfly diagram. It shows that the spots in a new cycle begin to appear at high latitudes, and as the cycle progresses the mean latitudes tend to decrease. The number of spots reach maximum about five years after the commencement of a cycle. The appearance of the diagram suggests its name.

B–V. ◇COLOUR INDEX.

C

Canals of Mars. Narrow linear markings on the surface of the planet MARS which were first seen in 1877 by the Italian astronomer Giovanni Schiaparelli. These features became the focus of considerable controversy, as it was suggested that they might be literally canals (or strips of vegetation along the banks of canals) constructed by advanced intelligent creatures inhabiting that planet. The dispute was further fuelled by the fact that some highly experienced observers could not see the canals – apart from a few rather broader features which looked reasonably natural – while other observers saw a whole network of them. In particular, the American astronomer Percival Lowell (who built the Flagstaff Observatory in Arizona, in 1884, in order to study these features) mapped about a thousand canals.

There is no doubt now that the majority of these so-called canals were illusory, their appearance probably being due to the tendency of the human eye to join up into lines disconnected features at the limit of visibility. Certainly the close-range mapping achieved by space-probes such as Mariner 9 has revealed no artificial structures on the planet's surface; but it may be that some of the observed 'canals' have a basis in reality, for there are certainly linear valleys and alignments of features on the Martian surface.

Captured rotation. ◊MOON.

Carbon cycle. The nuclear-fusion chain reaction thought to be the dominant energy-producing reaction in hot, highly luminous stars of spectral type earlier than A (◊SPECTRAL CLASSIFICATION). In this reaction, essentially four protons (hydrogen nuclei, denoted by $_1H^1$ where the subscript signifies atomic charge and the superscript atomic mass) are captured in a series of steps involving carbon (C) as a catalyst to form a helium nucleus ($_2He^4$). (◊ATOM.)

The various stages in the cycle are as follows, where C, N, and O are the symbols for carbon, nitrogen, and oxygen respectively, and e^+ denotes a POSITRON, ν a NEUTRINO and γ a quantum of gamma radiation ($\diamond$ GAMMA RAYS):

$$_6C^{12} + _1H^1 \rightarrow _7N^{13} + \gamma$$
$$_7N^{13} \rightarrow _6C^{13} + e^+ + \nu$$
$$_6C^{13} + _1H^1 \rightarrow _7N^{14} + \gamma$$
$$_7N^{14} + _1H^1 \rightarrow _8O^{15} + \gamma$$
$$_8O^{15} \rightarrow _7N^{15} + e^+ + \nu$$
$$_7N^{15} + _1H^1 \rightarrow _6C^{12} + _2He^4$$

Thus the $_6C^{12}$ in the first stage reappears at the end of the cycle, and the four $_1H^1$ build up the $_2He^4$ that appears in the final stage.

The carbon cycle is not thought to be a major contributor to energy production in the Sun, or in stars of type later than A. However, because the energy generation rate for the carbon cycle is much more strongly temperature dependent than is the PROTON–PROTON REACTION, it is thought to be the dominant energy generating process in the hotter early-type stars.

Cassegrain reflector. A type of reflecting TELESCOPE (see Figure 44b) which achieves a long effective FOCAL LENGTH within a quite compact instrument. In the instrument, light is reflected from a parabolic primary mirror, and is intercepted *before* the focus by a convex hyperbolic mirror which reflects the converging light cone (at the same time reducing its convergence) back through a hole in the centre of the primary, to an eyepiece mounting (see Figure 44b). Typically, the FOCAL RATIO of the primary might be f:5, with an effective focal ratio at the Cassegrain focus of f:15.

This is the most common optical system encountered in medium-sized telescopes. Medium- and large-sized telescopes normally combine a number of different optical systems (e.g. Newtonian–Cassegrain, or Cassegrain–coudé).

Cassini division. $\diamond$ SATURN.

Celestial coordinates. The coordinates of celestial bodies are normally measured on the celestial sphere using one of a number of systems. In each system there is a fundamental reference plane (i.e. a great circle on the celestial sphere) and position is expressed in terms of one coordinate measured parallel to this plane, and another measured perpendicular to the plane. The systems normally used are as follows:

The horizon system: the fundamental plane is the observer's *horizon*, and position is measured in terms of ALTITUDE (perpendicular to the horizon) and AZIMUTH. Due to diurnal rotation, both of these coordinates are continually changing.

The equatorial systems: the fundamental plane is the CELESTIAL EQUATOR, and position is measured in terms of DECLINATION (perpendicular to the celestial equator), and either HOUR ANGLE or RIGHT ASCENSION.

The ecliptic system: the fundamental plane is the ECLIPTIC, and position is measured in terms of CELESTIAL LATITUDE (perpendicular to the ecliptic) and CELESTIAL LONGITUDE.

Another system which may be encountered is galactic coordinates where the fundamental plane is the galactic equator (the plane of the MILKY WAY) and position is expressed in terms of GALACTIC LATITUDE (perpendicular to the galactic equator) and GALACTIC LONGITUDE.

Celestial equator. The great circle on the CELESTIAL SPHERE obtained by the intersection with the sphere of the plane of the Earth's equator (see Figure 9b).

Celestial latitude. The angular distance between the ECLIPTIC and a celestial body measured in a direction perpendicular to the ecliptic, and

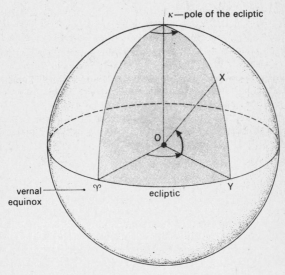

Figure 8. Celestial latitude and longitude. The observer, on the Earth, is imagined to lie at O in the centre of the celestial sphere. The celestial longitude, λ, of the star X is the angle ♈OY (which is equivalent to the spherical angle ♈κX), i.e. the angular distance between the vernal equinox, ♈, and the point Y, measured anticlockwise along the ecliptic (the angle ♈YX being a right angle). The celestial latitude, β, of X is the angle YOX, i.e. the observed angle between the ecliptic and the star, measured perpendicular to the ecliptic.

43

taking values between 0 and 90 degrees. The position of a celestial body may be expressed in terms of celestial latitude (denoted by β) and CELESTIAL LONGITUDE (see Figure 8). ($\Diamond$CELESTIAL COORDINATES.)

Celestial longitude. The angle between the great circle passing through the poles of the ECLIPTIC and the VERNAL EQUINOX, and the great circle passing through these poles and a celestial object, measured in an anticlockwise (i.e. eastward) direction from the vernal equinox. In other words, it is the angular distance measured along the ecliptic between the vernal equinox and the point on the ecliptic such that the angle between the vernal equinox, this point, and a star is a right angle (see Figure 8). Planetary positions are sometimes expressed in terms of celestial longitude (denoted λ) and CELESTIAL LATITUDE. ($\Diamond$CELESTIAL COORDINATES.)

Celestial mechanics. The study of the motions of celestial bodies moving in gravitational fields.

Celestial poles. The points on the CELESTIAL SPHERE at which the projected axis of the Earth intersects the sphere (see Figure 9b). The north celestial pole is thus vertically above the terrestrial north pole, and the south celestial pole vertically above the south terrestrial pole; the ALTITUDE (1) of the north celestial pole is equal to the latitude of an observer on the Earth's surface, and since there is a star (Polaris, the Pole Star) close to the north celestial pole, it is possible for an observer in the northern hemisphere to obtain a rough estimate of his latitude simply by measuring the altitude of the Pole Star. Due to the rotation of the Earth, stars appear to move in circles centred on the celestial poles.

Celestial sphere. An imaginary sphere of very large radius, centred on the Earth, and to which the stars are considered to be fixed for the purposes of position measurement (see Figure 9). Due to the rotation of the Earth on its axis, the celestial sphere appears to rotate round the Earth once a day, and it is convenient to imagine that it is the Earth which is stationary, and the sphere which rotates. The sphere is therefore considered to rotate about an axis joining north and south CELESTIAL POLES in an east to west direction (i.e. clockwise) at a rate of 15 degrees per hour (of SIDEREAL TIME). At any instant, an observer at a particular point on the Earth's surface can see only one half of the sphere; if he is located at one of the poles, one hemisphere is permanently above the horizon, while at the opposite extreme, if he is located at the equator, then each part of the sphere is visible at some time. ($\Diamond$CIRCUMPOLAR STARS.)

In ancient times, and up to the seventeenth century, it was widely accepted that the stars really were attached to such a sphere which

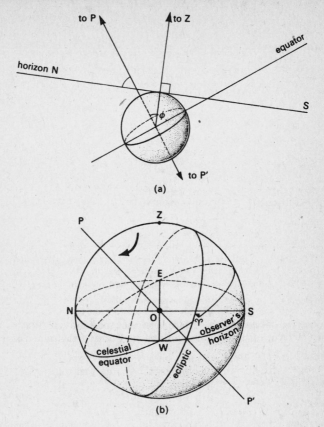

Figure 9. Celestial sphere. (a) An observer, O, is located at a particular latitude (denoted by angle ϕ) on the surface of the Earth. Vertically above him lies the zenith, Z. The celestial sphere is an imaginary sphere having the Earth as its centre and being very large compared to the Earth. The axis of the Earth projected outwards meets the celestial sphere in the north and south celestial poles, P and P' respectively in (b), and the equator projected cuts the sphere in the celestial equator. For the observer in question, the plane of the horizon bisects the sphere; at any instant he can see only one hemisphere.

The vernal equinox, ♈, is the point of intersection of the celestial equator and the ecliptic. The altitude of the north celestial pole (angle NOP) is equal to the observer's latitude on the Earth. N, E, S and W are the north, east, south and west points of the observer's horizon. The Earth rotates from west to east so that the celestial sphere *appears* to rotate from east to west.

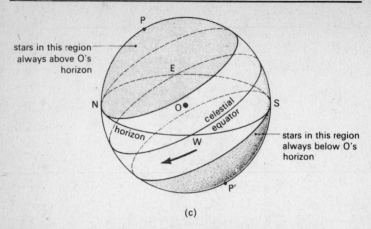

(c)

Figure 9. (c) Circumpolar stars. As the sphere rotates, stars in the region of the sphere bounded by the arc PN lie permanently above the observer's horizon and are called circumpolar stars. Stars in the region bounded by the arc P'S never rise above his horizon. Stars which are circumpolar for a particular observer depend upon his latitude.

rotated round the Earth. Although we know that the stars lie at very different distances and that the celestial sphere has no real existence, it is still convenient to retain the concept for positional astronomy.

Central force. A force which is always directed towards a particular point or centre. An example of this is the gravitational attraction of the Sun on a planet; this force is always directed towards the Sun.

Centre of mass. ♢BARYCENTRE.

Centrifugal force. That 'force' experienced by a revolving body which tends to propel it away from the point around which it is revolving. It is equal in magnitude but opposite in direction to the centripetal force, the force attracting the body towards the centre and preventing its flying away. A familiar example of centrifugal force is the sideways force apparently experienced by the occupant of a car which is turning a sharp corner; or, again, it is the force exerted on a string to which a revolving weight is attached. We usually say that the weight maintains a circular motion because the inward pull exerted by the string (the centripetal force) is equal and opposite to the outward-acting centrifugal force resulting from the motion of the weight. For a body of mass, m, revolving at speed, V, at distance, R, from the centre, we can say that,

$$\text{centrifugal force} = mV^2/R.$$

In these terms we can say that a satellite in a circular orbit round the Earth remains in that orbit because it is moving at such a speed that the centrifugal force exactly balances the gravitational attraction of the Earth on the satellite (⟡CIRCULAR VELOCITY).

Strictly speaking, centrifugal force is not a 'force' in the sense that we regard, say, gravitational attraction. It is an apparent force which arises as a consequence of the INERTIA – i.e. resistance to acceleration – of all massive bodies. A body which is subject to a constant acceleration towards a centre (such as a revolving weight, or an artificial Earth satellite in circular orbit) will move in a circular path, and the constant centrifugal force experienced by it arises because of its resistance to this acceleration. According to NEWTON'S LAWS OF MOTION, a body continues in a state of uniform, straight-line motion unless acted upon by a force. If the centripetal force were removed (e.g. by cutting the string holding the weight) the body would fly off in a straight line in the direction in which it was heading at the instant the force ceased, i.e. in the tangential direction. The body does *not* fly off in the radial direction (i.e. directly away from the centre) as would be expected if centrifugal force were a 'real' force.

Although, in strict terms, centrifugal force is an 'apparent' force rather than a 'real' one, the fact remains that the concept of centrifugal force allows us to describe the motion of orbiting bodies in very simple terms, and to obtain useful formulas to describe such motion.

Centripetal force.   ⟡CENTRIFUGAL FORCE.

Cepheid variable. A type of VARIABLE STAR named after Delta Cephei, the first star of this type to be recognized. Cepheids vary in a very regular way over periods of one to sixty days, and for classical Cepheids (there are several categories of Cepheids) the variation in ABSOLUTE MAGNITUDE amounts to between 0·5 and 1 magnitude. During the variation, the star expands and contracts, and the effective temperature and spectral class vary too. Such stars are giants and highly luminous, with absolute magnitudes of from -2 to -6.

What makes Cepheids particularly important is a relationship between their luminosities and their periods of variation – the period–luminosity relation discovered in 1908 by Miss Henrietta Leavitt. Basically, the longer the period, the more luminous the star (the period–luminosity relationship differs for Cepheids of Population I and Population II (⟡STELLAR POPULATIONS) since the former type are intrinsically more luminous than the latter, for a given value of period). This means that by measuring the period of a Cepheid one can obtain its absolute magnitude from the period–luminosity relationship and, by comparing this with its observed apparent magnitude, deduce the distance of the star (⟡DISTANCE MODULUS). Since Cepheids are highly luminous, they can be seen over great distances and have proved to be vital 'standard candles' for distance measurement in the universe. For example, the distance to the ANDROMEDA GALAXY was first established by observing Cepheid variables within it.

Ceres. The largest of the ASTEROIDS, and the first one of these to be discovered. It was first detected on 1 January 1801 by G. Piazzi working at the Palermo Observatory, Sicily. It has a diameter of about 800 km, and moves round the Sun in an elliptical orbit of semi-major axis 2·77 astronomical units, eccentricity 0·08, and period 4·61 years. (◊ BODE'S LAW.)

Chandrasekhar limit. ◊ STELLAR EVOLUTION.

Chemical element. ◊ ATOM.

Chromatic aberration. A fundamental defect of simple lenses. Due to the fact that different wavelengths of light are refracted by differing amounts in a glass lens – long-wave light (red) is refracted least, short-wave light (blue) is refracted most – each wavelength of light is focused at a different distance from the lens (see Figure 10a). Since white light is made up of a combination of all colours, it follows that any image formed by the lens will be surrounded and to some extent blurred by coloured fringes produced by out-of-focus light.

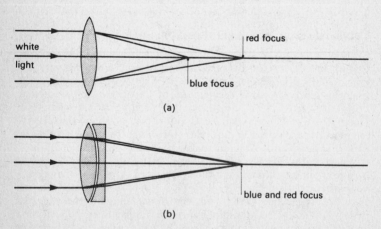

Figure 10. Chromatic aberration and the achromatic lens. In the simple lens (a) all different wavelengths of light are focused at different distances behind the lens. Thus, the blue focus is closer to the lens than is the red focus. The achromatic lens (b) is a compound lens, consisting of two components ground from different types of glass. By careful selection of the refractive indices of the glass and the curvatures of the surfaces of the lenses, two colours can be brought to the same focus.

This defect severely limited the performance of the early astronomical refractors ($\diamond$ TELESCOPE), but it can be overcome to a considerable extent by the use of compound ACHROMATIC LENSES (see Figure 10b).

Chromosphere. That layer of the Sun's atmosphere which lies directly above the visible surface or PHOTOSPHERE ($\diamond$ SUN, Figure 43). It is a rarefied region, the lower part of which is relatively cool (about 4200 K); the temperature increases to 8000 K at an altitude of 1500 km, and rapidly thereafter until the layer merges with the CORONA. The lower part of the chromosphere is known as the reversing layer, and it is here that the dark absorption lines in the solar SPECTRUM are produced ($\diamond$ KIRCHHOFF'S LAWS OF SPECTROSCOPY; FRAUNHOFER LINES). The layer cannot normally be seen visually without special equipment except during a total eclipse of the Sun; it is a brilliant red colour.

Circular velocity. The velocity of a body moving in a circular orbit round a massive body, e.g. a satellite in circular orbit round the Earth, or a planet in circular orbit round the Sun ($\diamond$ ORBIT, Figure 28). For a satellite at distance, R, from the centre of a body of mass, M, the circular velocity, V_c, is

$$V_c = \sqrt{(GM/R)}$$

where G is the GRAVITATIONAL CONSTANT.

For a satellite in close orbit round the Earth, $V_c = 7.8$ km per second. Clearly, circular velocity diminishes with distance; thus a SYNCHRONOUS SATELLITE at a distance of 42000 km requires a velocity of 2.9 km per second; while the Moon, at a mean distance of 384000 km, moves at 1 km per second.

The formula for circular velocity is easily deduced by equating the gravitational attraction experienced by a satellite of mass, m, GmM/R^2, to the CENTRIFUGAL FORCE, mV_c^2/R.

Circumpolar stars. Stars which are permanently above the horizon for an observer located at a particular latitude on the surface of the Earth, i.e. they do not rise and set. The apparent daily rotation of the CELESTIAL SPHERE causes stars to appear to trace out a circular path in the sky, centred on the celestial pole (see Figure 9c). For an observer whose latitude is ϕ, the altitude of the celestial pole above his horizon is ϕ degrees; it follows that any stars which lie within ϕ degrees of the celestial pole will trace out circles which never touch the horizon. For an observer located at the north pole, the celestial pole will be vertically overhead, and the stars will trace out circles parallel to the horizon; thus half of the celestial sphere is permanently visible, and the other half remains permanently below the horizon. For an observer at the equator, the north and south celestial poles lie on the horizon and no stars are circumpolar (as the year progresses all parts of the celestial sphere will be seen at one time or another). For intermediate latitudes, some stars are circumpolar, some rise and set, and the remainder are never seen.

Clusters of galaxies.   Galaxies tend to be found in clusters containing from a few to a few thousand member galaxies. Our own Galaxy is a member of a small cluster, the LOCAL GROUP. It has been argued that the Local Group together with other clusters form a supercluster. (See Plate 24.)

Colour index.   An indication of the colour of a star obtained by measuring the difference in brightness of the star when it is observed through different colour filters. For example, if measurements of a star's APPARENT MAGNITUDE are made through a filter which transmits blue (B) light and through a yellow (V) filter, the difference between these two magnitudes is the B–V colour index. By convention, the B filter is chosen to transmit a band of light centred on a wavelength of 0·44 micron (4.4×10^{-7} m), and the V filter is centred on a wavelength of 0·55 micron.

The B–V colour index is defined to be 0 for a star of spectral type A0 (◊SPECTRAL CLASSIFICATION), such as the star Vega; SIRIUS also has B–V = 0. A very hot blue star will emit most of its radiation in the blue and ultra-violet part of the spectrum; consequently it will emit *more* radiation in the B waveband than in the V band. Since we define magnitude in such a way that the brighter the object, the lower the value of magnitude, it follows that this star will have a *lower* value of magnitude at the B waveband than at the V band. The B–V colour index will therefore be negative. Stars cooler than those of spectral type A0 will emit more radiation at the V band than in the B band; such stars will have positive values of B–V (◊HERTZSPRUNG–RUSSELL DIAGRAM, Figure 24). Examples of B–V colour indices are given below:

Star	Colour	B–V	Spectral type
Spica	blue	−0·23	B1 V
Vega	white	0	A0 V
Sun	yellow	+0·65	G2 V
Betelgeuse	red	+1·86	M2 I

Other colour indices are defined by different filters. For example the U (ultra-violet) filter, which transmits around a wavelength of 0·36 micron, is used to define the U–B colour index. For fuller details of filters, ◊PHOTOMETRY.

Combustion. The process whereby a substance is combined with oxygen with the production of heat. Burning is a familiar example of this process. The energy required to propel chemical rockets is provided by the combustion of fuel with an oxidant (⬦OXIDIZER) at very high temperatures.

Comet. A minor and rather insubstantial member of the Solar System, usually revolving round the Sun in a highly elliptical orbit, which *may* become a bright extensive object when near PERIHELION (see Figure 11a). Although we now regard comets merely as cosmic debris, until comparatively recently they were regarded as portents of impending disaster.

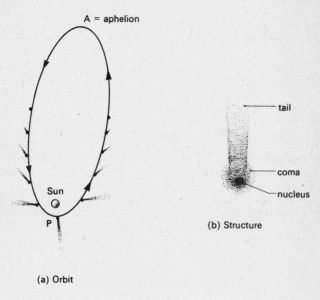

(a) Orbit

(b) Structure

Figure 11. Comet. (a) Most comets move in highly elliptical orbits and only become conspicuous when near perihelion, P, the point of closest approach to the Sun. The tail begins to develop as the comet approaches the Sun, and declines as it recedes. The tail (or tails) always points more or less directly away from the Sun.
(b) A bright comet usually consists of three principal parts, the compact nucleus, the surrounding gas and dust cloud, the coma, and the tenuous tail.

A typical comet consists of three parts, nucleus, coma and tail (see Figure 11b). The nucleus is small, probably no more than a few kilometres across, and contains virtually all the mass of the comet; the most popular theory regards it as being made up of ices of various kinds together with a proportion of small solid particles. The coma is a cloud of gas and dust surrounding the nucleus while the tail is a feature which becomes apparent only when the comet is relatively close to the Sun (usually within 2 astronomical units). There are two main types of tail, type I, usually fairly straight and made up of ionized molecules driven from the coma by the SOLAR WIND, and type II, usually curved, and made up of dust driven out by solar-radiation pressure. In either case, the tail points away from the Sun, following the head of the comet during the approach, and preceding it as the comet recedes.

A popular view is that there exists round the Solar System a vast cloud of comets extending to a radius of about a light year. The number of comets in the cloud has been estimated at between 10^{10} and 10^{11} (the combined mass of which is likely to be less than the mass of Jupiter), and it is thought that they represent condensations of matter from the original solar nebula ($\diamond$SOLAR SYSTEM, ORIGIN OF). Certainly, the composition of comets is similar to that of INTERSTELLAR MATTER.

It is thought that perturbations cause some of these comets to enter orbits which take them close to the Sun to appear as 'new' comets; in some cases, perturbations by the planets place them into elliptical orbits of relatively short period (less than a few hundred years). Such comets, known as periodic comets, lose mass each time they make a close approach to the Sun, and it is evident that the periodic comets which we now observe cannot have been in their present orbits since the formation of the system. The existence of a comet cloud would allow for the 'topping up' of a dwindling population of comets.

When a comet is discovered (or recovered in the case of a periodic comet), it is designated by the year and a letter (a, b, etc.) in order of discovery for the year (e.g. 1977 b). When the orbits of comets have been computed, they are given a number in order of perihelion passage consisting of the year (of perihelion passage) followed by a Roman numeral (thus 1977 II would be the second comet to pass perihelion in 1977). (See Plate 13.)

Comet family. A group of comets, each member of which has a similar value of APHELION distance; this value being close to the mean distance of a particular planet from the Sun. For example, the mean distance of Jupiter from the Sun is 5·2 astronomical units, and the maximum distance from the Sun reached by a considerable number of comets is similar to that value. Since comets have very small masses compared to planetary masses, their orbits may be considerably altered as a result of close encounters with planets; comet families are believed to arise as a result of such encounters. Jupiter, being the most massive planet, has the largest comet family.

Conic. $\diamond$CONIC SECTION.

Conic section. The curve obtained by cutting a right circular cone with a plane which does not pass through the apex of that cone (see Figure 12). If the plane makes an angle relative to the base which is less than the angle of slope of the side of the cone, an ELLIPSE is obtained; if the plane is parallel to the base, the special case of a circle arises. A plane parallel to the side produces a PARABOLA, while a plane making an angle with the base greater than that made by the side produces the HYPERBOLA.

Conic sections are important in astronomy and astronautics as they represent the various forms of orbit which may be followed by a body moving in a gravitational field.

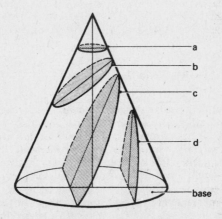

Figure 12. Conic sections. The cone shown here has a circular base and the axis of the cone is perpendicular to the base.

a – a plane parallel to the base cuts the cone in a circle.

b – a plane making an angle with the base less than that made by the side of the cone cuts the cone in an ellipse.

c – a plane parallel to the side of the cone cuts the cone in a parabola.

d – a plane making an angle with the base greater than that made by the side of the cone cuts the cone in a hyperbola.

Conjunction. The alignment or close alignment of two or more astronomical bodies; thus, for example, if the planet Mars and the Moon lie very close together in the sky, Mars is said to be 'in conjunction' with the Moon. (✩ INFERIOR CONJUNCTION; SUPERIOR CONJUNCTION.)

Constellation. A grouping of stars which, in some cases at least, make up a recognizable pattern, and that area of the CELESTIAL SPHERE associated with it. The original constellations were named by ancient civilizations after mythological creatures or inanimate objects; Ptolemy (◊ PTOLEMAIC SYSTEM), in the second century A.D., listed forty-eight constellations and these names are still in use today, although others have since been added (particularly in the southern sky). By international agreement, the celestial sphere has been divided into eighty-eight constellations separated by arcs of circles parallel to and perpendicular to the CELESTIAL EQUATOR.

Perhaps the most conspicuous constellation is Orion (the Hunter), strikingly obvious in the winter sky for observers located in the northern hemisphere (and therefore in the summer sky for southern-hemisphere observers), but the best known is Ursa Major (the Great Bear), the seven brightest stars of which make up the shape known as the Plough (or Big Dipper). Such a group of stars within a constellation is known as an asterism.

It is important to note that the stars making up a constellation are not physically close together, but just happen to lie in more or less the same direction in space as seen from the Earth; thus, some of the stars making up the Plough are further from each other than we are from some of them.

Contamination. A possible danger associated with space exploration is the possibility of contaminating the Earth's environment with living (or toxic) material accidentally brought back from another celestial body by a spacecraft. Although it was fairly certain that the airless Moon was completely sterile, nevertheless precautions were taken to quarantine the returning astronauts of the Apollo 11 to 14 missions to guard against this possibility (◊ APOLLO PROJECT). By Apollo 14 it had become apparent that no such threat existed in the case of the Moon, but it is by no means certain that such a hazard might not exist in the cases of spacecraft returning from Venus or Mars.

The contamination problem certainly exists in the other direction: all planetary spaceprobes are thoroughly sterilized before launch, but even so there remains a small but finite chance of contaminating a planetary environment. In the case of the Moon it has been estimated that the amount of gases added to any tenuous residual atmosphere which the Moon may possess by the Apollo lunar modules' rocket motors may amount to as much as 10 to 20 per cent of the total atmosphere. Due to the rapid rate at which certain terrestrial bacteria can multiply, it is possible that contamination of, say, the atmosphere of Mars by such bacteria (assuming that conditions permitted reproduction) could in a very short time reach such a level that it would become extremely difficult to separate these from any indigenous bacteria.

Continental drift. ◊ EARTH.

Continuous spectrum. ◊ SPECTRUM.

Continuum. ◊SPECTRUM.

Convergent point. ◊HYADES.

Copernican system. The heliocentric (i.e. 'sun-centred') theory proposed by the Polish astronomer Nicolaus Copernicus (1473–1543), and published by him in 1543 in his book, *De Revolutionibus Orbium Coelestium*. In this system Copernicus placed the Sun at the centre of the universe and regarded the Earth and the planets as moving around it in circular orbits. Because of his retention of the notion of circular motion, the theory did not give a perfect description of the apparent motion of the planets in the sky (◊KEPLER'S LAWS), but it did offer some slight improvement over the geocentric PTOLEMAIC SYSTEM.

The idea that the Earth might move round the Sun had been suggested earlier, for example by the Greek philosopher Aristarchus in the third century B.C., but had not then been treated seriously. Despite some quite strong objections by the religious authorities of the period, by the end of the seventeenth century, heliocentric theory was widely accepted.

Corona, Solar. The 'outer atmosphere' of the SUN (see Figure 43), visible to the unaided eye only during a total ECLIPSE of the Sun, when it gives the appearance of a 'halo' round the Sun's obscured disc, extending out to as much as three times the Sun's radius. The corona extends beyond this, merging into the interplanetary medium, but even close to the solar surface its density is very low, less than one million millionth of the density of the Earth's atmosphere at ground level. The mean temperature (which is a measure of the speed at which the particles in the corona are moving) is nearly 2 000 000 K, but the total amount of mass in the corona is very small compared to the mass of the Sun. Most of the visible light from the corona is reflected light originating from the PHOTOSPHERE, but the total amount of light reaching the Earth from the corona is only about one millionth of that received from the photosphere. The corona is also a source of ultraviolet and X-ray emission.

The corona exhibits considerable structure: for example, streamers (regions of higher than average density) and coronal holes (regions of much lower density), and the general shape and structure change throughout the SOLAR CYCLE. The corona may be studied under very good conditions from the Earth by means of the coronagraph, or directly from spacecraft (one of the principal objectives of the Skylab programme was to study the corona). (◊FREE–FREE RADIATION.)

Cosmic rays. Atomic particles (generally protons and atomic nuclei) reaching the Earth from space and travelling at very high speeds, approaching that of light. Such particles cannot penetrate the atmosphere to reach the surface, but they interact in the upper atmosphere giving rise to secondary particles (neutrons, mu-mesons, etc.) which can reach ground level. It is not known where these particles originate (although a small proportion of them come from the Sun), but it has been proposed that they stem from violent events in the GALAXY (2), such as SUPERNOVAE or PULSARS. Alternatively, they may come from beyond the Galaxy, possibly from such enigmatic objects as QUASARS.

Cosmic year. The period of time taken for the Sun to complete one orbit of the galactic centre; this is approximately equal to 225 000 000 years. Since its formation, the Sun has completed about twenty-two circuits round the Galaxy.

Cosmogony. The study of, or theories concerning, the origin of the universe or of its constituent components.

Cosmology. The study of the universe as a whole, its origin, evolution and future development.

There are many cosmological theories. One approach to the problem is to take a theory of the nature of space and time, and on this basis construct a theoretical model of the universe. Most theories today are based on the GENERAL THEORY OF RELATIVITY which indicates that space itself may be curved by the presence of matter. Although this concept is hard to visualize, it implies that the universe could have a finite volume without having a boundary, just as the surface of the Earth has a finite area without having an edge (as Christopher Columbus set out to show). If this is the case then it may be that a ray of light could circumnavigate the universe and return to its original point of emission. On the basis of such models it was shown quite early in this century that the universe is likely either to be expanding or contracting.

For cosmological theories to have any real value, they must be testable, i.e. they must make definite statements about aspects of the universe which can be checked by observation. One of the fundamental observations is of the recession of the galaxies (♢ RED-SHIFT; HUBBLE'S CONSTANT), i.e. that apart from members of the LOCAL GROUP, all the galaxies in the universe are moving away from us with velocities proportional to their distances (e.g. if galaxy A is twice as distant as galaxy B, it will be receding at twice the velocity of B). This does not imply that we lie at the centre of the universe; in fact every galaxy (or cluster of galaxies) is receding from every other one, and whichever galaxy you were observing from, you would see the others appear to be rushing away from you. A helpful analogy is to imagine a balloon covered in spots; as the balloon is blown up each spot moves away from every other one, but no one spot is the centre of the expansion.

If the universe is expanding, and the galaxies are getting further apart, it follows that they must have been closer together in the past. If we continue to look further back in time, we should arrive at a time when all the galaxies were clumped together; on current estimates, this state of affairs occurred between ten and twenty thousand million years ago (the 'age' of the universe may be estimated from Hubble's constant, H; in fact, 'age' = 1/H).

A current theory embodying this concept is the so-called BIG-BANG THEORY, according to which the universe originated as an extremely dense hot FIREBALL (of matter and radiation) which exploded, and, as it expanded, cooled sufficiently for matter to form (⊳HELIUM PROBLEM) into galaxies; the observed expansion of the universe, according to this theory, is a result of its explosive origin.

An alternative theory, put forward in 1948 by Bondi, Gold and Hoyle, was the Steady-State theory. This was built around the 'perfect cosmological principle' that the overall appearance of the universe is everywhere the same in space *and* time. The implication was that the universe never had a beginning and will never end; as old galaxies evolve and move apart, new galaxies are formed from matter which was supposed to be *continuously created* in space.

There are a number of ways in which astronomers can attempt to distinguish between rival theories. An important point is that the further we look into space, the further back in time we are seeing (for example, light from a galaxy at a range of a thousand million light years has taken that length of time to reach us). According to the Steady-State theory, the appearance of the universe thousands of millions of years ago should be essentially the same as now, while the Big-Bang theory would suggest that the appearance would be different (the galaxies being closer together). In principle, by observing distant objects, it should be possible to eliminate one of these possibilities.

In practice, the types of observation which have been undertaken have been *source counts*, where the number of galaxies or radio sources above certain values of brightness are counted and compared with the predictions of the theories. These observations indicate fairly conclusively that the universe is evolving with time; this implies that the Steady-State theory is untenable (at least in its original form) and that the Big-Bang theory is more acceptable.

Of the utmost importance was the discovery in 1965 of the MICRO-WAVE BACKGROUND RADIATION (weak cool BLACK-BODY radiation approaching us from all directions); the existence of such radiation is just what would be expected if the universe had a Big-Bang origin.

Although the Big-Bang theory is quite widely accepted, there is considerable controversy over the future of the universe. Either the expansion will continue forever or, if the amount of matter in the universe is sufficiently great, mutual gravitational attraction will slow the expansion to an eventual halt. Thereafter, the galaxies would begin to rush together again until, once more, they were packed

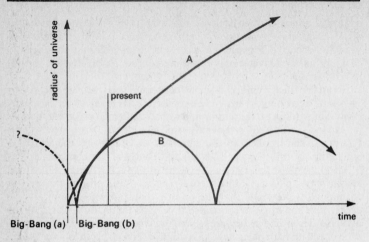

Figure 13. Expanding and oscillating universe. At present we believe that the universe is expanding; its 'radius' therefore is increasing with time. If the mean density of the universe is less than the critical density, the rate of expansion should tend to a steady value and the universe will expand forever (curve A). If the mean density is greater than this value, the expansion will slow down and eventually cease, to be followed by a contraction phase. It may be that the universe expands and contracts in a cyclic way (B) and may, indeed, have been doing so in the past – this is the oscillating universe theory. According to this theory the big bang occurred more recently than theory A suggests. Current evidence tends to support A.

together again. It has been suggested that this would be followed by a new 'Big-Bang' and a new expansion phase. This is the oscillating universe theory, which supposes that the universe expands and contracts in a cyclic fashion and may continue to do so in the future and may have been doing so in the past, too (see Figure 13).

Observations are being made to try to distinguish between these possibilities. One approach is to try to measure the rate at which the expansion is slowing down (the *deceleration parameter*), but results to date are inconclusive. Another approach is to try to estimate the mean density of matter in the universe. There is a *critical density* which, if exceeded, implies that the expansion must eventually cease (and would support the oscillating universe concept); if we accept the current value of Hubble's constant, this critical density is about 5×10^{-27} kg m^{-3} (this value depends upon H^2, so that each revision of Hubble's constant has a marked effect on the value). Current observations indicate that the mean density of the universe is less than a tenth of the critical density, and this implies that the universe may expand without limit.

However, it is still too early to make such a definite assertion, as our uncertainty in our knowledge on the amount of matter in the universe is very high (e.g. ♢INTERGALACTIC MATTER).

In conclusion, the current status of theory and observation favours a Big-Bang universe which is likely to expand indefinitely. The Steady-State theory (which was in many ways philosophically satisfying, as it had no need of a 'beginning' for the universe) is untenable as it stands, but the oscillating universe remains a possibility. The oscillating universe is satisfying in the sense that it, too, need not have a *unique* beginning, and it allows a universe which is finite yet unbounded (circumventing the awkward concept of infinite space). We should not be dogmatic, however; it may well be that none of the present theories stand up to the test of future observations.

Cosmos series. A blanket title covering the series of artificial Earth satellites which embraces the major part of Soviet space activity. The Cosmos series includes scientific satellites (studying, for example, the EXOSPHERE, the space environment of the Earth, GEODESY, etc.), and satellites devoted to, for example, meteorology, military reconnaissance and prototypes of manned spacecraft. A considerable degree of standardization has been achieved, particularly with the smaller scientific satellites and their launch vehicles, these satellites being constructed from standard basic modules.

The first of the series, Cosmos 1, was launched on 16 March 1962, and since that time – although some years have seen considerably more launchings than others – the average rate of launching Cosmos satellites has been one per week. By February 1976, the number of launchings had passed 800.

Coudé focus. A fixed-focus position, usually of very long effective FOCAL LENGTH, used with large reflectors. With such a focus, it is possible to have a spectrograph (of high dispersion) permanently mounted. (♢TELESCOPE, Figure 44b.)

Crab Nebula. A turbulent expanding cloud of gas which is a source of visible light, radio waves and most forms of ELECTROMAGNETIC RADIATION. Also known as M1 (i.e. the first object in the catalogue of nebulae and star clusters produced in the eighteenth century by Charles Messier), its name stems from a comment on its appearance made by the third Earl of Rosse who observed it in the nineteenth century with his 1·8-metre (72-inch) reflecting telescope. The nebula is located in the constellation Taurus, and lies at a distance of about 5000 light years.

The Crab Nebula coincides in position with a SUPERNOVA which was observed by Chinese astronomers in the year 1054 as a 'guest star' which appeared in the sky, became temporarily bright enough to be seen in daylight, then faded from view in a few months; there is little doubt that the observed gas cloud represents the remnants of a star which exploded. Within the nebula is located a PULSAR, emitting pulses in the radio, optical and X-ray regions of the spectrum, which, with a period of 0·033 seconds, is the fastest known pulsar. Pulsars are now considered to be due to highly compact and rapidly rotating NEUTRON STARS; the discovery of a pulsar in the Crab Nebula strengthens the view that neutron stars are the collapsed remnants of supernovae. (See Plate 18.)

Craters. ⟡MOON.

Critical density. ⟡COSMOLOGY.

Culmination. ⟡TRANSIT.

Cyclops Project. A project carried out in the USA in 1971 which was directed towards the optimization of techniques for the detection of signals from extraterrestrial technological civilizations, assuming such to exist (⟡INTELLIGENT LIFE IN THE UNIVERSE). The results suggested that the optimum frequencies for INTERSTELLAR COMMUNICATION lie in the microwave region of the spectrum where the background noise from astronomical sources is at a minimum.

If the assumption is made that advanced civilizations will wish to advertise their presence to the rest of the universe by having a beacon transmitting at such frequencies, then it should be possible, with existing techniques, to construct an array of radio dishes, covering an area 5 km in diameter, which could detect a 1000-megawatt beacon out to a range of about 1000 light years. Within that range there are about one million stars similar to the Sun and likely to have planets. However, the cost of such a project would be comparable with the entire Apollo programme.

Cygnus A. A radio galaxy, the second strongest radio source in the sky, which lies in the constellation of Cygnus. It was discovered in 1946, and was the first discrete cosmic radio source to be detected. It is associated with a galaxy at a distance of nearly 1000 million light years, the radio source being much larger than the visible galaxy, and presumably due to radiation emitted from a cloud of matter expelled from the galaxy.

Cygnus X-1. A powerful X-ray source in the constellation Cygnus which was originally discovered by the US satellite UHURU, and later identified as coinciding in position with a visible star, HDE 226 868. Investigation showed that the visible star, itself a hot, highly luminous star of spectral type O9 or B0 (⟡SPECTRAL CLASSIFICATION) and with an estimated mass of 30 solar masses (C. T. Bolton, 1972), was orbiting an invisible object in a period of 5·6 days. The mass of the invisible object has been estimated at between 6 and 15 solar masses. Such a massive invisible object cannot be a normal star, white dwarf or neutron star, and it has been postulated that it is a BLACK HOLE. The rapid fluctuation in intensity of the X-ray source indicates that the source is small, while spectroscopic evidence suggests that matter is flowing from the visible star. A popular model suggests that the X-rays are being emitted from a disc of gas, drawn from the visible star, and orbiting close to the event horizon or boundary of the black hole (⟡X-RAY ASTRONOMY, Figure 48). Although Cygnus X-1 is the best current candidate for being a black hole, other explanations may be possible and, although the evidence is compelling, we should be wary of considering the evidence as definite proof of the existence of black holes.

D

Daedalus Project. A study undertaken by the British Interplanetary Society to investigate the feasibility of producing a design for an interstellar spacecraft capable of reaching the nearer stars in periods of a few decades, and using only existing or foreseeable technology. The initial conclusions were that it might be possible to employ a nuclear pulse rocket (i.e. a rocket propelled by a series of controlled thermonuclear explosions) to achieve an effective EXHAUST VELOCITY of the order of 10000 km per second (thousands of times better than existing rockets).

With a MASS RATIO (2) of the order of 150, it would then be possible to reach a velocity of one-sixth of the speed of light; a proposed payload of 500 tonnes would imply an initial mass of some 150000 tonnes (constructed in orbit above the Earth).

A possible target for such a mission might be BARNARD'S STAR, at a range of 6 light years, which is thought to have a planetary system, and which could be reached in about 40 years. The probe would pass through the system at one-sixth the speed of light, and radio data back to Earth.

Clearly there are many practical and economic difficulties in the way of such a project; although such a craft is unlikely to be constructed in the foreseeable future, the concepts discussed are interesting and realistic ones.

Dark nebula. A cloud of gas and small solid particles (◊INTERSTELLAR MATTER) in which the dust particles absorb and scatter light from stars lying beyond the cloud. The cloud therefore appears as a dark patch against the starry background. The mean density of dust particles in such clouds is very low, only about 10^{-21} kg m^{-3}, but the volume of these clouds is such that they may contain many times the mass of the Sun in the form of absorbing material. Perhaps the best-known example of a dark nebula is the 'Coal Sack', a dark patch in the Milky Way, clearly visible to the naked eye near the Southern Cross. This particular cloud is about 25 light years in diameter and contains about 15 solar masses in the form of absorbing material.

Deceleration parameter. ◊COSMOLOGY.

Declination. The angular distance of a celestial body north or south of the CELESTIAL EQUATOR; i.e. the angle between the celestial equator and a star, measured in a direction perpendicular to the celestial equator. Declination may take values between 0 and 90 degrees, and is taken to be positive for an object north of the celestial equator, and negative for an object south of the celestial equator. Declination is often abbreviated to dec, or denoted by δ. The position of a star is normally expressed in terms of RIGHT ASCENSION (see Figure 36) and declination. (⟡ CELESTIAL COORDINATES.)

Deferent. ⟡ EPICYCLE.

Degenerate matter. ⟡ WHITE DWARF.

Deimos. The smaller of the two tiny moons of the planet Mars. It was discovered by Asaph Hall in 1877 and is now known to be an irregular rocky body only about 12 km in diameter. The first detailed photograph, showing its cratered surface, was obtained by the US spaceprobe Mariner 9 in 1971. At its mean distance from the planet of 23 000 km, it takes 1·26 days to complete an orbit, a period only five and a half hours longer than the AXIAL PERIOD of Mars itself. From the surface of Mars, Deimos would be seen to move across the sky very slowly from east to west, taking four and a half days between successive risings.

Density. The amount of mass contained within a unit volume of material. The mean density of an astronomical body, such as a star or a planet, is simply equal to its mass divided by its volume; in practice, however, the density of such a body increases towards the centre. Thus, for example, the density of the surface rocks on the Earth is about half the mean density, while the central density is about two and a half times the mean value. Astronomical bodies exhibit a wide range of densities; examples are given below, taking the density of water (1000 kg per cubic metre) as unity.

Object	Mean density (water = 1)	Mean density ($kg\ m^{-3}$)
Neutron star (typical)	10^{15}	10^{18}
White dwarf (typical)	10^{5}	10^{8}
Earth	5·5	$5·5 \times 10^{3}$
Jupiter	1·3	$1·3 \times 10^{3}$
Sun	1·4	$1·4 \times 10^{3}$
Red giant (typical)	10^{-4}	10^{-1}
Red supergiant (typical)	10^{-7}	10^{-4}
Interstellar gas cloud	10^{-23}	10^{-20}

The current estimated value for the mean density of matter in the universe, based on observations of galaxies, is of the order of 10^{-28} kg m^{-3}, i.e. about 10^{-31} times the density of water.

Deuterium. A heavy isotope of hydrogen; a deuterium nucleus, or deuteron, contains one proton and one neutron and is denoted as either $_1H^2$ or $_1D^2$. Nuclear FUSION reactions involving deuterium (available in water) should release about ten times as much energy per unit mass of fuel as is released by the fission reactions employed in nuclear power stations.

Diamond ring effect. An effect observed at the onset and end of the totality phase in a total eclipse of the Sun. Just as the extreme edge of the Sun's disc is about to disappear behind (or emerge from behind) the Moon's disc, a bright flash of sunlight is seen, giving the impression of a diamond ring.

Diffraction grating. A plate ruled with a series of finely spaced parallel lines (usually about 6000 or 12000 lines per centimetre) which by reflection (reflection grating) or by transmission (transmission grating) produces a spectrum of incident light. One of the greatest advantages of the diffraction grating over the conventional prism is that the dispersion (i.e. the spread of wavelengths of light) is uniform. (◊SPECTROGRAPH.)

Direct and retrograde motion. Figure 14 illustrates the motions of the planets Earth and Mars round the Sun, and the apparent motion of Mars in the sky as seen from the Earth. Most of the time Mars moves in a west–east (i.e. right to left) direction in the sky; this is direct motion. However, as the Earth overtakes Mars (positions 3 to 5) Mars appears to move retrograde (i.e. east to west, or left to right) relative to the background stars.

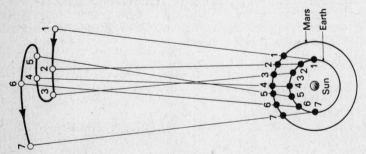

Figure 14. Direct and retrograde motion.

Discrete radio source. ◊RADIO SOURCE.

Distance determination in the universe. There are many methods of distance determination employed by astronomers; essentially, though, the greater the distance, the more steps are required in the chain of reasoning needed to obtain a value of distance, and the greater the possible errors in the results.

Within the Solar System, planetary PARALLAX (see Figure 30) and, more recently, radar techniques ($\Diamond$RADAR ASTRONOMY) are employed, and these have led to the determination of the ASTRONOMICAL UNIT to an accuracy of the order of one part in 10^8. Beyond the Solar System, distances to the nearest stars may be obtained with good accuracy by the method of trigonometrical parallax; however, the best possible measurements are limited to an accuracy of ± 0.01 seconds of arc, and beyond 100 parsecs are wholly unreliable. In fact, the results are only really good out to about 30 parsecs (about 100 light years).

Measurements of MOVING CLUSTERS of stars, and the technique of statistical parallaxes, extend the possible range of measurement to some 500 parsecs. For large distances there are two basic methods: the DISTANCE MODULUS (comparison of the observed brightness of an object with its theoretical luminosity; $\Diamond$CEPHEID VARIABLES); and the comparison of apparent and theoretical diameters (e.g. if a bright luminous nebula has a diameter of, say, forty light years, and its apparent angular size is 1 second of arc, we can calculate that its distance must be about 8 000 000 light years).

Distances to the nearer galaxies are calculated by means of the distance modulus applied to individual objects (such as Cepheid variables) within them. With larger distances, either of the two methods may be employed, depending on the individual objects which can be recognized. Beyond a few hundred million light years, it becomes necessary to look at the properties of individual galaxies or clusters of galaxies in order to estimate distance.

Finally, the velocity of recession of galaxies, as indicated by their RED-SHIFTS, can be used to give a value of distance based on HUBBLE'S CONSTANT. By this means it has been estimated that the most distant objects so far observed lie at distances in excess of ten thousand million light years.

Distance modulus. The difference between the absolute magnitude, M, and apparent magnitude, m, of a star, $M-m$, is an indicator of the distance of that star. Since we know that the apparent brightness of a star diminishes as the square of its distance (i.e. if we double the distance, brightness is reduced to one-quarter), and absolute magnitude is defined to be the apparent magnitude which a star would have if it were at a distance of 10 parsecs, it can be shown that:

$$M - m = 5 - 5 \log_{10} d$$

where d is the distance of the star in parsecs.

This relationship is of fundamental importance in the determination of distance in the universe. Beyond about 100 parsecs, PARALLAX cannot be determined with any accuracy, and indirect distance-measuring techniques must be employed. If the absolute magnitude of a star can be estimated (e.g. by looking at the spectrum of the star), then a comparison of this with its observed apparent magnitude yields the distance.

The distances to galaxies, for example, can be obtained in this way. The distance to the Andromeda Galaxy (M31) was first obtained by identifying stars in it of the CEPHEID VARIABLE type, estimating their absolute magnitudes from their periods of variation, and comparing these with the apparent magnitudes.

Doppler effect.   The wavelength of radiation received from a source of light which is moving relative to the observer differs from the wavelength of the emitted light (λ) by an amount, $\varDelta\lambda$, which depends upon the relative radial velocity of the source and the observer. If the source is approaching, the received radiation will be of shorter wavelength (i.e. 'bluer') than the radiation that would be received from a stationary source, while if the source is receding, the observed radiation will have a longer wavelength (i.e. it will appear 'redder') ($\lozenge$ SPECTROSCOPIC BINARY, Figure 40). This principle was first suggested by the German mathematician Christian Doppler in 1842. In 1848, the French physicist, Hippolyte Fizeau, showed that the wavelengths of lines in the spectrum of a moving source would be affected in the same way; thus, for example, absorption lines in the spectrum of a receding star would be shifted towards the long-wave (red) end of the spectrum, compared to the same lines produced from a stationary source (i.e. the lines would be 'red-shifted'). Thus, the RADIAL VELOCITY of a source of radiation may be determined from the displacement ($\varDelta\lambda$) of the spectral lines.

For values of velocity, v, which are small compared to the speed of light (c), we have

$$\varDelta\lambda/\lambda = v/c.$$

If the relative velocity of source and observer is an appreciable fraction of the speed of light, the relativistic expression

$$\varDelta\lambda/\lambda = [(c+v)/(c-v)]^{\frac{1}{2}} - 1$$

must be used.

The Doppler effect provides the means in astronomy of determining the velocities of stars and galaxies, rotational velocities, and so on.

Double star.   A pair of stars close together in the sky. There are two types, optical doubles and binaries. An optical double is made up of two stars which appear to be close together only because they happen to lie in almost exactly the same direction as seen from the Earth. The individual stars may lie at very different distances from the Earth and do not form a physically linked system. A BINARY consists of two stars which are close together and which move round their common centre of mass subject to their mutual gravitational attraction.

Drag.　Frictional force opposing motion. Generally speaking, the term is applied to the aerodynamic drag exerted by a planetary atmosphere on a spacecraft. It is this drag effect which causes the decay of the orbits of close Earth satellites; the resistance of the tenuous outer layers of the atmosphere, even at altitudes of a few hundred kilometres, is sufficient to reduce the kinetic energy of a spacecraft and eventually cause it to descend into denser layers and burn up. Aerodynamic drag is also used as a deliberate means of braking a re-entering spacecraft prior to a soft-landing with the aid of parachutes, RETRO-ROCKETS or a combination of both.

E

Early-type star. ▷SPECTRAL CLASSIFICATION.

Earth, The. The third planet in order of distance from the Sun. The Earth is unique in the Solar System in having 70 per cent of its surface covered in water. The internal structure, determined by seismic techniques, is thought to be as follows: there is a central solid nickel–iron inner core of some 1300 km radius, above which lies the liquid nickel–iron outer core, a layer some 2200 km thick. Above this, and extending to within about 30 km of the surface, is the mantle, composed of basic rocks. The outermost layer is the crust, made up of such familiar materials as granite, basalt, etc. At the surface, mean values of temperature and density are 287 K and $2 \cdot 6 \times 10^3$ kg m^{-3} (2·6 times water) respectively, while at the centre, the estimated values are 6400 K and $1 \cdot 3 \times 10^4$ kg m^{-3}.

The distribution of surface features, land masses, mountain chains, etc., is subject to change. Volcanic activity and erosion are obvious examples of this, but in the longer term, convection in the mantle (i.e. the slow circulation of mantle material) exerts a strong influence. The crust is considered to be made up essentially of plates which 'float' on top of the mantle, and which are capable of moving relative to one another. Over hundreds of millions of years this gives rise to the motion of the continents relative to each other (continental drift), while collisions between plates may give rise to the folding of crustal material resulting in the formation of mountain chains, etc.

The atmosphere of the Earth is composed, by volume, of 78 per cent nitrogen, 21 per cent oxygen, and 1 per cent of other constituents (of which water vapour, argon and carbon dioxide are the main contributors). The Earth has a magnetic field (a dipole field such as would be expected if a bar magnet were embedded in the core) which has a strength of about 0·6 gauss near the magnetic poles. The magnetic axis does not exactly coincide with the rotation axis, and is subject to slow changes. The field is believed to be sustained by the circulation of material in the liquid metallic core causing the core to act like a dynamo. The region of influence of the field in the space surrounding the Earth is known as the MAGNETOSPHERE. The Earth has one natural satellite, the MOON.

The Earth remains the only planet on which there is definite evidence of the existence of life.

Earth data

Mean distance from the Sun	149 600 000 km
Orbital eccentricity	0·0167
Orbital inclination	zero (by definition)
Sidereal orbital period	365·2564 days
Axial rotation period	23h 56m 04s
Axial inclination	23° 27′
Mass	$5·976 \times 10^{24}$ kg
Radius (equatorial)	6378·16 km
Mean density	$5·52 \times 10^3$ kg m^{-3}
Surface gravity	9·82 m s^{-2}

Earthshine. The illumination of the dark side of the Moon by light reflected from the Earth; this phenomenon may be seen with the un-aided eye when the Moon is a narrow crescent, and is sometimes referred to as 'the old moon in the new moon's arms'. Because the Earth is larger in area than the Moon and has a higher ALBEDO, the amount of light cast by the 'full Earth' on the Moon exceeds the amount of moonlight received on Earth at full moon by a factor of about one hundred.

Eclipse. The passage of one celestial body through the shadow of another; the eclipsed body then becomes wholly or partly invisible. An eclipse of the Moon occurs when the Moon passes into the shadow cone of the Earth (see Figure 15a) while the term 'eclipse of the Sun' is applied to the obscuring, wholly or partially, of the Sun's disc by the disc of the Moon (Figure 15b); the observer, in fact, lies within the shadow cone of the Moon during such an event as the Moon passes between the Sun and the Earth.

A partial eclipse of the Sun occurs when, seen from a point on the Earth, the Sun is only partly obscured by the Moon's disc; the observer lies within the PENUMBRA of the Moon's shadow. A total eclipse occurs when the Sun is wholly obscured by the Moon's disc, and the observer lies within the UMBRA of the Moon's shadow. Because the Sun and Moon have virtually the same apparent size (the Sun is 400 times larger but 400 times further away than the Moon), the lunar umbra only just reaches to the Earth, so that the region of the Earth's surface from which a total eclipse may be observed is very narrow. The maximum duration of totality, seen from a fixed observing point, is about 7 minutes 40 seconds. If an eclipse occurs with the Moon at APOGEE, the Moon is then sufficiently far away to appear marginally smaller than the Sun, and an annular eclipse (where the rim of the

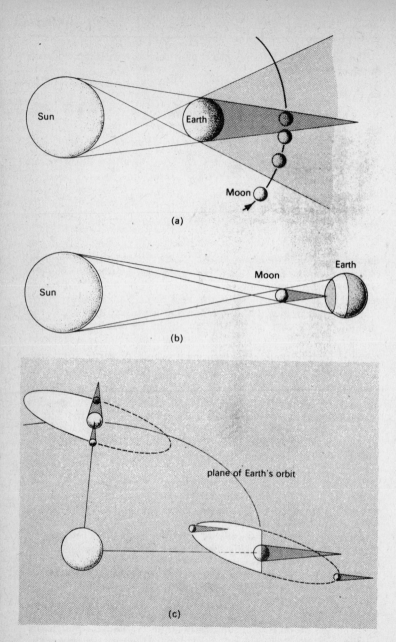

(a)

(b)

plane of Earth's orbit

(c)

Sun's disc remains visible round the dark disc of the Moon) may be observed.

An eclipse of the Moon occurs when the Moon enters the umbra of the Earth's shadow (the Earth's shadow is much wider than the Moon), a total eclipse occurring if the Moon wholly enters the umbra, and a partial eclipse if the Moon partly enters the umbra. When the Moon passes through the penumbra of the Earth's shadow, a penumbral eclipse is said to occur; however, such phenomena are hard to see as the observed appearance of the Moon does not change appreciably.

If the plane of the Moon's orbit lay exactly in the ECLIPTIC, an eclipse of the Sun would occur once every 29·3 days (at each new moon) and an eclipse of the Moon would occur approximately 14 days later, at each full moon. The Moon's orbit is inclined to the ecliptic by about 5° 9′, so that an eclipse can take place only when new or full moon occurs with the Moon near a NODE of its orbit (see Figure 15c). There must be at least two, and up to five, solar eclipses each year, and up to three (and rarely less than two) lunar eclipses each year. As a lunar eclipse can be seen from an entire hemisphere of the Earth, an observer at a particular point is likely to see more lunar eclipses than solar ones.

Eclipsing binary. A BINARY in which the two stars revolve round each other in a plane which lies in the line of sight as seen from the Earth with the result that each star alternately eclipses the other, i.e. passes in front of the other, obscuring it, wholly or partly, from view (see Figure 16). As the stars are too close together to be seen indivi-

Figure 15. Eclipses. (a) An eclipse of the Moon occurs when the Moon enters the shadow of the Earth. The Earth's shadow consists of the dark, central umbra and the lighter, outer penumbra. The Sun is totally obscured for an observer located within the umbra, and partially obscured for an observer within the penumbra. If the Moon enters only the penumbra, a penumbral eclipse occurs with little apparent diminution of the brightness of the Moon. If the Moon partially enters the umbra, it becomes partially eclipsed; while if it wholly enters the umbra, a total eclipse occurs.

(b) A partial eclipse of the Sun is observed from any point on the Earth's surface which lies in the penumbra of the Moon's shadow. A total eclipse of the Sun is observed from within the lunar umbra. The area of the Earth's surface covered by the umbra is very small; therefore total eclipses of the Sun are seen very rarely from any given point on the Earth.

(c) Eclipses of Sun or Moon occur only when new moon or full moon takes place at or near one of the nodes of the Moon's orbit. For example, on the right at new moon, the Moon's shadow passes above the Earth, while at full moon, the Moon passes below the Earth's shadow: no eclipses occur.

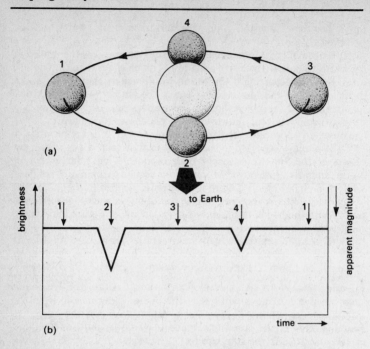

Figure 16. Eclipsing binary. In this hypothetical example we assume, for simplicity, that the brighter star is stationary and that the fainter (shaded) star moves round it (a). In fact the two stars would move round their common centre of mass. Because the two stars lie so close together in the sky, the Earth-based observer sees only the combined light of the two stars appearing as one star which apparently varies in brightness. In this particular example the eclipses are partial. The light-curve (b) shows the apparent brightness of the eclipsing binary: the primary eclipse (2) occurs when the fainter star passes in front of the brighter, this resulting in a greater drop in brightness than when the fainter passes behind the brighter (4) giving rise to the secondary eclipse.

dually, we see what appears to be a single star which periodically fades in brightness as each eclipse occurs. If, as is frequently the case, one star is more luminous than the other then the diminution in brightness will be greater when the faint star eclipses the brighter. The first star of this type to be recognized was Algol, the variation of which may be seen with the naked eye.

Eclipsing binaries are of importance in astronomy, particularly if the spectra of both stars can be observed (i.e. if the star is also a

SPECTROSCOPIC BINARY), for it is then possible in principle to determine the orbital parameters, the masses and diameters, of the member stars.

Ecliptic. A great circle on the CELESTIAL SPHERE which represents the apparent annual path of the Sun in its motion relative to the background stars (see Figure 9b). Due to the motion of the Earth round the Sun, the Sun appears to move across the celestial sphere, completing one full circuit in a YEAR ($\diamond$ZODIAC, Figure 49). The ecliptic, in fact, represents the intersection of the orbital plane of the Earth with the celestial sphere and, because the equator of the Earth is inclined by an angle of approximately $23\frac{1}{2}°$ to the orbital plane, it follows that the ecliptic is inclined to the celestial equator by the same amount (the obliquity of the ecliptic). The ecliptic intersects the celestial equator at two points, the vernal equinox and the autumnal equinox ($\diamond$EQUINOX).

Ecosphere. The region of space around the Sun, or another star, in which the external conditions are suitable for life-bearing planets to exist.

Such a concept has to be defined rather arbitrarily since an all-embracing definition of life and the conditions necessary for it does not exist. In the case of the SOLAR SYSTEM we can regard the ecosphere as a zone within which the Earth could be located and the level of incident heat and other radiations would allow certain forms of life (as we know it) to exist. If we take as limiting conditions a level of radiation up to double and down to half of that which the Earth receives at present, then the ecosphere extends roughly from the orbit of Venus to the orbit of Mars. Ecospheres can be defined similarly for other stars.

The existence of planets within the ecosphere does not necessarily imply that life *will* exist on all or even any of them; the atmospheric and surface conditions on these planets may not be suitable. For example, in the Solar System space probes have shown that the conditions on Venus are utterly hostile to terrestrial life. Nevertheless, the concept of an ecosphere is a useful one when we are trying to estimate the probability of life existing elsewhere in the universe ($\diamond$LIFE IN THE UNIVERSE).

Effective temperature. The surface temperature of a star, expressed in the following way: the effective temperature of a star is the temperature of a black body (a perfect emitter of radiation) which has the same luminosity (i.e. total output of radiation) and radius as the star. Real stars are not perfect black bodies but most approximate reasonably well to these idealized concepts. Where temperature values for stars are quoted without qualification, it is usually effective temperature that is implied. The effective temperature of the Sun is 5800 K. Most stars have effective temperatures in the range 40000 K to 2000 K. ($\diamond$HERTZSPRUNG–RUSSELL DIAGRAM, Figure 24.)

Electromagnetic radiation. Radiation, consisting of an electric and a magnetic disturbance, which travels in a vacuum at a characteristic speed known as the velocity of light (approximately $300\,000$ km s^{-1}); i.e. a light wave consists of periodically varying changes in electric and magnetic fields (see Figure 17). Visible light, radio waves, etc. (◊ELECTROMAGNETIC SPECTRUM), are examples of electromagnetic radiation.

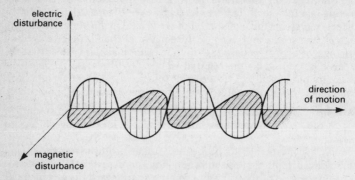

Figure 17. Electromagnetic wave. For many purposes it is convenient to regard electromagnetic radiation as being made up of a periodically varying electrical disturbance and a periodically varying magnetic disturbance travelling like a wave in a direction perpendicular to the direction of the disturbance (i.e. a transverse wave.)

Electromagnetic radiation is usually thought of as a wave motion, the distance between successive crests being the wavelength; thus, for example, visible light has a wavelength of a few hundred nanometres (a nanometre $= 10^{-9}$ metres), while a radio wave has a wave-length of the order of metres. The number of wavecrests passing a fixed point in one second is the frequency, which equals the velocity of light divided by wavelength; thus short wavelength corresponds to high frequency.

Electromagnetic radiation may be described in terms of quanta or photons ('packets' or 'particles' of energy); the energy associated with electromagnetic radiation is inversely proportional to wavelength and directly proportional to frequency (thus, the shorter the wavelength, the more energetic the photon).

The human eye responds to different wavelengths of light by recognizing different colours (red light has a longer wavelength than blue light).

Most of our information about the universe has been obtained by measurements of electromagnetic radiation of one kind or another reaching us from space.

Electromagnetic spectrum. The complete range of ELECTROMAG-NETIC RADIATIONS from the shortest to the longest WAVELENGTH. The electromagnetic spectrum is conventionally divided into a number of sections, the boundaries of which are really quite arbitrary; beginning with the shortest wavelength radiation we have gamma rays, X-rays, ultra-violet, visible, infra-red, microwave and radio. Further subdivisions are sometimes encountered: thus very short wavelength ultra-violet may be referred to as X U V; very long wavelength infra-red as 'sub-millimetre', and so on. The principal regions of the electromagnetic spectrum are shown in the table below, the characteristics of the radiation being described in terms of wavelength, λ, frequency, f, and energy, E. These quantities are related to each other by the following,

$$E = hc/\lambda = hf$$

where c is the velocity of light and h is Planck's constant.

The Electromagnetic Spectrum

	Wavelength (λ) in metres	Frequency (f) in hertz	Energy (E) electron-Volts
Gamma rays	10^{-14}	3×10^{22}	8×10^{7}
	10^{-12}	3×10^{20}	8×10^{5}
	10^{-10}	3×10^{18}	8×10^{3}
X-rays	10^{-8}	3×10^{16}	8×10^{1}
Ultra-violet			
Visible	10^{-6}	3×10^{14}	8×10^{-1}
Infra-red	10^{-4}	3×10^{12}	8×10^{-3}
Microwave	10^{-2}	3×10^{10}	8×10^{-5}
	1	3×10^{8}	8×10^{-7}
Radio	10^{2}	3×10^{6}	8×10^{-9}
	10^{4}	3×10^{4}	8×10^{-11}

Electron. An atomic particle, having one unit of negative charge ($= 1 \cdot 602 \times 10^{-19}$ coulomb) and a mass equal to 1/1837 times the mass of a proton (i.e. $9 \cdot 108 \times 10^{-31}$ kg, or $5 \cdot 486 \times 10^{-4}$ atomic mass units). In the simple (Bohr) model of the ATOM, the electron is visualized as being allowed to orbit the nucleus in specific orbits only. If an electron drops down from an orbit of large radius to one of smaller radius, it is said to make a downward transition, and releases a quantum of energy in the form of radiation. Conversely, if an electron in an atom absorbs the appropriate quantity of energy, it may make an upward transition. The electron is sometimes referred to as the beta particle, and a stream of electrons, beta radiation. (◊SPECTRUM, Figure 41.)

Electron volt (eV). A unit of energy used to describe the energies of sub-atomic particles, or the energies of short wavelength photons (◊ELECTROMAGNETIC RADIATION). One electron volt is equal to the energy gained by an ELECTRON in falling through a potential difference of 1 volt, and is equivalent to $1 \cdot 602 \times 10^{-19}$ joules. Common multiples are keV (1000 eV) and MeV (10^6 eV).

Elements of an orbit. ◊ORBITAL ELEMENTS.

Ellipse. The CONIC SECTION obtained by cutting a right circular cone by a plane which makes an angle relative to the base of the cone less than the angle made by the side (see Figure 12). It is an oval curve having within it two points or foci (singular: focus) such that the sum of the distances from each focus to any point on the curve is a constant. The greatest diameter of an ellipse is the major axis (half of this is the semi-major axis), and the least diameter the minor axis.

The greater the separation of the foci, the more flattened the ellipse. A measure of the separation of the foci is given by the eccentricity, e, which can take values between 0 (the circle) and 1 (the case of the parabola).

The orbits of the planets are elliptical in nature.

Elliptical galaxy. ◊GALAXIES, CLASSIFICATION OF.

Elongation. The angle between the Sun and a celestial body such as a planet when observed from the Earth (◊PLANETARY CONFIGURA- TIONS, Figure 32). For an inner planet (◊INFERIOR PLANET) the maximum possible angle between it and the Sun occurs when the line of sight from the Earth to the planet makes a tangent to the planet's orbit, and this angle is greatest elongation. Maximum values of greatest elongation for Mercury and Venus are 28° and 48° respectively. When a planet is located east of the Sun in the sky, it is said to be at eastern elongation and, since its sets after the Sun, is referred to as an 'evening star'; a planet located west of the Sun rises before the Sun, is said to be at western elongation and is sometimes referred to as a 'morning star'.

Emission line. ⟡ KIRCHHOFF'S LAWS.

Emission nebula. ⟡ NEBULA.

Ephemeris (pl: Ephemerides). A table of the computed positions of a celestial body on given dates and times.

Ephemeris time. A time system with a constant rate defined by reference to the motions of the Sun, Moon and planets. Most astronomical time systems (sidereal time, universal time, etc.) are based on the rotation of the Earth; the Earth does not rotate at a constant rate, there being a slow increase in the Earth's rotation period due to tidal friction and, in addition, small abrupt and unpredictable changes. Consequently, time systems based on the Earth's rotation are not perfectly uniform. Ephemeris time is an attempt to overcome this problem. At present (1976) Ephemeris time is ahead of universal time by about 46 seconds.

Epicycle. A circle on which, according to, for example, the Ptolemaic theory of the universe, a planet was supposed to move while the centre of that circle itself moved in a circular path around some centre (the Earth, in the case of that particular theory) (see Figure 18). The circle upon which the centre of the epicycle moved was known as the deferent. The use of the epicycle in planetary theory was first discussed by Appolonius in the third century B.C.

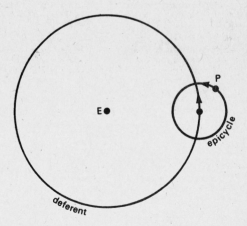

Figure 18. Epicycle and deferent. According to the Ptolemaic theory, a planet was supposed to move on a small circle, the epicycle, the centre of which revolved round the Earth, E, on another circle, the deferent.

Epoch. A particular instant of time used for reference purposes. Thus, for example, because of the effects of PRECESSION and PROPER MOTION the positions of stars (in terms of celestial coordinates) are slowly changing; any star chart or catalogue of stellar positions must be drawn up giving the positions at a particular epoch (e.g. 1950.00 would refer to zero hours on 1 January 1950). To obtain precise positions for particular times thereafter, allowance must be made for the changes in position since the epoch of the catalogue.

Equation of time. An equation giving the difference between apparent solar time (or sundial time) and mean time (i.e. clock time). Thus,

equation of time (E) = apparent solar time (AT) − mean time (MT).

A positive value of E means that apparent time is ahead of mean time while a negative value of E means that apparent time is lagging behind mean time.

The difference arises for two reasons. Firstly, since the Earth moves round the Sun in an elliptical orbit, when the Earth is near PERI-

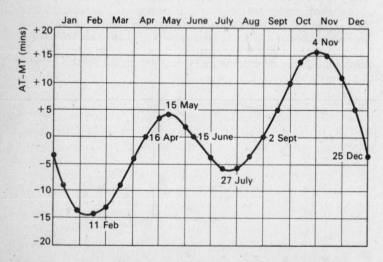

Figure 19. Equation of time. Due to the elliptical nature of the Earth's orbit (resulting in non-uniform motion of the Earth relative to the Sun) and to the fact that whereas the real Sun moves along the ecliptic, the mean sun (the basis of mean time) moves along the celestial equator, apparent solar time (sundial time) and mean time differ from each other by an amount which varies throughout the year. The difference between apparent time and mean time is given by the equation of time as shown above.

HELION it moves faster than when it is near APHELION; consequently, the apparent motion of the Sun relative to the background stars is more rapid near perihelion than near aphelion. This variation in the Sun's apparent motion affects the length of the apparent solar day. Secondly, although the real Sun's apparent motion is along the ECLIPTIC, the variation in the length of the apparent solar day depends upon the daily change in the RIGHT ASCENSION of the Sun. This change in RA is equal to the projection of the Sun's ecliptic motion onto the celestial equator, and is maximum near the SOLSTICES and minimum near the EQUINOXES.

As a result of the combination of these two effects, mean time and apparent solar time can differ by up to 16·3 minutes (see Figure 19).

Equatorial mounting. A method of mounting a telescope with one axis of rotation parallel to the Earth's axis, so enabling the apparent diurnal rotation of the celestial sphere to be followed by rotating the telescope about this axis only. With such a mounting, once the telescope is pointing towards a star, the star may be kept in the field of view by driving the telescope round this, the polar axis, at a rate of one revolution in twenty-four hours of SIDEREAL TIME. (See Figure 20.)

Equinox. An instant at which the Sun crosses the CELESTIAL EQUATOR; the Sun is then vertically overhead at the equator, and day and night have equal duration at every point on the Earth's surface. The apparent annual path of the Sun on the CELESTIAL SPHERE is inclined to the celestial equator and intersects it at two points; the terms vernal equinox and autumnal equinox are applied to these points (see Figure 9b).

Eros. An ASTEROID, catalogue number 433, which was discovered in 1898 by Witt. It is one of a number of asteroids known as 'Earth-grazers' which can approach the Earth relatively closely; in fact Eros can approach to within 23 million km. In 1931 it was used for PARALLAX measurements which yielded the best value of the ASTRONOMICAL UNIT which had been obtained up to that time. It is a small irregular body with a radius of about 7 km; variations in its brightness suggest that it is roughly ellipsoidal in shape (the variations occurring as it spins). It moves round the Sun in an elliptical orbit of semi-major axis 1·46 a.u., eccentricity 0·177 and sidereal period 642 days.

Escape velocity. The minimum velocity required in order to leave the vicinity of a massive body and not return to the body. Thus the escape velocity of the Earth is the minimum velocity at which some object must be projected in order that it continues to move away and never falls back again. An object which has this velocity will move away from the massive body along a PARABOLIC TRAJECTORY (⟡ORBIT, Figure 28).

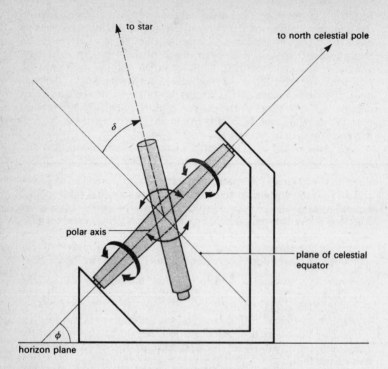

Figure 20. Equatorial mounting. The equatorial mounting may take a wide variety of forms, but consists essentially of a polar axis aligned parallel with the axis of the Earth (the polar axis points towards the celestial poles) and a declination axis at right angles to it. The telescope is attached to the declination axis and rotation about this axis allows the telescope to be pointed at a star at any desired declination, δ. Rotation about the polar axis allows the telescope to be directed towards the appropriate hour angle or right ascension. Because the polar axis is parallel to the Earth's axis, if the telescope is pointed at a particular object and the polar axis driven so that it rotates at the same rate as the Earth, the object will remain in the field of view. (The angle, ϕ, is equal to the latitude of the telescope on the Earth.)

The term is sometimes taken to imply that the projected object literally 'escapes' from the gravitational field of the body. This is not so; as the projectile moves away, its velocity is reduced by the gravitational attraction of the body, but will fall to zero only when the projectile has moved out to an infinite distance. In terms of energy, we can say that the initial KINETIC ENERGY of the projectile is exactly equal to the POTENTIAL ENERGY which it has gained by the time it has reached an infinite distance. Conversely, an object which is allowed to fall from an infinite height will hit the surface of a massive body with a speed exactly equal to escape velocity.

The value of escape velocity, V_e, at a distance R from the centre of a massive body, of mass M, is easily calculated from:

$$V_e = (2GM/R)^{\frac{1}{2}}$$

where G is the GRAVITATIONAL CONSTANT.

Examples of values of escape velocity at the surfaces of the following bodies are: Earth 11·2 km s⁻¹; Moon 2·4 km s⁻¹; Jupiter 61 km s⁻¹; Sun 617·7 km s⁻¹; white dwarf 6000 km s⁻¹; neutron star 150000 km s⁻¹.

Ether (or aether). A transparent, weightless medium which was imagined by nineteenth-century physicists to fill all space, and to provide the medium through which electromagnetic waves (◇ELECTRO-MAGNETIC RADIATION) could propagate. Conventional physical ideas of the time did not admit of waves that could travel through 'nothingness'. The concept of the ether came to be associated with the idea of absolute space, the ether providing a background to the universe against which all motion could be measured.

Experiments were devised, notably the MICHELSON–MORLEY EXPERIMENT, to try to measure the motion of the Earth through the ether, and these all failed to detect any such motion, however small. The null result of these experiments was explained by the theory of relativity, first published in 1905. The ether, being undetectable, became an unnecessary hypothesis, and has been abandoned (along with the Newtonian concept of absolute space). (◇SPECIAL THEORY OF RELATIVITY.)

EVA – Extra-Vehicular Activity. Activity undertaken by an astronaut outside the confines of his spacecraft. The first EVA was a 'spacewalk' of 12½ minutes' duration carried out by Alexei Leonov in 1965 (◇VOSKHOD).

Evening star. Term sometimes applied particularly to the planet Venus when it is visible in the evening sky after sunset. The term is also applied to any planet when it is visible in the evening sky and reaches culmination (◇TRANSIT) before midnight. (◇MORNING STAR.)

Event horizon. A boundary such that no knowledge of events which may occur on one side can be communicated to the other side. The term is applied to the boundary of a BLACK HOLE, in which case the event horizon is a one-way membrane – light can enter the black hole, but nothing can emerge; i.e. no knowledge of an event inside a black hole can cross the event horizon to the outside world.

Exhaust velocity. The velocity at which the hot gases are expelled from the combustion chamber of a ROCKET motor. For a given MASS RATIO, the higher the exhaust velocity, the greater the final velocity of the rocket. Unfortunately, existing chemical rockets achieve exhaust velocities only of the order of 3 km per second. However, ION ROCKETS, it is hoped, will achieve much higher values. (◊ DAEDALUS PROJECT.)

Exobiology. The study of biological systems which may exist beyond the Earth. At present there is no direct evidence of the existence of living matter elsewhere in the universe, but it does seem likely that life of some kind exists elsewhere (◊ LIFE IN THE UNIVERSE). The problem of exobiology may be approached: (a) by sampling materials from other planets (soil samples from the Moon reveal no trace of living material; the results from Martian soil are still unclear (◊ VIKING)) or METEORITES, some of which appear to contain organic matter; (b) by detecting signals transmitted by other technologies, if they exist (◊ INTELLIGENT LIFE IN THE UNIVERSE); and (c) by laboratory experiment (trying to simulate the processes which lead to the formation of life on Earth, or testing living matter in simulated planetary environments). At present work continues in area (a) with unmanned space probes and in area (c); preliminary observations have been carried out in area (b) with radio telescopes, so far without success. (◊ OZMA PROJECT; CYCLOPS PROJECT; LIFE, ORIGIN OF.)

Exosphere. The outermost part of the Earth's atmosphere, which blends into the interplanetary medium. It lies well above the IONOSPHERE and is nominally taken as starting at an altitude of 1000 km, where the density is less than one thousand million millionth (10^{-15}) that of air at ground level.

Explorer. A continuing series of US scientific satellites covering a wide range of applications. The first of the series, Explorer 1, was the first US satellite to be placed in orbit (on 31 January 1958). Its major achievement was the discovery of the inner VAN ALLEN BELT. By 1976, the number of successful Explorer launchings was well over fifty, and the scientific objectives of these satellites have included studies of the upper atmosphere, interplanetary medium, micro-meteorites, and X-ray, gamma-ray and radio-astronomy, etc.

Eyepiece. ◊ TELESCOPE.

F

Faculae. Bright patches on or immediately above the visible surface (PHOTOSPHERE) of the SUN (Figure 43), normally seen only near the edge of the visible disc where the apparent brightness of the photosphere is less than at the centre of the disc. They are normally associated with sunspot groups but may occur in their absence. (◊ PLAGES.)

Filaments. ◊ PROMINENCES.

Filter. A device which transmits the required part of a signal and rejects the rest. For example, a colour filter might transmit only blue light; such filters are used in astronomical PHOTOMETRY (◊ COLOUR INDEX). An electronic filter ideally will reject all but the required frequency signal.

Fireball. An extremely bright METEOR which leaves a bright trail lasting at least several seconds and which may appear larger than the Moon in the sky. There is no precise definition, but it is convenient to talk in terms of a fireball for a meteor phenomenon brighter than magnitude −5 (◊ APPARENT MAGNITUDE). Occasionally fireballs may be brighter than the full moon.

First point of Aries. An alternative term for VERNAL EQUINOX. At one time (some 2000 years ago) the vernal equinox lay in the constellation of Aries but, due to PRECESSION, this is no longer the case.

First point of Libra. An alternative term for the autumnal equinox (◊ EQUINOX). Due to PRECESSION, this point no longer lies in the constellation of Libra.

Fission. Literally 'breaking apart'; the term is applied to the fragmenting of a heavy atomic nucleus, a process which results in the release of nuclear energy. The mass of the nucleus prior to fission is greater than the combined masses of the fragments, the difference in mass, ΔM, being released as energy, ΔE ($\Delta E = \Delta Mc^2$, where c is the velocity of light).

For example, the capture of a NEUTRON by a uranium nucleus (U^{235}) results in that nucleus breaking into two fragments plus two neutrons together with energy. Because the reaction liberates additional neutrons a chain reaction is possible in a mass of uranium; if this reaction is allowed to build up unchecked, a nuclear explosion results (this is the basis of the atomic bomb), while if the rate of the reaction is controlled by regulating the supply of neutrons, a steady output of energy is achieved (this is the basis of the nuclear power station). (⟡ATOM.)

Fixed stars. Until comparatively recent times the stars were thought to be fixed and immovable (the planets moved relative to this starry background). The stars were envisaged as being attached to a huge sphere, the CELESTIAL SPHERE which rotated each day round the Earth. We know, of course, that the stars actually lie at different distances, and that they are all in motion relative to one another, but because of their great distances this motion is not readily apparent. For many purposes (such as plotting the motion of a comet) they can be regarded as a fixed frame of reference. The 'frame of the fixed stars' is a term sometimes used to describe a frame of reference which may be regarded as being fixed for the purpose of making measurements; for example, instead of 'stars' we might make reference to the distant background of galaxies.

Flare star. A faint red star which suffers short-lived major outbursts from localized areas of its surface, these causing the total light output of the star to increase temporarily. The outbursts appear to be similar in nature to SOLAR FLARES. A typical flare star would be about a thousand times less luminous than the Sun (with an ABSOLUTE MAGNITUDE of about 12) and of spectral type M (⟡SPECTRAL CLASSIFICATION); on the HERTZSPRUNG–RUSSELL DIAGRAM these stars are located in the lower part of the main sequence. A flare will, on average, enhance the brightness of the star by two magnitudes (i.e. a factor of about 6); the rise in brightness takes, typically, about one minute, and the duration of the outburst is, on average, some twenty minutes. The average frequency of outbursts on a flare star is about one per day.

Flares. ⟡SOLAR FLARES.

Flash spectrum. The emission-line SPECTRUM of the solar CHROMO-SPHERE visible during a total eclipse of the Sun. The normal spectrum of the Sun consists of a continuum together with dark absorption lines, the absorption lines being produced in the REVERSING LAYER in the lower chromosphere. Atoms in the chromosphere are also emitting radiation at the same wavelengths at which absorption takes place, but under normal circumstances these weak emission lines cannot be observed; however, when the bright surface of the Sun (the photo-sphere) is hidden during a total eclipse, these lines are revealed.

Flattening. ⟡OBLATENESS.

Flocculi. ⟡PLAGES.

Flying saucer. Term sometimes used to describe an unidentified flying object (⟡UFO), the implication of this description being that the UFO is an alien spacecraft visiting the Earth. While such a possibility cannot absolutely be ruled out (for example, ⟡INTELLIGENT LIFE IN THE UNIVERSE or INTERSTELLAR COMMUNICATION) it seems highly implausible.

Flux density. A term, used particularly by radio astronomers, as a measure of the amount of power per unit interval of frequency incident on unit area of the flux collector (e.g. per square metre of the surface of a radio telescope). Flux density is usually denoted by S, and expressed in units of watts (W) per square metre (m^{-2}) per hertz (Hz^{-1}). This definition is adequate for a point source of radiation such as a star. For an extended source, such as a radio galaxy, covering a finite area of sky, it is usual to describe the brightness of a given area of the source in terms of the flux density per unit solid angle, i.e. $W\ m^{-2}\ Hz^{-1}$ per steradian (sr^{-1}).

Focal length. For a lens or a mirror, this is the distance between the centre of that lens or mirror and the focal point or focus, this being the point at which an image of a distant object (i.e. an object which is at an effectively infinite distance) is formed.

Focal ratio. The ratio of the FOCAL LENGTH of the objective (for a refracting telescope) or the primary mirror (for a reflecting telescope) to its clear diameter, or aperture. Thus an instrument of 10 metres focal length and 2 metres aperture would have a focal ratio of 5; this would be denoted as f:5. The focal ratio of a camera lens may be altered by adjusting the aperture by means of a variable diaphragm.

Forbidden lines. Emission lines corresponding to transitions (between energy levels) which under normal conditions are extremely impiobable. Under the conditions of extremely low density and pressure found in gaseous nebulae (for example, the density of gas in the Orion nebula is about 10^{-17} times that of air at sea level), such transitions can occur much more frequently than at normal laboratory densities, and many of the emission lines in nebulae are forbidden lines.

Forces of nature. There are four different types of force which are known to operate in nature. They are:

1. GRAVITATION;
2. the weak nuclear interaction, which governs radioactive decay;
3. the electromagnetic force;
4. the strong nuclear interaction, which binds together the atomic nuclei.

Of these, the weakest force is gravitation, but 2 and 4 are only effective over short ranges.

Foucault's pendulum. A freely swinging pendulum mounted in such a way as to reduce its physical contact with the Earth to an absolute minimum. An ideal pendulum of this type would, if set swinging in a particular plane at one of the Earth's poles, continue to swing in that same plane relative to the 'fixed stars', and the Earth would rotate underneath it. To the observer on the Earth's surface, the pendulum would be seen to rotate its plane of swing through 360 degrees each day. The period of rotation of the plane of the pendulum increases with decreasing latitude on the Earth's surface; no rotation is observed for a pendulum at the equator. Observation of the behaviour of such a pendulum is direct evidence of the fact that the Earth rotates on its axis. This type of pendulum is named after the French physicist, Léon Foucault (1819–68).

Fraunhofer lines. Dark lines in the SPECTRUM of the Sun, first studied in detail by Joseph von Fraunhofer in 1814. He labelled the most prominent of these by the letters A to K, ranging from the red end of the spectrum to the violet. These are absorption lines due to the absorption of light by atoms in the outer regions of the Sun; for example, a prominent pair of close dark lines in the yellow part of the solar spectrum are the 'D' lines of the element sodium. ($\Diamond$ SPECTROSCOPY.)

Frame of fixed stars. $\Diamond$ FIXED STARS.

Free–bound radiation. The radiation emitted by a free electron as it is accelerated and captured by an ion.

Free fall. The state of falling freely under gravitational attraction. A freely falling body is in no way resisting the acceleration due to gravity, and because of this a person inside a freely falling container feels no weight ($\Diamond$ WEIGHTLESSNESS). For example, a person inside a freely falling lift will be accelerating at the same rate as the lift itself; therefore there will be no relative acceleration (and therefore no force) between the floor of the lift and his feet and he feels no sensation of weight (see Figure 21a). An orbiting satellite is in a state of free fall, being accelerated towards the Earth by gravity, but not hitting the surface because of the transverse motion of the satellite relative to the Earth (see Figure 21b). Spacecraft, when not operating their motors, are in a state of free fall.

Free–free radiation. The radiation emitted by a free electron as it is accelerated in the electrostatic field of an ion; the electron is not captured by the ion in the encounter. Free–free (or '*bremsstrahlung*') emission is an important radiation source in ionized gas clouds or PLASMAS such as the solar CORONA.

Frequency. The rate at which specific events occur. In the context of electromagnetic radiation, the term is taken to mean the number of

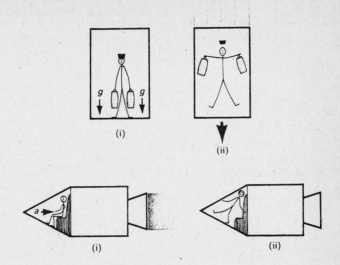

Figure 21. Free fall. (a) (i) A luggage porter stands in a stationary lift burdened by the full weight of the suitcases which are being attracted to the Earth by a force in each case equal to the mass of the suitcase times the acceleration due to gravity, *g*. (ii) If the lift is allowed to fall freely, without any resistance to acceleration by gravity, the porter, suitcases and lift will be accelerated at the same rate and the suitcases will appear to be weightless.

(b) Likewise (i), a spacecraft firing its rocket motor is accelerated at a rate *a*. The astronaut's inertia (resistance to acceleration) results in his being pushed against the couch by a force equal to his mass times the acceleration, *a*, of the spacecraft. (ii) When the motor is not operating, there is no acceleration of the spacecraft relative to the astronaut, and he floats freely in a weightless or free-fall condition.

wavecrests per second passing a particular point. For light of WAVE-LENGTH λ, since the speed of light $= c$, then frequency, $f = c/\lambda$.

The unit of frequency measurement is the HERTZ (Hz).

Fusion. The combination of nuclei of lighter elements to form heavier nuclei. Fusion reactions involving nuclei lighter than iron (Fe^{56}) release energy; if heavier elements are to be built up by fusion, energy must be supplied. For most of its lifetime, a star produces energy by fusion reactions involving the conversion of hydrogen to helium ($\Diamond$ STELLAR EVOLUTION; PROTON–PROTON REACTION; CARBON CYCLE).

Strenuous efforts are being made to obtain sustained power outputs from fusion reactions here on Earth but there are tremendous technical problems (e.g. the containment of PLASMA at temperatures of the order of 10^8 K) which are still some way from solution. If these problems can be overcome, then the way is open for the production of energy from, for example, DEUTERIUM in sea water, by essentially the same process as powers the Sun.

G

g. The acceleration due to gravity. The letter '*g*' is usually taken to imply the value of acceleration experienced by a freely falling body at the Earth's surface (which is equal to the gravitational force experienced by a body of unit mass at the Earth's surface; ⟡SURFACE GRAVITY). The standard value of *g* is 9·8067 m s^{-2} (i.e. a freely falling body will accelerate by 9·8067 metres per second for each second that it continues to fall), but the value of *g* differs at different latitudes on the Earth's surface due to the effects of rotation (⟡CENTRIFUGAL FORCE) and the shape of the Earth (since the Earth is not spherical, points at its surface lie at slightly different distances from the centre).

Acceleration is sometimes expressed in terms of *g*, or 'gees'. Thus a rocket accelerating away from the Earth's surface at $3 \times 9·8067$ m s^{-2} is accelerating at three times *g*. Any occupants of such a vehicle will experience a 'gee' force due to this acceleration which will make them weigh four times as much as they would normally weigh on the Earth (their normal weight plus the effect of three gees).

Galactic centre. ⟡GALAXY (2).

Galactic clusters. Clusters of stars (otherwise known as open clusters) which lie in the galactic disc, and contain up to a few hundred member stars; they are Population I (⟡STELLAR POPULATIONS) objects. With time, such clusters tend to disperse since the mutual gravitational attraction of the member stars is insufficient to resist the effects of gravitational perturbations (which might accelerate a star to beyond the ESCAPE VELOCITY of the cluster) and the differential rotation of the Galaxy.

Galactic clusters are thought to originate from the fragmentation of large gas clouds into smaller clouds which themselves form stars; thus all members of a cluster are assumed to be of more or less the same age. Most galactic clusters are relatively young objects, a few tens or hundreds of million of years old. Examples of such clusters visible to the unaided eye are the PLEIADES and the HYADES. (⟡HERTZSPRUNG–RUSSELL DIAGRAM.)

Galactic latitude. The angular distance between the galactic equator (⟡GALACTIC PLANE) and a celestial body, measured perpendicular to the galactic equator, and taking values between 0 and 90 degrees. It is denoted by b^{II} to signify that the value of galactic latitude relates to the galactic equator defined in 1959 by the International Astronomical Union; the previous system is denoted b^{I}. (◇ CELESTIAL COORDINATES.)

Galactic longitude. The angular distance between the direction of the galactic centre (◇ GALAXY (2)) and the point on the galactic equator (◇ GALACTIC PLANE) perpendicularly below (or above) a celestial body; it is measured in an anticlockwise direction, and takes values between 0 and 360 degrees. Galactic longitude is denoted by l^{II} to signify that it is referred to the position of zero longitude agreed in 1959 by the International Astronomical Union (and presumed to coincide with the galactic centre). The old system (denoted l^{I}) was referred to a presumed direction of the galactic centre which was in error by some 30 degrees. (◇ CELESTIAL COORDINATES.)

Galactic plane. The plane of the disc of our GALAXY (2). It follows a line running more or less through the centre of the MILKY WAY, and is inclined to the CELESTIAL EQUATOR by an angle of 62°.

Galaxies, Classification of. Galaxies were originally classified according to their shapes by Hubble in 1925 and his system, with some modification, is still widely used. The Hubble classification recognizes three basic types of galaxy, elliptical, spiral and irregular (see Figure 22).

Ellipticals: apparently elliptical in shape, these range from spherical to highly flattened systems; they are denoted by the letter E, followed by a numeral between 0 and 7 (inclusive) according to the degree of ellipticity. For an En galaxy, n is obtained from $n = 10[(a-b)/a]$ where a is the greater diameter and b the lesser; thus E0 galaxies are spherical ($a = b$) and E7 galaxies have a ratio of $a:b$ of about 3:1.

Spirals: these are subdivided into normal spirals and barred spirals. Normal spirals have a central ellipsoidal nucleus from which emerge spiral-shaped arms of stars and interstellar material; they are denoted by Sa, Sb, or Sc according to the degree of openness of the spiral arms. Thus, Sa galaxies have tightly wound arms, while Sc galaxies are open and S-shaped (our Galaxy is of type Sb). Barred spirals are essentially similar, except that the spiral arms emanate from the ends of a luminous bar of material which straddles the nucleus. They are denoted by SBa, SBb, SBc, again according to the openness of their arms.

Irregulars: these have no definite discernible structure, and are denoted Irr I if made up predominantly of Population I objects and Irr II if made up predominantly of Population II objects.

In addition, there is a class of lens-shaped galaxies which show some evidence of a central nucleus and the beginnings of a disc and which

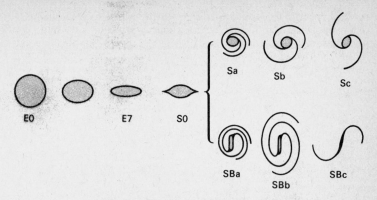

Figure 22. Classification of galaxies. The more common types of galaxy having regular structure are classified as shown. Elliptical galaxies are denoted by the letter E followed by a numeral having values from 0 to 7 depending on the flattening of the ellipse. Spiral galaxies are denoted Sa, Sb or Sc according to how open is the pattern of the spiral arms. Barred spiral galaxies are denoted SBa, SBb, SBc. S0 denotes a class intermediate between elliptical and spiral. Irregular galaxies are denoted by Irr.

appear to be intermediate between elliptical and spiral; these are denoted by S0.

On average, spirals are the most luminous, and irregulars the least luminous of galaxies, but there are many exceptions. For example, although ellipticals are generally fainter than spirals, a few ellipticals are exceptionally luminous and appear to be the most massive of all galaxies. Of the brighter galaxies, about 75 per cent are spiral, some 20 per cent elliptical, and 5 per cent irregular; however, when allowance is made for the fainter galaxies, the relative proportions of spiral:elliptical:irregular are more like 30:60:10. For galaxies with particular or peculiar characteristics, ◊ACTIVE GALAXIES; SEYFERT GALAXY; RADIO GALAXY; QUASAR.

Galaxy (1). A large massive star system. Galaxies may contain, typically, between 10^6 and 10^{12} stars, and differing proportions of interstellar material (gas and dust). Our own GALAXY (2) contains about 10^{11} (one hundred thousand million) stars and is, therefore, among the largest systems. (◊GALAXIES, CLASSIFICATION OF.)

Galaxy (2). The star system of which the Sun is a member; sometimes called the Milky Way Galaxy, or the Home Galaxy. The Galaxy is a disc-shaped system of some 100 000 000 000 stars, having an overall diameter of just under 100 000 light years (there is some controversy at present over this value, and there are estimates which make the diameter appreciably less). The Sun is located about three-fifths of the way from the centre to the outside edge of the galactic disc, at a distance of about 32000 light years from the centre.

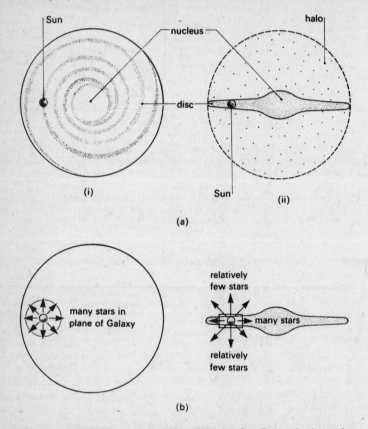

Figure 23. The Galaxy and the Milky Way. (a) Our Galaxy is shown in plan (i) and in cross-section (ii). The nucleus, halo and disc are shown together with a schematic representation of the spiral structure of the disc and the position of the Sun.

(b) The Milky Way, which appears in the night sky as a relatively narrow band of starlight extending round the celestial sphere arises because of our observing position in the Galaxy. If we look in a direction close to the plane of the galactic disc, then many stars are seen; in a direction away from this plane, fewer stars are seen. The concentration of stars towards the plane gives rise to the appearance of the Milky Way.

The Galaxy can be divided into three principal regions, the central nucleus, the disc, and the halo (see Figure 23a). The nucleus is ellipsoidal in shape, being about 15000 light years thick (measured across the vertical, minor, axis); this region is heavily obscured by interstellar dust (◊INTERSTELLAR MATTER) lying between it and us, but radio and infra-red studies are possible. The stars in the nucleus are predominantly Population II objects (◊STELLAR POPULATIONS) and there appears to be little, if any, neutral hydrogen gas in this region; there does seem to be a strong compact energy source at the galactic centre the nature of which is uncertain. The disc is a flattened system some 50000 light years in radius but only a few thousand light years thick. Virtually all the neutral hydrogen gas, nebulae, young stars (Population I objects) are located in this region (◊MILKY WAY). The halo is a roughly spherical distribution of stars and GLOBULAR CLUSTERS centred on the galactic centre and extending out to some 50000 light years. The stars in this region are very thinly spread out, and belong to Population II (see Figure 23b).

The Galaxy is rotating, the Sun taking some 220 million years to complete one circuit and, like many other galaxies, it exhibits a spiral structure in its disc. The total mass of the system is estimated at 1.8×10^{11} solar masses, about 10 per cent of which is in the form of interstellar matter.

Galilean refractor. The type of simple refracting TELESCOPE employed by Galileo in his early astronomical observations. It consists of an object glass, a convex lens, with a concave lens acting as eyepiece; the same principle is employed in opera glasses. Such a telescope produces an erect image but a small field of view, and like all simple refractors, suffers from CHROMATIC ABERRATION (see Figure 10).

Galilean satellites. The four major satellites of the planet JUPITER, namely Io, Europa, Ganymede and Callisto. They move in orbits which are practically circular and parallel to the planet's equator. All four are clearly visible in small telescopes and were first observed in 1610 by Galileo Galilei (1564–1642), the Italian physicist and astronomer who is thought to have made the first recorded astronomical telescopic observations. It has been suggested that his observations of the motions of these satellites round Jupiter helped to convince him of the validity of the Copernican theory (◊COPERNICAN SYSTEM) that the Earth and planets move round the Sun.

Measurements carried out by the space probes Pioneer 10 and Pioneer 11 indicate that the two innermost satellites, Io and Europa, are basically rocky bodies while the outer two, Ganymede and Callisto, have much lower densities and may be made up largely of various ices and water.

Galileo Galilei. ⟡GALILEAN SATELLITES.

Gamma-ray astronomy. That branch of astronomy concerned with the detection and measurement of astronomical GAMMA-RAY sources. Due to atmospheric absorption (by, for example, oxygen, ozone and nitrogen) gamma-ray sources cannot be studied from ground level, and although some measurements can be made from high-altitude balloons, the development of this branch of astronomy did not begin until well into the era of artificial satellites. Some pioneering measurements were carried out by the ORBITING SOLAR OBSERVATORIES, OSO-3 and OSO-7, and the later Apollo flights 15 to 17 (⟡APOLLO PROJECT) carried gamma-ray spectrometers, but the first satellite to be devoted wholly to the study of cosmic gamma rays was the US Explorer 48 (also known as SAS-B) launched on 16 November 1972. A number of European satellites have carried gamma-ray experiments.

Detectors employed to receive gamma radiation include the spark chamber, but although the sensitivity of gamma-ray detectors has been improved by a factor of a thousand in the past decade, the majority of sources are so weak that detection remains a problem. Among the astronomical gamma-ray sources so far identified are the CRAB NEBULA, the galactic centre (⟡GALAXY (2)), and a number of extragalactic sources such as the SEYFERT GALAXY 3C120. Although this branch of astronomical science has not yet generated the excitement that X-RAY ASTRONOMY has achieved, it may well prove to be a fascinating development area in the next decade.

Gamma rays. Term applied to the shortest wavelengths of ELECTROMAGNETIC RADIATION; although the boundary between X-rays and gamma rays is somewhat arbitrary, the latter are generally described as having WAVELENGTHS shorter than about 0·01 nanometres (10^{-11} metres). Since the energy of a photon is inversely proportional to the wavelength of radiation, it follows that gamma rays are the most energetic of the electromagnetic radiations, and as such are extremely harmful to living tissue.

Gemini Project. A series of US two-man space missions, undertaken between 1965 and 1966, as a follow-up to the Mercury programme, and which preceded the Apollo lunar missions. Among the objectives of the series were the study of man's adaptation to a weightless environment and the development of techniques for orbital rendezvous and docking. The conical Gemini spacecraft had an overall length of 5·6 metres and a maximum diameter of 3 metres; the pressurized crew compartment (the re-entry module) seated two astronauts side by side.

The first manned mission of the series, Gemini 3, was launched on 23 March 1965 and completed three orbits. Highlights of the series are listed opposite:

Gemini 4 (launched 3 June 1965): first 'spacewalk' by a US astronaut, E. H. White;

Gemini 6 and 7 (launched 15 December and 4 December 1965): first rendezvous of two manned spacecraft, approach being made to within 2 metres. Gemini 7 made the longest flight of the series, 206 orbits in 13 days 18 hours 35 minutes;

Gemini 8 (launched 16 March 1966): first docking of a manned spacecraft with an unmanned target vehicle.

The final flight in the series was Gemini 12, launched on 11 November 1966.

Throughout the series, large numbers of photographs were taken of the Earth; these focused public attention on the potentialities of surveying the Earth from space.

General theory of relativity. The theory dealing with observers in accelerated frames of reference developed by Albert Einstein following on the SPECIAL THEORY OF RELATIVITY; general relativity is in fact a theory of gravitation which is in some ways superior to Newtonian GRAVITATION.

A central postulate of the theory is the principle of equivalence, that 'all freely-falling (non-rotating) laboratories are fully equivalent for the performance of all physical experiments'. It follows from this that an observer in a windowless spacecraft is unable to distinguish between the effects of acceleration (which gives him apparent weight) and the effects of a gravitational field (which also gives him weight) (⊳ACCE-LERATION; FREEFALL; WEIGHT; WEIGHTLESSNESS). A freely falling laboratory can be regarded as a *local* INERTIAL FRAME.

General relativity embodies the idea that the three dimensions of space (length, breadth, height) and the dimension of time are not independent, but are linked together as four-dimensional spacetime. The effect of a lump of matter is to bend (i.e. introduce curvature to) spacetime in its vicinity. Particles (including rays of light) follow curved paths (⊳GEODESIC) in spacetime; thus the planets move round the Sun in the way which they do because of the curvature of spacetime in the Sun's vicinity (the Sun being a very massive body). General relativity therefore regards gravitation as the effects of the curvature of spacetime rather than as a force acting directly between two massive bodies (as in Newton's theory).

Under certain extreme situations, general relativity is superior to Newton's theory. For example, rays of light (from stars) are deflected when passing the edge of the Sun by an amount which is predicted by the general theory, but not by Newtonian theory. Other tests to date have tended to support general relativity as being the best theory of gravity currently available. The theory has wide application in COSMOLOGY, the theory of BLACK HOLES, and so on.

Geocentric coordinates. Coordinates as measured from the centre of the Earth.

Geodesic. A line of minimum length between two points on a curved surface (for example, the shortest distance between two points on the Earth's surface is an arc of a great circle). In the GENERAL THEORY OF RELATIVITY the path in spacetime of a free particle subject only to gravitational forces is a geodesic. A ray of light, which takes the shortest possible time to travel between two points, follows a null-geodesic.

Geodesy. The study of the shape and gravitational field of the Earth. This science has been greatly advanced by the advent of artificial satellites, for a detailed study of their motion provides precise information on the shape of the Earth and the distribution of matter in it. The first geodetic satellite was the US Vanguard 1 launched on 17 March 1958, and this discovered the 'pear-shape' of the Earth's equator. Since that time, the study has advanced to the extent that satellites (such as GEOS-3) should be able to map the topography of the ocean floor to an accuracy of better than 5 metres.

Geodetic. Relating to the shape of the Earth, i.e. to the GEOID.

Geoid. The precise figure of the Earth. The shape of the Earth has been established to a high degree of accuracy by the analysis of the motion of artificial satellites in their orbits round the Earth; these orbits are influenced by any departure in spherical symmetry in the Earth's globe. The basic shape of the geoid is an oblate spheroid (i.e. the figure obtained by rotating an ellipse about its minor axis) with polar radius 6356·779 km and equatorial radius 6378·164 km. The equator itself is not quite circular, but is basically elliptical, differing from circular shape by a maximum of about 100 metres.

Giant. A star having a radius and a luminosity which is large compared to a main-sequence star of the same spectral class ($\Diamond$SPECTRAL CLASSIFICATION). ($\Diamond$RED GIANT; HERTZSPRUNG–RUSSELL DIAGRAM and Figure 24.)

Glide path. The path through the atmosphere followed by a re-entering spacecraft such as the SPACE SHUTTLE which has the ability to glide and effect a landing in a controlled fashion.

Globular cluster. A roughly spherical cluster of stars, containing from a few tens of thousands to over 1 000 000 stars within a relatively small volume of space. These clusters, of which more than 120 are known, are distributed in a roughly spherical 'halo' round the GALAXY (2); the

1. *Above:* The 200-inch (5-metre) Hale reflector. The primary mirror is clearly visible and the observer can be seen in the prime-focus 'cage'.

2. *Right:* The UK 48-inch (1.2-metre) Schmidt telescope at Siding Spring, Australia.

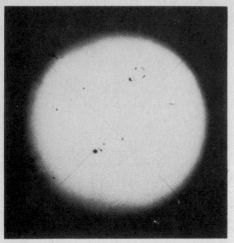

3. The Sun, photographed on 25 September 1928, showing several complex sunspot groups.

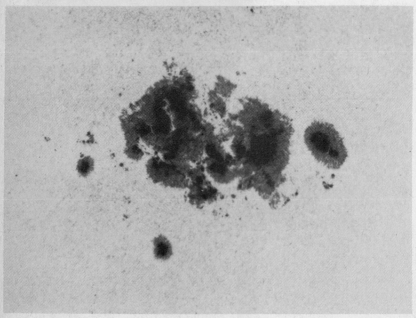

4. Large sunspot group of 17 May 1951. The complex umbra and penumbra regions are seen together with the granulation of the photosphere.

5. The Moon, aged ten days (i.e. ten days after new moon). The principal features, dark maria, craters and mountain chains are well seen, and features are thrown into sharp relief near the terminator (north is at the top).

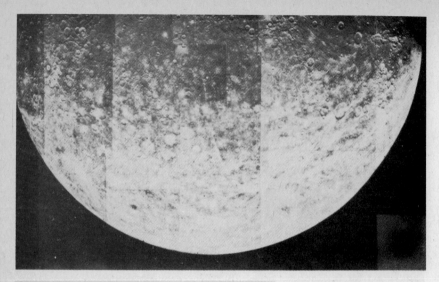

6. *Above:* Mercury. Photomosaic constructed from eighteen photographs taken by the spaceprobe Mariner 10 from a range of 210 000 kilometres on 29 March 1974. The similarity to the Moon is quite striking.

7. *Left:* Venus. An ultra-violet photograph taken in 1974 by Mariner 10 and showing the cloud structure.

8. *Right:* Jupiter photographed in December 1973 by the spaceprobe Pioneer 10 from a range of about 1 800 000 kilometres. Apart from the zones and dark belts, of particular interest are the white ovals in the southern hemisphere, these being rising cloud columns.

9. *Below:* Saturn and its ring system photographed with the 100-inch (2.5-metre) Hooker reflector. The Cassini division between rings A and B is well shown.

10. The surface of Mars, photographed from Viking 1. The martian soil and rock are shown, the horizon being about 3 kilometres distant.

11. Olympus Mons, the great martian volcanic structure, photographed on 31 July 1976 by the Viking 1 orbiter. The 24-kilometre high mountain extends over a base of 600 kilometres diameter, while the summit crater is about 80 kilometres across. The photograph taken at mid-morning (local Mars time) shows extensive cloud cover up to an altitude of 19 kilometres.

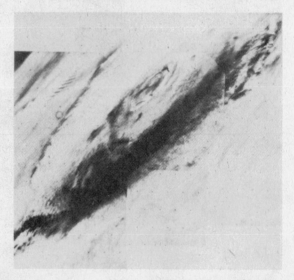

12. *Opposite:* A series of Viking photographs :
1. Yuty crater in the Chryse Planitia. It has a large central peak and is surrounded by ejecta flows.
2. Part of Valles Marineris, an equatorial canyon some 2 kilometres deep. Evidence of landslides is apparent and a large crater has partially fallen into the valley.
3. A mosaic of six photographs showing drainage channels around Shawnee crater in the Chryse Planitia. Material appears to have been deposited in a 'tail' behind Shawnee.
4. A crater 40 kilometres in diameter and having a complex, cracked floor.
5. A region 250 kilometres square in Capri, an area near the martian equator. The valley may have been created by collapse following the melting of the sub-surface ice.
6. View looking west from the Viking 1 lander.

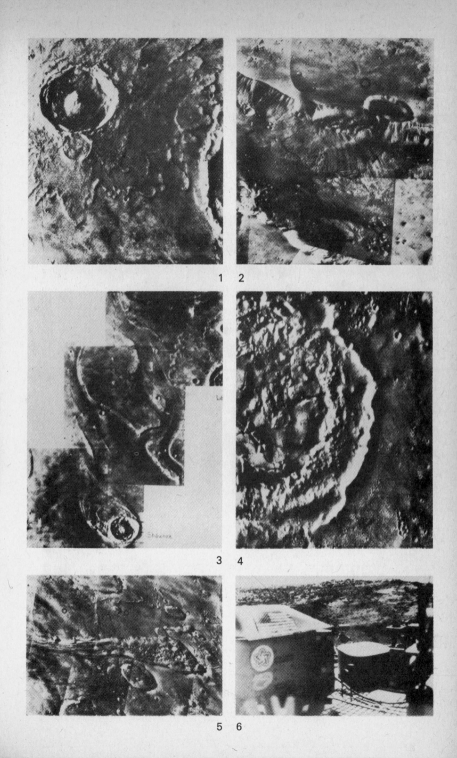

1 2

3 4

5 6

13. Comet Bennett photographed on 4 April 1970 by M. J. Hendrie at
R. L. Waterfield's Observatory, Woolston. Two tails are visible. Because the
camera was made to follow the motion of the comet during the 40-minute
exposure, the stars appear as short trails.

majority of them are seen to lie in regions of the sky away from the plane of the MILKY WAY as a result of this. They appear to be old star systems (older than the Sun), the brightest member stars being RED GIANTS and supergiants. It seems likely that they represent some of the oldest star systems in the Galaxy, most of them probably formed when the Galaxy was more nearly spherical in shape, before it assumed its present disc-shape. However, the evolution of the Galaxy is not well understood at present.

A typical globular cluster is M13 in the constellation Hercules. It lies at a distance of some 25 000 light years, and within a radius of approximately eighteen light years, contains some 300 000 stars.

Gnomon. A vertical stick or column used to measure the altitude of the Sun. If measurements are made of the length of the solar shadow cast by the stick, then, when the shadow is shortest, the Sun's altitude is greatest and it is then noon. Measurements carried out over the year enabled the date of midsummer and midwinter to be determined (the noon shadow having a minimum length in the first case and a maximum length in the second). Hipparchus, in the second century B.C., made use of the gnomon to determine the length of the year and hence to discover the phenomenon of PRECESSION.

Grand Tour. A term applied to a series of theoretically possible space missions designed to take advantage of the convenient alignment of the outer planets which takes place towards the end of the 1970s. Between about 1977 and 1981, Jupiter, Saturn, Uranus and Neptune will be lined up in such a way that a single space probe could be sent on a trajectory that flies by all four planets. For example, a mission launched in 1978 could take in the four planets, reaching Neptune in just over nine years, while a 1977 launch could take in Jupiter, Saturn and Pluto.

The key to the Grand Tour concept lies in the gravitational field of the most massive planet, Jupiter, which can be used to accelerate a passing spacecraft. For example, a spacecraft launched from the Earth with sufficient velocity to reach the orbit of Jupiter (but not far beyond) will be moving more slowly than Jupiter by the time it gets out to that distance. As the spacecraft passes behind the planet, it will be swept along by the gravitational attraction of Jupiter, and as it moves away again it will have picked up additional speed (in the direction of Jupiter's motion) sufficient to send it further out in the Solar System. In principle the same sort of effect would occur (although to a lesser extent) at each successive planetary encounter as, for example, the spacecraft moves past Saturn, Uranus and Neptune. As a result of these encounters, the amount of energy (and hence fuel) which must be supplied to the spacecraft at launch is considerably reduced, and the total flight time for the mission is less, too.

Any plans NASA may have had for attempting the full Grand Tour were cancelled as a result of cutbacks in space expenditure following the first few Apollo flights ($\Diamond$APOLLO PROJECT); this seems a great pity, as the alignment will not recur for some 180 years. However, the basic principle has already been used in a number of space missions. Thus in November 1973, the US probe Pioneer 10 by-passed Jupiter and was accelerated to a velocity in excess of solar ESCAPE VELOCITY so that it will eventually leave the Solar System and move into interstellar space. Again, Pioneer 11, in December 1974, was deflected by Jupiter into a path which should take it to Saturn in 1979. The principle was also used in 1974 to deflect Mariner 10 past Venus towards Mercury ($\Diamond$MARINER SERIES). Future missions of this type include a Jupiter–Saturn fly-by (launch date 1977) and a Jupiter–Uranus flight (launch date 1979).

Gravitation. In 1687 Isaac Newton (1642–1727) published his Law of Universal Gravitation in his book, *De Philosophiae Naturalis Principia Mathematica*. It stated essentially that every particle of matter in the universe attracts every other particle with a force which is directly proportional to the product of their masses and inversely proportional to the square of the distance between them. In other words, for two bodies, of masses m_1 and m_2, the gravitational force of attraction, F, between them is given by

$$F = Gm_1m_2/r^2,$$

where r is the separation of the two bodies and G the GRAVITATIONAL CONSTANT. If the separation is doubled, the force is reduced by a factor of four. (Note that an equal and opposite force acts on each particle, or body; thus the force experienced by m_1 is the same in magnitude but opposite in direction to that experienced by m_2.)

According to Newtonian theory, gravity is a force which acts instantaneously between bodies and particles; Newtonian gravitation has proved satisfactory to account for the motions of planets, stars, galaxies, etc., and for almost all purposes, the theory works perfectly. However, under certain extreme conditions (e.g. in the vicinity of BLACK HOLES) Newtonian theory turns out to be inadequate and it is necessary to use the GENERAL THEORY OF RELATIVITY to describe these situations. This does not imply that Newtonian theory is 'wrong', simply that, under certain circumstances, general relativity is more adequate.

The real nature of gravitation is still something of a mystery. It is an extremely weak force compared to the other known forces of nature (electromagnetic force, and the weak and strong nuclear interactions), but where large masses are concerned (which tend to be more or less electrically neutral) it is the dominant one.

Gravitational constant (G). The constant which determines the magnitude of the gravitational attraction between two massive bodies, according to Newton's theory of gravity. According to Newtonian theory, the magnitude of the force (F) acting between two bodies of masses m_1 and m_2, separated by distance r, is given by:

$$F = Gm_1m_2/r^2.$$

The value of G in SI units is 6.67×10^{-11} N m² kg⁻² (newton square metre per kilogramme squared). G is a universal constant and, we believe, applies equally everywhere in the universe.

However, although G is regarded as a fundamental constant, there have been suggestions made that G changes with time, and that possibly the value of G declines in a way that is related to the rate of expansion of the universe. If this is so, then the value of the gravitational constant must have been greater in the past than it now is. The evidence for and against this proposal is not yet sufficiently clear-cut. If the value of G does decline with time, then among the interesting consequences, we should expect the Sun to decline in luminosity with time, and the Earth to expand. A changing gravitational constant would have far-reaching implications for COSMOLOGY.

Gravitational waves. According to the GENERAL THEORY OF RELATIVITY, a disturbance in a gravitational field should be propagated through space as a wave (analogous to ELECTROMAGNETIC RADIATION) travelling at the speed of light. Because gravity is a very weak force compared to the other FORCES OF NATURE, we would expect gravitational radiation to be very difficult to detect.

Possible sources of gravitational radiation include rapidly rotating objects which are distorted from spherical shape, explosive events such as SUPERNOVAE, and material falling into BLACK HOLES.

Attempts to detect gravitational waves have been going on for nearly two decades, but the first reported results were published as recently as 1969 by Professor J. Weber of the University of Maryland. Weber's detectors take the form of aluminium cylinders (about $1\frac{1}{2}$ metres long by 1 metre in diameter) which would be set into vibration if a gravitational wave of the right frequency should pass by. In order to eliminate spurious effects he used a number of widely spaced detectors. His results appear to indicate gravitational waves approaching from the direction of the galactic centre. If his results are interpreted as indicating that there is a source of gravitational waves at the centre of the Galaxy, then, because gravitational waves are so weak, and the galactic centre so far away, the amount of energy required to produce detectable waves must be colossal. If the gravitational radiation were produced by stars falling into a massive black hole at the galactic centre, then the results appear to indicate that several thousand stars per annum must be swallowed up to account for the observed radiation.

Attempts to duplicate Weber's results have failed so far, and there is now considerable doubt as to the validity of his observations. Therefore there is no undisputed evidence of the detection of gravitational waves. However, the search for these waves is continuing, and it may, for example, prove possible to detect gravitational waves by studying perturbations in the motion of deep-space probes.

Great circle. The circle obtained on the surface of a sphere by the intersection with the surface of a plane which passes through the centre of the sphere. Any plane which intersects the sphere but does not pass through the centre meets the sphere in a small circle. A great circle is, in fact, the largest possible circle which can be drawn on the surface of a sphere. The shortest distance between two points on a sphere is an arc of a great circle passing through those points. Examples of great circles on the Earth are the equator and lines of longitude; on the CELESTIAL SPHERE, the celestial equator, the meridian, ecliptic, etc. (see Figure 9).

Great Red Spot. The only feature in the atmosphere of JUPITER which is of a permanent or semi-permanent nature. It appears as a large oval reddish patch (with a surface area comparable to that of the Earth) in the south tropical zone of the planet, and the earliest records of its appearance date back at least to the astronomer Cassini in 1665. It became prominent in 1878 and has remained fairly conspicuous since. Several theories have been advanced to account for it; for example, it was suggested that it might represent a solid 'raft' of material floating in the atmosphere. An alternative possibility was that it might be the top of a 'Taylor column', a column of stagnant air formed by the flow of the atmosphere above a 'surface' obstruction. Photographs taken by the US space probes Pioneers 10 and 11 indicate a circulation of gas within the spot suggestive of a massive cyclone. It may well be, therefore, that the Great Red Spot is a weather system, the coloration being due to the chemical composition of the material contained in the circulation.

Greatest elongation. ◊ELONGATION.

Greenhouse effect. The effect whereby a planetary atmosphere acts to maintain the surface temperature of a planet well above the temperature that would be expected if the planet were a BLACK BODY, i.e. absorbing all the incoming solar radiation and re-emitting it again. A particular case is the planet Venus which has a dense carbon-dioxide atmosphere; carbon dioxide is largely opaque to infra-red radiation. Incoming radiation of shorter wavelength passes through the Venusian atmosphere and is absorbed at the planetary surface, so heating up the ground; the heat re-radiated by the ground (infra-red radiation) does not readily escape through the atmosphere, with the result that the temperature of the planet is maintained at a high level (almost 500°C, compared to the expected black-body temperature of some 90°C).

The effect is analogous to that which is conventionally thought to operate in a terrestrial greenhouse, the glass transmitting visible light, but limiting the amount of re-radiated heat from the ground which can escape; the effectiveness of this process in greenhouses has been questioned.

Gregorian calendar. ⬦YEAR.

Gregorian reflector. A type of reflecting telescope designed by the Scottish mathematician James Gregory in 1663. It employed a concave primary mirror and a concave secondary which was placed outside the focus of the primary; light reflected from the secondary passed back down the telescope tube through a hole in the primary to the eyepiece (⬦TELESCOPE, Figure 44b). Such an optical system produces an erect image, but the field of view is very restricted. Gregory did not construct such a telescope, the first reflector actually to be built being the NEWTONIAN REFLECTOR in 1671.

H

H II region. A region of ionized ($\Diamond$IONIZATION) hydrogen gas; the term is applied to the region of ionized emission nebula ($\Diamond$NEBULA) found around hot, highly luminous stars embedded in gas clouds. Around the hottest stars (of spectral type O; $\Diamond$SPECTRAL CLASSIFICATION), H II regions can extend out to a radius of as much as 100 parsecs.

Half-life. In the context of radioactive decay ($\Diamond$RADIOACTIVITY) this is the time required for one-half of the radioactive atoms ($\Diamond$ATOM) in a sample of material to decay. Thus, for example, the isotope of uranium, U^{238}, has a very long half-life of $4 \cdot 5 \times 10^9$ years, while polonium-212 has a half-life of 3×10^{-7} seconds. From a knowledge of its half-life it is possible to estimate the age of a sample of radioactive material.

Halley's comet. Probably the most famous COMET, it is named after Edmond Halley (Astronomer Royal from 1719 to 1742, the year of his death) who first showed that comets move round the Sun in elliptical orbits, and are in fact members of the Solar System. In particular he noted that the comets which had been seen in 1531, 1607 and 1682 had very similar orbits, and he suggested that they were one and the same object returning at intervals of between seventy-five and seventy-six years. He predicted that the comet would return in 1758, as indeed it did. Record's of Halley's comet stretch back over hundreds of years (for example, it is depicted in the Bayeux tapestry as it made an appearance in the year 1066, prior to the Battle of Hastings); its last appearance was in 1910, and it is due to return in 1986. Details of its orbit are: period 76·1 years; orbital eccentricity 0·97; semi-major axis 17·8 a.u.; perihelion distance 0·6 a.u. (closer to the Sun than Venus); aphelion distance 35 a.u. (beyond Neptune).

Heaviside layer. A layer in the IONOSPHERE which reflects radio waves of the frequencies generally used for long-distance communication on Earth. It is otherwise known as the E layer.

Heliocentric coordinates. Coordinates specifying the position of an object as seen from the centre of the Sun. Heliocentric coordinates are usually referred to the plane of the ECLIPTIC – thus the position of a planet in its orbit at any instant is often specified in terms of heliocentric ecliptic coordinates. (◊ELEMENTS OF AN ORBIT.)

Helium (He). The second lightest element which, after hydrogen, is the second most abundant in the universe. The neutral helium ATOM consists of a nucleus made up of two protons and two neutrons around which revolve two electrons; the atomic mass is 4, and the atomic number (i.e. charge on the nucleus) is 2. The nucleus of a helium atom is also known as an alpha particle. (◊HELIUM PROBLEM.)

Helium problem. In terms of volume, nearly 8 per cent of all the matter in the universe is helium, and in terms of mass (since helium atoms are four times as massive as hydrogen atoms, hydrogen being the most common element in the universe), 25 per cent of all the mass in the universe appears to be helium. If, as is generally agreed, the heavier elements have been built up from the lighter ones (starting with hydrogen) in a chain of nuclear reactions, the problem is to account for this observed abundance of helium. Helium is being produced from hydrogen by means of nuclear reactions inside stars, but this process is not adequate to account for the amount of helium actually observed. If the BIG-BANG THEORY of the origin of the universe is correct, then the observed quantity of helium could have been produced in the first few minutes of the existence of the universe, while the temperature lay in the region of 10^{10} to 10^9 degrees kelvin. The observed abundance of helium is one of many factors which at the moment favour the Big-Bang theory.

Hermes. A tiny ASTEROID, less than 1 km in diameter, which can occasionally approach the Earth to within twice the Moon's distance (as it did in 1937). It is sometimes called an 'earth-grazer'.

hertz (Hz). The SI unit of measurement of frequency (i.e. the number of waves passing a fixed point per second). Thus, 1 wave per second would correspond to a frequency of 1 Hz, 100 000 waves per second to 100 000 Hz, etc. Common multiples are kilohertz (kHz) – 1000 Hz, megahertz (MHz) – 1 000 000 Hz, and gigahertz (GHz) – 1 000 000 000 Hz. An older unit of frequency is cycles per second (c/s); 1 Hz = 1 c/s.

Hertzsprung–Russell diagram. A diagram, originally devised in the early part of the twentieth century as a result of the work of H. N. Russell and E. Hertzsprung, which plots luminosity (or an equivalent quantity) against temperature (or an equivalent) for stars.

As shown in Figure 24, in the vertical direction one plots either ABSOLUTE MAGNITUDE or the logarithm of LUMINOSITY (or, under certain circumstances, APPARENT MAGNITUDE), while in the horizontal direction one plots spectral class (◊SPECTRAL CLASSIFICA-

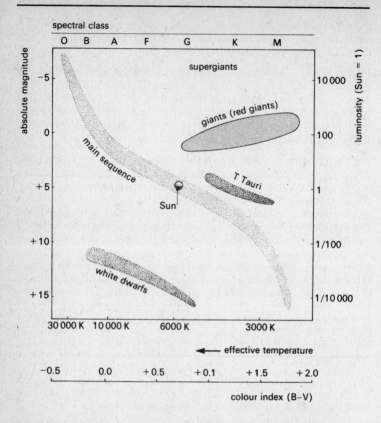

Figure 24. Hertzsprung–Russell Diagram. The diagram here illustrates schematically different types of coordinates which may be used in various forms of the Hertzsprung–Russell (or H–R) Diagram and the principal regions of the diagram in which most stars are to be found. In the vertical direction may be plotted absolute magnitude or luminosity, while on the horizontal axis is plotted spectral class, colour index, or effective temperature (note that temperature *increases* from right to left).

TION), COLOUR INDEX or the logarithm of EFFECTIVE TEMPERATURE (note that in this diagram temperature increases from right to left). We can denote the Sun as a point on the diagram, knowing its absolute magnitude (+4·8) and spectral class (G2). If this is done for a large cross-section of stars, it is found that the positions of stars are not distributed at random on the diagram, i.e. any random value of luminosity is not associated with any random value of temperature. Instead the majority of stars lie in a few well-defined regions of the diagram; the largest group forming the main sequence, a band which slopes from the upper left to the lower right of the diagram. This basically implies that, for main-sequence stars, the hotter the star, the more luminous it is.

Two other important groups are the RED GIANTS and the WHITE DWARFS. The former are cool red stars which, because of their very large surface areas, emit large quantities of radiation; they are much more luminous than main-sequence stars of the same spectral class. The latter are stars which may be very hot but which are so small that their luminosities are much lower than those of main-sequence stars of the same spectral class.

The applications of the diagram are many and varied: for example, the changes in temperature and luminosity of a star throughout its lifetime may be plotted as an evolutionary track (◊STELLAR EVOLUTION, Figure 42c). It has proved to be a particularly valuable aid to the study of star clusters, stellar evolution, effect of interstellar extinction, etc.

The name is usually abbreviated to H–R diagram. A form of the diagram in which magnitude is plotted against colour index is referred to as a colour–magnitude (or C–M) diagram.

Hohmann orbit. The TRANSFER ORBIT which allows a spacecraft to move from one orbit to another with the minimum expenditure of energy (see Figure 45). For example, the Hohmann orbit from the Earth to Mars is an ellipse for which the PERIHELION distance is equal to the radius of the Earth's orbit and the APHELION distance is equal to the radius of the orbit of Mars; in other words, the orbit is an ellipse which just touches the orbits of Earth and Mars (but does not cross either) at opposite ends of the major axis. Although the Hohmann orbit requires the least expenditure of energy to get from one orbit to another, it has the disadvantage of requiring long flight times; to reach Mars in this way would require some ten months. In practice faster transfer orbits, requiring more energy, tend to be used for interplanetary space probes.

Hour angle. The angle between an observer's MERIDIAN and a celestial body measured westwards (i.e. clockwise) from the meridian in a direction parallel to the CELESTIAL EQUATOR (see Figure 25). Hour angle is usually expressed in terms of time units (hours, minutes and seconds, where one hour is equivalent to 15 degrees) since the value of hour angle increases due to the apparent daily rotation of the CELESTIAL SPHERE. Thus the hour angle of a star is zero when it crosses the meridian (at upper TRANSIT); six hours later, the celestial sphere has rotated through 90°, and the value of hour angle is six hours. Thus, the hour angle is equal to the time which has elapsed since the

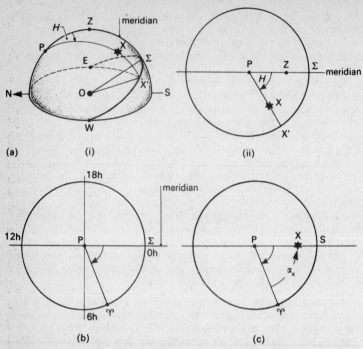

Figure 25. Hour angle and sidereal time. (a) (i) The hemisphere of the celestial sphere visible to the observer, O, is shown. His meridian passes through N (north point of the horizon), P (north celestial pole), Z (zenith) and S (south point of the horizon). It intersects the celestial equator at the point Σ. The hour angle, H, of star X is the angle $\Sigma OX'$ = angle ZPX measured on the celestial sphere. The apparent east to west rotation of the celestial sphere causes the hour angle of the star to increase steadily from zero hour when the star crosses the meridian, until after twenty-four hours it again returns to the meridian.

(a) (ii) A view of the celestial sphere from vertically above P; again, angle ZPX (= angle ΣPX) is the hour angle H.

(b) The sidereal time at any instant is defined to be the hour angle of the vernal equinox, Υ; i.e. it is the angle $\Sigma P\Upsilon$ expressed in time units where 24h = 360°.

(c) If a star of right ascension α_x is on the meridian, then the sidereal time is equal to the right ascension of that star.

last occasion on which the star crossed the meridian. After twenty-four hours, the star returns to the meridian once more. ($\Leftrightarrow$ CELESTIAL COORDINATES; SIDEREAL TIME.)

Hour circle. A great circle on the celestial sphere passing through a celestial body and the north and south celestial poles; it intersects the celestial equator at right angles.

Hubble's constant (H). The constant of porportionality relating the velocity of recession of a galaxy (V) to its distance from us (D); thus $V = HD$. In the 1920s E. E. Hubble showed that the galaxies beyond the LOCAL GROUP are receding from us with velocities proportional to their distances, i.e. a galaxy at twice the distance of a nearer one will be receding at twice the velocity of the nearer one. Hubble's original observations indicated that a galaxy at a distance of, say, 10 megaparsecs would be receding at a velocity of 5500 km s^{-1}; i.e. his observations indicated that H = 550 km s^{-1} per megaparsec. In subsequent years, revised determinations have altered the accepted value of H considerably and, at present, it is thought to lie between 100 km s^{-1} Mpc^{-1} and 50 km s^{-1} Mpc^{-1}; the consensus of opinion is that the true value lies close to the lower limit, and a widely quoted value is 55 km s^{-1} Mpc^{-1}, which is smaller than Hubble's original value by a factor of 10.

The value of Hubble's constant is crucial to a determination of the 'age' of the universe, the mean density of matter in the universe, and the future development of the universe ($\Diamond$ COSMOLOGY).

Hyades. A GALACTIC CLUSTER of stars, the brightest members of which form a fairly conspicuous V-shaped formation visible to the naked eye in the constellation Taurus. The cluster is located at a distance of some 140 light years and contains about 100 stars within a diameter of 16 light years. The age of the cluster is estimated to be about 500 million years.

It is an example of a moving cluster; i.e. all members of the cluster share the same motion through space (apart from their individual random motions within the cluster) and because of this their individual PROPER MOTIONS converge towards a point on the celestial sphere (in the same way that parallel railway lines appear to converge at a distant point) – the convergent point. If this point can be determined for a cluster, this information can be combined with measurements of the RADIAL VELOCITY and proper motion of member stars to reveal the distance of the cluster.

Hydrogen (H). The lightest and most common element in the universe; about 92 per cent by volume of all the matter in the universe is hydrogen. The hydrogen ATOM consists of one positively charged particle, the proton, and one negatively charged particle, the electron, which orbits the proton ($\Diamond$ SPECTRUM, Figure 41a); the atomic mass is 1 and the atomic number (i.e. charge on the nucleus) is also 1. Regions of neutral hydrogen are referred to as H I regions, while regions of ionized hydrogen are H II regions.

Hyperbola. The CONIC SECTION obtained when a right circular cone is cut by a plane which makes an angle with the base greater than that made by the side of the cone (see Figure 12). It is an *open* curve, i.e. it does not close on itself like an ellipse.

Hyperbolic trajectory. The open path (◇HYPERBOLA) followed by a body moving in excess of ESCAPE VELOCITY (◇ORBIT, Figure 28). For example, a spacecraft leaving the Earth on such a trajectory will never return, but will continue to move away at a speed which diminishes (because of the Earth's gravitational attraction) but tends towards a finite value. Thus, in principle, no matter how far the spacecraft travels it will still continue to move away from the Earth at a finite velocity. It follows that any body in the vicinity of the Sun which is observed to be pursuing a hyperbolic trajectory cannot remain a member of the SOLAR SYSTEM.

I

Icarus. An ASTEROID just over 1 km in diameter, and remarkable because of its highly elliptical orbit (eccentricity = 0·83) which takes it at perihelion to within 28 000 000 km of the Sun (less than half the mean distance of Mercury from the Sun), while at aphelion it passes beyond the orbit of Mars.

IGY – International Geophysical Year. A period of concerted international study of the Earth and its environment in which some fifty nations participated between 1 July 1957 and 31 December 1958. This period coincided with a period of maximum activity in the sunspot cycle (◊SOLAR CYCLE), and it was during this time that the first artificial Earth satellites were launched by the USSR and USA.

Image tube. A device containing a sensitive surface on which a pattern of charge is built up according to the intensity of light in an image which falls on it; amplification of the resulting signals enables a faint image to be enhanced. The image tube is finding wide application in astronomy today, for example in studying faint spectra. (◊SPECTRO-GRAPH.)

Inclination. The angle at which one plane is tilted to another. For example:

(a) the inclination of a planetary orbit is normally taken to mean the angle between the plane of the orbit and the plane of the Earth's orbit (i.e. the ECLIPTIC) (◊ORBITAL ELEMENTS, Figure 29b);

(b) equatorial inclination of a planet is the angle between the plane of its equator and its orbit plane;

(c) the inclination of the orbit of an artificial Earth satellite is the angle at which its orbit plane intersects the plane of the equator.

Inertia. The resistance of a massive body to any change in its velocity. Any body will continue in a state of rest or of uniform straight-line motion unless acted upon by a force (◊NEWTON'S LAWS OF MOTION). Thus a spacecraft, when its rocket motors are switched off, follows a ballistic trajectory because of its inertia. In Newton's second law of motion, the relationship between the acceleration, a, of a body and the applied force, F, is $F = ma$, where m is the inertial mass of the body. As far as can be determined, the inertial mass of a body is exactly equal to its gravitational mass, which determines its gravitational attraction. There does not seem to be any *a priori* reason why these two masses should be exactly equal, and there is still considerable debate on the question of the nature of inertia ($\diamond$ MACH'S PRINCIPLE).

Inertial frame. A frame of reference, or coordinate system, which is in uniform motion, i.e. it is not subject to acceleration.

Inertial mass. $\diamond$ INERTIA.

Inferior conjunction. A planet is said to be at inferior conjunction when the Sun, planet and Earth are in a straight line such that the planet lies between the Sun and the Earth ($\diamond$ PLANETARY CON-FIGURATIONS, Figure 32). This situation can occur only for the planets Mercury and Venus. ($\diamond$ TRANSIT.)

Inferior planets. Term applied to those planets whose orbits lie closer in to the Sun than the orbit of the Earth, namely, Mercury and Venus. ($\diamond$ PLANETARY CONFIGURATIONS, Figure 32.)

Infra-red astronomy. That branch of astronomy concerned with the measurement of infra-red radiation from celestial sources. Some pioneering work was done in this field by means of the thermocouple, a device which produces an electric current when subjected to heat, in the nineteenth century by Lord Rosse, and in the 1920s by such workers as Pettit and Nicholson. Most of the developments in this field have come in the last decade. The atmosphere transmits to ground level only a limited amount of infra-red radiation with wavelengths within particular wavebands, and water vapour, for example, is a major absorber of this radiation. It is because of the effect of the atmosphere, the faintness of infra-red sources (apart from the Sun), and the fact that it is only in recent years that efficient detectors have been developed, that infra-red astronomy has been rather a slow starter.

It is now an exciting and developing branch of astronomy. Among the sources under study are the planets (maps of the temperature distribution over their surfaces can be produced), young stars in the process of formation (protostars; $\diamond$ STELLAR EVOLUTION) which may not emit measurable amounts of visible light, but can be detected in the infra-red, the galactic centre, and extra-galactic objects such as QUASARS.

Infra-red astronomy can be carried out by means of suitable detectors placed at the focus of ordinary reflecting optical telescopes, but a number of purpose-built infra-red telescopes (or flux-collectors) have been constructed, such as those installed on mountain sites in Tenerife and Hawaii. Because the wavelength of infra-red radiation is longer than visible light, the reflecting surfaces of the telescope mirrors do not need to be formed so precisely as for conventional optical telescopes (⟡RESOLVING POWER). Like other branches of astronomy, it is best performed from above the Earth's atmosphere and, although there has not yet been a satellite devoted exclusively to infra-red observations, a design is under active consideration.

Infra-red radiation. Electromagnetic radiation of wavelength longer than that of visible light (literally, 'beyond red') which we may detect as 'heat'. Although the boundaries drawn between different kinds of radiation are rather arbitrary, infra-red can be taken as lying between wavelengths of 0·75 MICRON (i.e. $0·75 \times 10^{-6}$ metres) and 1000 micron (1 millimetre). The longest wavelength infra-red is sometimes referred to as sub-millimetre radiation. The existence of infra-red radiation was first demonstrated experimentally in 1800 by William Herschel; his experiment consisted of passing sunlight through a prism to produce a spectrum in order that, with a thermometer, he could determine which wavelengths of light carried the greatest quantity of heat. In fact, he discovered that the thermometer rose in temperature by the greatest amount when it was placed *beyond* the red end of the spectrum, and deduced that invisible radiation of longer wavelength must carry heat from the Sun.

Inner planet. ⟡INFERIOR PLANET.

Intelligent life in the universe. At present there is no direct evidence for the existence of intelligent life elsewhere in the universe but, because there is a substantial body of opinion that life in some form is quite commonplace, then the possibility of intelligent life cannot be ignored. If the possibility of intelligent life is admitted then one must also admit the possibility of the existence of advanced technologies, possibly with the ability to communicate over interstellar distances. Opinions differ widely on the probability of advanced technological civilizations existing at present in the Galaxy, estimates of the number of such civilizations ranging from one (i.e. we are unique, a view quite strongly held by a number of authorities) to 10^6. Although there are no results available, nevertheless there is a substantial body of published theoretical work on this topic, and a measure of the scientific respectability which this subject has achieved is the number of conferences which have already been devoted to it; of particular note was the international conference held at Byurakan Astrophysical Observatory in the USSR in 1971.

In an attempt to specify the principal questions which must be answered in order to estimate the number of advanced technologies in the Galaxy the following equation, proposed in its original form by F. D. Drake, provides a useful basis for discussion:

$$N = R_* f_p n_e f_l f_i f_c L$$

where

N = the number of advanced technologies capable of interstellar communication *at this time*,

R_* is the mean rate of star formation over the lifetime of the Galaxy,

f_p is the fraction of stars in the Galaxy which have planetary systems,

n_e is the average number of planets per system where conditions are suitable for life,

f_l is the fraction of those suitable planets on which life actually appears,

f_i is the fraction of life-bearing planets on which intelligence develops,

f_c is the fraction of such planets on which communication technology (e.g. radio astronomy) develops, and,

L is the average lifetime of such a communicative technology.

The degree of certainty with which such factors can be estimated diminishes rapidly as we proceed down the list; thus R_* is known to be about ten stars per annum, but the value of L is a matter of sheer speculation. The product of the first six factors on the right-hand side of the equation gives the mean rate of emergence of communicative technologies in the Galaxy. This may be denoted by R, in which case we have $N = RL$.

For the sake of argument, let us make the following estimates of the various factors:

$R_* = 10$ (fairly well established)

$f_p = 0\cdot1$ (this may well be an underestimate)

$n_e = 0\cdot1$ (if there is an average of ten planets per system, this means that one planet in a hundred may be ecologically suitable for life)

$f_l = 1$ (there is a strong body of opinion to the effect that, if conditions *are* right, life *will* develop)

$f_i = 0\cdot1$ (we do not know how intelligence originated on Earth, but we assume that it originated by natural processes likely to occur elsewhere)

$f_c = 0\cdot1$ (for the sake of argument).

Taking these figures, we find that $R = 10^{-3}$ (i.e. one new technology appears in 1000 years), and so, $N = 10^{-3}L$.

What is L? The only technology we know about is our own, and we have possessed radio communication for less than 100 years; the current trend in the behaviour of the human species does not allow us to be particularly confident that the species will survive much beyond the year 2000. Will the same be true of other technologies (if they exist)? If so, then $L = 10^2$, and $N = 0.1$; i.e. at the present time we are the *only* advanced technology in the Galaxy. However, if other species can overcome the problems of resources and social organization, L may be quite large. A value which is often discussed is $L = 10^8$ years, in which case $N = 10^5$, and there is a reasonable chance of other advanced technologies existing at present within a range of 1000 light years.

All of the factors estimated above may be grossly in error, with the exception of R_* and, possibly, f_p, so that little faith can be placed in the value of N. Nevertheless, the figures are sufficiently interesting to make it worthwhile considering projects to attempt to detect evidence (such as artificial radio emissions) of the civilizations which *may* exist elsewhere in the Galaxy. At least the possibility of intelligent life existing elsewhere in the universe appears quite a strong one. ($\Diamond$ LIFE IN THE UNIVERSE; LIFE, ORIGIN OF; PLANETS OF OTHER STARS; UFO; INTERSTELLAR COMMUNICATION.)

Intensity interferometer. $\Diamond$ INTERFEROMETER.

Interference pattern. The pattern of light and dark obtained when two beams of light combine or interfere with each other (see Figure 26a and b). If two waves of the same wavelength and amplitude have the same phase (i.e. their crests and troughs are in step), then the crests will enhance each other to produce a bright fringe of light; if they are exactly out of phase, then the crests of one wave and the troughs of the other will cancel each other out, so producing a dark fringe. These patterns are also referred to as interference fringes. Such patterns may be formed with any type of electromagnetic radiation (or with other types of waves, water waves, for example), and the interpretation of these interference patterns forms the basis of the technique of interferometry ($\Diamond$ INTERFEROMETER).

Interferometer. A device which makes use of the phenomenon of the interference of electromagnetic waves ($\Diamond$ INTERFERENCE PATTERN) arriving at two separate detectors to attain more precise position measurements or better RESOLVING POWER than could be achieved with a single telescope or detector (see Figure 26c and d).

Consider, for example, the radio interferometer. In this device, two radio telescopes, separated by a known distance, are used to study the same source; because of the separation of the two receivers, there is a small delay between the arrival of a given radio wave at the first and second radio telescope (i.e. the waves arriving at any instant at the two receivers will be out of phase, in general, and will interfere with each other if they are combined). The combined signal is analysed and, for example, as the source moves across the sky, the analysis of the changing interference pattern will yield a precise position for the source.

For a given wavelength of radiation, the greater the separation of the telescopes, the higher the resolving power achieved. The most precise position measurements in radio astronomy have been made by long-baseline interferometry, combining signals from two radio telescopes separated by thousands of kilometres. The longest baseline so far achieved is between California and Australia, some 10 600 km, by means of which, in 1970, a resolving power of 0·001 seconds of arc was obtained at a wavelength of 13 cm.

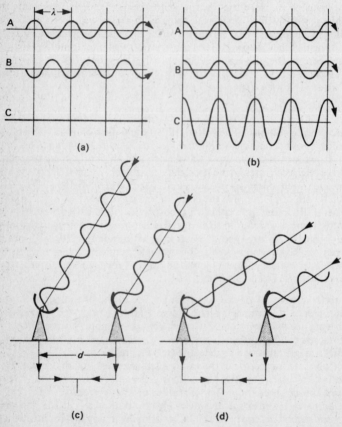

(a)

(b)

(c)

(d)

The Michelson stellar interferometer is a device which combines in one telescope two lightbeams reflected from mirrors separated by a distance greater than the aperture of the telescope to produce an interference pattern. By this means, the diameters of a few giant stars were measured. The intensity interferometer is a more recent device involving two telescopes, each of which measures the intensity of light from the same star, and the resulting signals are then combined. In this way the instrument at the Narrabri Observatory, Australia, can measure the angular diameters of stars as small as 2×10^{-4} seconds of arc; this has allowed the diameters of main-sequence stars ($\diamond$ HERTZSPRUNG–RUSSELL DIAGRAM) to be measured directly for the first time.

Intergalactic matter. It is uncertain how much rarefied matter exists in the space between the galaxies. Although there is no evidence for the intergalactic extinction of starlight due to solid matter, the existence of gas cannot be ruled out, and there is a number of different observations which hint strongly at the existence of intergalactic gas in clusters of galaxies.

First, there are some clusters of galaxies in which the amount of matter in the member galaxies does not provide sufficient mass to prevent the member galaxies from dispersing, i.e. escaping from the clusters; since these clusters still exist, it would seem that there must be a considerable quantity of invisible mass in these clusters. It may be that much of this 'missing mass' is contained in intergalactic gas.

Secondly, there are some RADIO GALAXIES – where the radiation appears to be coming from expanding clouds of matter moving out from these galaxies – which give the impression from their appearance that the expanding matter is experiencing resistance to its motion, such as might be expected if this matter were expanding into gas clouds.

Figure 26. Interferometer and interference. (a) Two waves have the same wavelength, λ, but wave B is 180° out of phase with wave A (i.e. the crest of one coincides with the trough of the other). If the waves combine they cancel each other out (C).

(b) If waves A and B are in phase (crests coinciding) then the crests and troughs amplify each other (C). The effect of combining two out-of-phase light waves is to produce a dark patch; two in-phase waves produce a bright patch.

The interference of waves has a number of applications in astronomy: Illustrated here is the use of two radio telescopes, separated by a known distance, d, as an interferometer. In (c) the waves arriving from a source are out of phase, combining to give zero signal, while in (d) the waves are in phase, producing a strong signal. Analysis of the interference patterns obtained from astronomical sources allows high resolving power to be achieved, so that the position of a source, or its detailed structure, may be deduced.

Third, a number of extended X-ray sources ($\Diamond$ X-RAY ASTRONOMY) coincide with clusters of galaxies, and it has been suggested that the X-rays are emitted by hot intergalactic gas in these clusters. In the case of the Perseus cluster, all three of the above phenomena have been noted, and the case for intergalactic gas must be strong.

International Geophysical Year. $\Diamond$ IGY.

Interplanetary matter. The rarefied gas, PLASMA and distribution of solid particles which exist within the SOLAR SYSTEM. The solid particles range in size from METEOROIDS to particles of less than 0·1 micron (10^{-7} metres) across. Visible evidence for such material includes the ZODIACAL LIGHT, but much of our knowledge of the interplanetary medium comes from interplanetary space probes. The interplanetary gas is largely ionized, and so may be regarded as a plasma; it is made up of atomic particles expelled from the Sun ($\Diamond$ SOLAR WIND) and has an average density in the vicinity of the Earth of about 5×10^6 protons per cubic metre (about 10^{-19} times the density of air at ground level). The density of solar-wind plasma diminishes with the square of distance from the Sun.

Interstellar communication. The view is quite widely held that the difficulties of physically travelling over interstellar distances are so great that we are unlikely to be able to travel to the stars in the remotely foreseeable future (but $\Diamond$ DAEDALUS PROJECT), if ever, and so if we are to communicate with other technological civilizations in the Galaxy ($\Diamond$ INTELLIGENT LIFE IN THE UNIVERSE), if any exist, then it must be by some other means.

The consensus of opinion is that the most logical means of communication is by means of microwave transmissions ($\Diamond$ CYCLOPS PROJECT). A question under debate at present is whether or not more advanced technologies than our own would be willing to take the trouble to advertise their presence to newer civilizations such as our own; if this were so, the chances of picking up such a signal would be much greater than those of simply 'eavesdropping' on two-way communications between advanced technologies.

It is furthermore assumed that basic messages can be exchanged between widely differing civilizations by utilizing fundamental mathematical principles which are taken to be universal. Whether or not this would work out in practice remains to be seen.

Interstellar dust. $\Diamond$ INTERSTELLAR MATTER.

Interstellar extinction. The absorption of starlight in space by the interstellar dust ($\Diamond$ INTERSTELLAR MATTER) which causes stars to appear fainter than they ought to be for their distances. This effect was first noted in the 1920s, and the realization of the existence of this effect greatly altered our understanding of the scale of the Galaxy. On average the effect of extinction is to make a star appear fainter by about 0·8 magnitudes ($\diamond$APPARENT MAGNITUDE) for each kiloparsec of distance; i.e. in round figures, a star at 3000 light years appears only half as bright as it would do if no dust were present.

Interstellar matter. The rarefied gas and small particles (interstellar dust) distributed through interstellar space in the GALAXY (2). The gas is principally hydrogen and helium, having an average density of about 10^{-21} kg m^{-3}; this corresponds to about 500000 hydrogen atoms per cubic metre, an extremely low density (much lower than any terrestrial vacuum). Other gases exist in smaller quantities and in recent years more than twenty different molecules have been identified. ($\diamond$INTER-STELLAR MOLECULES).

The dust consists of particles, or 'grains', which are typically 0·1 micron (10^{-7} metres) in radius, and which are thought to be composed of carbon (in the form of graphite) or silicates; in some cases, the grains are thought to have icy mantles. The effect of the dust is to scatter starlight, so that distant stars appear fainter than they would appear in the absence of dust; furthermore, since blue light is more strongly scattered than red, stars appear redder than they really are ($\diamond$INTER-STELLAR REDDENING). The extinction of starlight in space limits the distance to which we can observe in the plane of the Galaxy, the dust being heavily concentrated towards the galactic plane, and prevents our seeing the galactic centre. It was not until the 1920s that the effects of interstellar extinction were realized. Longer wavelength radiation, infra-red, microwave and radio, is not significantly affected by the dust ($\diamond$21-CENTIMETRE RADIATION).

The total mass of interstellar material is about 10 per cent of the mass of the Galaxy, and about 10 per cent of the interstellar matter is in the form of dust grains.

Interstellar molecules. In recent years, emission-line radiation from a wide variety of molecules in interstellar clouds has been detected. These molecules emit mostly in the microwave region of the spectrum ($\diamond$ELECTROMAGNETIC SPECTRUM), and may be detected by means of radio telescopes.

Well over thirty different types of molecule, many of them organic, have been identified. They include hydroxyl (OH), water (H_2O), hydrogen cyanide (HCN), formaldehyde (H_2CO), and more complex molecules such as ethyl alcohol (CH_3CH_2OH). The origin of these molecules is uncertain, but they may form on the surfaces of dust grains ($\diamond$INTERSTELLAR MATTER), the dust clouds shielding them from stellar ultra-violet radiation.

Many of the interstellar molecules are basic to the formation of life, and the widespread existence of such material in the universe tends to support the view that life may be widespread ($\lozenge$LIFE IN THE UNIVERSE).

Interstellar reddening.   The apparent increase in the redness of stars with increasing distance, due to the effects of interstellar dust ($\lozenge$INTERSTELLAR MATTER). The interstellar dust grains are comparable in size with the wavelength of visible light, and as a result, the amount of scattering of starlight by the grains (and therefore the amount of starlight which is 'lost' in travelling through the dust) is inversely proportional to wavelength. The shorter wavelength radiation (e.g. blue light) is therefore more strongly affected than longer wavelength radiation (red light), and the light which we receive from a distant star has lost more of its blue component than its red component. The effect is to make the star appear redder than it really is.

Invariable plane.   A plane through the centre of mass of the Solar System forming a reference plane which does not change with time due to planetary perturbations. The plane of the ECLIPTIC does slowly change with time. Relative to the ecliptic (epoch 1975), the inclination of the invariable plane is 1° 37′, and the longitude of the ascending node, 107° 28′. The invariable plane is inclined to the Sun's equator by about 7 degrees.

Ion.   An atom which has lost (or gained) one or more electrons compared to the normal or 'neutral' atom (in which the number of negatively charged electrons is equal to the number of positively charged protons in the nucleus). An ion, unlike a neutral atom, has a net charge, positive if it is deficient in electrons (i.e. a positive ion) and negative if it possesses excess electrons (i.e. a negative ion). ($\lozenge$IONIZATION.)

Ion rocket.   A rocket motor in which thrust is produced by the ejection of charged atomic particles (ions; $\lozenge$IONIZATION) accelerated by an electric field, rather than by the expulsion of hot gases generated by chemical reactions as in a conventional rocket. The ion rocket has the great advantage that much higher EXHAUST VELOCITIES can be achieved than with chemical fuels. However, the amount of thrust generated by such motors is small because the mass of material ejected per unit time is small. Ion rockets are quite incapable (in the present state of technology) of lifting themselves off the ground, but they are ideally suited to the situation where a small amount of thrust is required for extended periods or, intermittently, for much longer periods (e.g. attitude-control thrusters in satellites or spacecraft). In the longer term, ion rockets operated in space may be used to provide a small continual thrust over long periods so as to accelerate interplanetary spacecraft to much higher final velocities than may be attained by chemical rockets at the present time.

In practice, an ion motor operates by passing gaseous propellant such as mercury or caesium into a discharge chamber where the gas is ionized; an electric field between two grids accelerates the positive ions and ejects them from the rear of the motor; the resulting REACTION (1) propels the vehicle forward. It is important to arrange to eject a stream of electrons too, so as to keep the spacecraft electrically neutral.

Ionization. The process by which ATOMS lose one or more electrons to become ions. An atom which has its full complement of electrons is said to be neutral (neutral hydrogen, for example, is denoted by H I), one which has lost one electron is singly ionized (ionized hydrogen would be denoted H II), an atom which has lost two electrons is doubly ionized, and so on. Ionization may occur in a number of ways, for example, by an electron absorbing a sufficiently energetic photon (◊ELECTROMAGNETIC RADIATION) of radiation to give it the energy required to escape from an atom, or by collisions. The ionization potential is the amount of energy required to remove an electron from a particular energy state in an atom. The very high temperatures in stellar interiors maintain matter in a wholly ionized state. In a gas, high temperature and low pressure and density are conducive to ionization.

Ionization potential. The energy required to ionize (i.e. to remove an electron from) an atom. This is usually expressed in ELECTRON VOLTS (eV). For example, the ionization potential of the hydrogen atom is the energy required to remove its electron from the ground state; this is equal to 13·6 eV. (◊IONIZATION.)

Ionized. ◊IONIZATION.

Ionosphere. That region of the Earth's atmosphere extending from an altitude of some 60 km to approximately 1000 km. It derives its name from the fact that this region contains a large proportion of ionized atoms, the IONIZATION being due to solar radiation. A number of ionized layers have been distinguished, the D, E (or Heaviside layer), F_1 and F_2 layers centred approximately on altitudes of 80, 120, 170 and 300 km respectively. These layers have the property of reflecting radio waves (for example, the E layer reflects signals with frequencies below about 6 MHz, i.e. wavelengths longer than about 50 metres); by 'bouncing' radio transmissions off these layers, radio broadcasts may be sent round the curvature of the Earth's globe. Because the level of ionization is controlled by solar radiation, it follows that any sudden influx of radiation due to solar activity (e.g. SOLAR FLARES) affects these layers so giving rise to interference in radio communication.

Isotope. ◊ATOM.

J

Jovian planets. Term applied to the four giant planets, Jupiter, Saturn, Uranus and Neptune, which share common characteristics that distinguish them from the smaller TERRESTRIAL PLANETS such as the Earth. They are gaseous bodies composed largely of hydrogen, are large compared to the Earth (their radii range from eleven to just under four Earth radii) and massive (318 to 14·5 Earth masses), but have low densities (0·7 to 2·3 times that of water). A further common feature of these planets is rapid axial rotation, their rotation periods lying in the range 9h 50m to 15h 50m. All lie further than 5 astronomical units from the Sun. They are sometimes known as the 'giant planets' or the 'gas giants'.

Julian calendar. The form of calendar ordered by Julius Caesar in 45 B.C., and used for the first time in 44 B.C. This calendar, which was constructed by the Alexandrian astronomer Sosigenes, was the first to utilize a twelve-month year of 365 days with the addition of an extra day every four years (i.e. every fourth year was a leap year) to compensate for the fact that the duration of the year is approximately 365¼ days. The Julian calendar remained in use for some 1600 years until the introduction of the Gregorian calendar (⬦YEAR).

Julian date (J.D.). The number of days, and the fraction of a day, which have elapsed since noon on 1 January 4713 B.C. Thus 1800 hours GMT on 1 March 1980 corresponds to J.D. 2 444 300·25. For certain purposes, for example, when analysing the frequency with which events occur over long periods of time, it is most convenient to use this system of dating.

Jupiter. The fifth planet in order of distance from the Sun and the largest and most massive planet in the Solar System. Although some eleven times the Earth's diameter and 318 times the mass of the Earth, the mean density of Jupiter is low, 1·34 times that of water (i.e. one-quarter of the mean density of the Earth). The axial rotation period is short, 9h 50m 30s at the equator (the period increases slightly at higher latitudes, and a mean figure of 9h 55m 41s is adopted for latitudes of greater than 10°), and because of this rapid rotation the planet bulges out at the equator to the extent that the ratio of equatorial radius to polar radius is 1·06:1. This flattened appearance is readily visible in quite small telescopes.

The visible disc shows parallel cloud belts in which considerable activity takes place. There are no permanent features other than the GREAT RED SPOT which appears to be a giant hurricane in the Jovian atmosphere (the adjective 'Jovian' applies to properties of Jupiter). The atmosphere of Jupiter is composed largely of hydrogen, helium, ammonia and methane, and the overall composition of Jupiter seems to be similar to that of the Sun: about 75 per cent hydrogen, 23 per cent helium and 2 per cent of everything else. As a gaseous planet it does not have a true solid surface, although it may have a small rocky core. It is believed that the structure of Jupiter is as follows: a small central core surrounded by a zone of liquid metallic hydrogen (under very high pressure, hydrogen behaves like a metal) extending out to a radius of some 45000 km, on top of which is a layer of liquid hydrogen some 25000 km thick. The atmosphere, about 1000 km thick, lies on top of this layer.

The mean temperature at the cloud tops is about 140 K (−173°C), but this increases rapidly with depth. Thus it is estimated that at a depth of 1000 km, the temperature may be 2000 K while at the centre of the planet it may reach 50000 K. In fact Jupiter emits between two and three times as much heat as it receives from the Sun.

Jupiter has fourteen satellites, four of which, the GALILEAN SATELLITES, are comparable with our Moon, the rest being small.

Much of our knowledge of Jupiter stems from the two fly-by missions Pioneer 10 and Pioneer 11 of 1973 and 1974 (⟡PIONEER). (See Plate 8.)

Jupiter data

		(Earth = 1)
Mean distance from Sun	778 300 000 km	5·2
Orbital eccentricity	0·048	—
Orbital inclination	1° 18′ 17″	—
Sidereal orbital period	11·86 years	11·86
Axial rotation period (equator)	9h 50m 30s	0·41
Mass	$1·9 \times 10^{27}$ kg	317·8
Radius (equatorial)	71 300 km	11·18
Mean density	$1·34 \times 10^3$ kg m^{-3}	0·242
Surface gravity	25·9 m s^{-2}	2·64

K

Kepler. ◊KEPLER'S LAWS.

Kepler's laws. The three basic laws governing the motion of the planets which were first enunciated in the early part of the seventeenth century by the German mathematician and astronomer Johannes Kepler (1571–1630). These laws were determined as a result of his investigation of planetary motion based on the precise observations of Tycho Brahe (◊TYCHONIC SYSTEM), and are as follows:

1. Each planet moves round the Sun in an elliptical orbit (◊ELLIPSE), with the Sun located at one focus of the ellipse in each case;

2. The radius vector (i.e. the line between the Sun and the planet) sweeps out equal areas of space in equal times; in other words, when the planet is far from the Sun it moves more slowly than when it is close (see Figure 27);

3. The square of the sidereal period (i.e. the time taken to complete one orbit of the Sun), P, is directly proportional to the cube of the mean distance, a, between the Sun and the planet (in fact, a is the semi-major axis of the orbital ellipse). If we measure P in years, and a in astronomical units, this relationship becomes: $P^2 = a^3$.

The third law is of considerable importance in that it allows the distances of all the planets to be determined in terms of astronomical units, provided that their orbit periods can be measured. It is sometimes referred to as the Harmonic Law.

Kepler's laws apply to the motion of any small body in the gravitational field of a massive one, e.g. artificial Earth satellites, interplanetary space probes, etc., and with slight modification, to the motion of two similar massive bodies under their mutual gravitational attraction.

Kinetic energy. The energy which a body possesses as a result of its motion. For a body of mass, m, moving at velocity, v, this is usually expressed as, kinetic energy $= \frac{1}{2}mv^2$. (◊POTENTIAL ENERGY.)

Kinetic theory of gases. The theory, developed in the nineteenth century, notably by Clausius and Maxwell, that the properties of a gas (temperature, pressure, etc.) could be described in terms of the motions

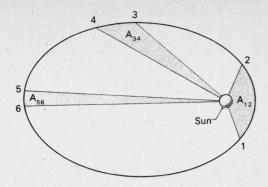

Figure 27. Kepler's Laws. The figure illustrates the first and second laws. The first law states that the planets move round the Sun in elliptical orbits with the Sun located at one focus of the ellipse. The second law states that the radius vector of a planet sweeps out equal areas of space in equal times. Thus in the same length of time the planet will move from 1 to 2, 3 to 4, and 5 to 6 such that areas A_{12}, A_{34} and A_{56} are equal, i.e. the planet moves faster when it is nearer the Sun than it does when farther away.

(and kinetic energy) of the molecules comprising the gas. The theory has wide applications in astrophysics; in particular, from this theory is derived the perfect gas law, relating the pressure, volume, temperature and number of molecules in a gas, which is fundamental to theoretical models of the interiors of stars.

Kirchhoff's laws of spectroscopy. Three basic laws of spectroscopy (⬦ SPECTRUM) first proposed by Gustav Kirchhoff in 1858.

1. Incandescent solids, liquids, and gases under high pressure emit a continuous spectrum (continuum) of radiation;

2. Incandescent gases under low pressure give out an emission-line spectrum (i.e. bright lines at particular wavelengths only);

3. When a continuous spectrum passes through a gas, the gas absorbs radiation at wavelengths which are identical to its own bright emission-line spectrum (case 2 above); this gives rise to dark lines superimposed on the bright continuous spectrum.

The dark lines in the spectrum of the Sun arise because of absorption of light in the solar CHROMOSPHERE which lies above the PHOTO-SPHERE from which a continuous spectrum is emitted.

Kirkwood gaps. Regions in the ASTEROID belt, between Mars and Jupiter, which are practically devoid of asteroids. The gaps arise as a result of the gravitational attraction of the planet Jupiter. If, for example, an asteroid had an orbit period exactly one-half that of Jupiter then after every two revolutions of the asteroid round the Sun it would be lined up with Jupiter, at its closest approach to that planet, and would be subject to the perturbing effect of Jupiter's gravitational attraction. At each of these occasions the asteroid would be subject to the same perturbation, and the cumulative effect of this after a large number of revolutions would be to divert the asteroid into an orbit which was no longer an exact fraction of Jupiter's orbit period. This is an example of the phenomenon of resonance, and the situation applies to asteroids with periods corresponding to other simple fractions of Jupiter's period; thus gaps exist at distances corresponding to periods of $\frac{1}{2}$, $\frac{2}{5}$, $\frac{1}{3}$ and $\frac{1}{4}$ of Jupiter's period.

L

Laika. The name of the first living creature to be placed in orbit round the Earth, a dog which was launched in the Soviet satellite Sputnik 2 on 3 November 1957. She lived for ten days in a space environment.

Large space telescope (LST). A 3-metre aperture reflecting telescope, due to be launched by means of the SPACE SHUTTLE in the 1980s. The LST should be capable of detecting galaxies 100 times fainter than the best that can be achieved by the largest ground-based instruments and should provide monitoring of atmospheric conditions on Venus, Mars, Jupiter and Saturn, as well as being adaptable to a wide variety of observing programmes. The structure will have a mass of some ten tonnes and is to be placed in orbit round the Earth at altitudes of between 648 and 778 kilometres. Its guidance system is designed to hold a target for extended periods to within 0·005 seconds of arc (equivalent to locking on to a human hair at a range of over three kilometres). Images will be relayed to the Earth by television.

Late-type star. ⟡SPECTRAL CLASSIFICATION.

Launch window. The period of time over which conditions are suitable for the launching of a satellite or spacecraft into the desired orbit. Many different conditions determine the duration and frequency of such windows. For example, it may be possible to launch a spacecraft to Mars on any day out of a period of several weeks (provided the rocket vehicle has sufficient reserves of fuel), and this period would constitute the launch window; but this window would only recur at intervals of about 780 days. The long interval arises because suitable *relative* configurations of the Earth and a target planet arise at times separated by the SYNODIC PERIOD of that planet.

Length contraction. ⟡SPECIAL THEORY OF RELATIVITY.

Librations. Apparent oscillations of the Moon which allow an Earth-based observer to see a total of 59 per cent of the surface of the Moon over a period of time. There are two basic librations:

Libration in latitude. Because the rotation axis of the Moon is tilted by

$6\frac{1}{2}°$ to the perpendicular to the plane of its orbit, at alternate times of the month the north or the south pole of our satellite is turned towards us, allowing us to see part of the far side beyond the pole.

Libration in longitude. Although the axial period of the Moon is exactly the same as its orbital period, because its orbit is elliptical, it moves across the celestial sphere faster when near PERIGEE than when at APOGEE. As a result, it is possible to see a little way first round one LIMB and then round the other as the angular rates of axial rotation and revolution periodically get a little out of step.

Life in the universe. The question of whether or not life exists elsewhere in the universe, other than on the Earth, is a subject of very wide interest and debate at present. At this time there is no direct evidence of life elsewhere in the universe, but the consensus of opinion is that life of some kind is likely to be quite common in the universe. Whether or not intelligent life or advanced technologies exist elsewhere at present is very much an open question.

Discussion of this topic is fraught with difficulties. We do not even know exactly what life is; there is no absolute definition of life which distinguishes unequivocally between inanimate and animate matter. We can at least consider those attributes which are necessary for life as we understand it. Life would appear to take the form of an organized system of molecules which is capable of growth and reproduction, and which takes energy from its environment to use for its own purposes; it would seem likely, too, that following the appearance of life, *evolution* to more complex and varied species is likely to occur. This definition of life may well be inadequate, but it is a broad one. It might well be argued that on this basis an advanced computer system, utilizing an energy source, and capable of controlling machinery such that it could extend and reproduce itself, would be 'alive' – possibly this would be so.

We are not certain what conditions are necessary for life to exist, and we only have the example of life on Earth to work from. In the case of the Earth, the conditions prevailing when life originated are quite different from present-day conditions ($\lozenge$ LIFE, ORIGIN OF). However, if we are considering life as we know it (and excluding exotic hypothetical possibilities), then the following conditions are probably necessary:

1. *A planet*: we believe that a planetary surface is the optimum place for life;

2. *Basic chemical elements*: living material built up largely out of the elements carbon (C), nitrogen (N), oxygen (O) and hydrogen (H), and these elements are among the most common in the universe;

3. *Water* (or an equivalent solvent): all species of life on the Earth appear to require at least intermittent exposure to water, which makes up about 80 per cent of the content of most cells;

4. *Temperature*: it may be that life can exist anywhere where water is available in liquid form; for Earth-like planets this would indicate a temperature which was not permanently below freezing point (0°C) or above boiling point (100°C);

5. *Energy source*: for the Earth the prime energy source is the Sun, and we assume that, for a planet, the star around which it moves will be the energy source;

6. *Atmosphere*: for Earth-type life this is necessary to provide protection from short-wave, X- and ultra-violet radiation, which is harmful to living tissue, as well as (in the case of animals) providing oxygen to breathe. However, for some forms of life free oxygen is not required, and there are living organisms which thrive in environments of, for example, ammonia, methane and hydrogen sulphide. Pressure does not seem to be critical (living material in the depths of the oceans survive 1000 atmospheres of pressure, while other material can survive for periods in 10^{-11} atmospheres).

The above serves only as a guide to the requirements for life; it is by no means an exhaustive list of conditions.

Within the SOLAR SYSTEM there are nine planets, including the Earth. It is possible to define a zone round the Sun, the ECOSPHERE, within which the level of radiation from the Sun could sustain a suitable temperature for life (although the atmospheric conditions on planets modify this). The planet VENUS lies just inside and the planet MARS at the outer boundary of this zone. Of these planets Venus appears to be far too hot while Mars also appears to be rather hostile to life as we know it. However, at the Martian equator, temperatures rise well above the freezing point of water and, although there do not appear to be appreciable quantitites of water or oxygen, there are features which indicate that water may have been present in the past. It is just possible that life exists or has existed on Mars, and exploration of the surface by unmanned space probes may soon provide the answer to this problem. (◊ VIKING PROJECT.)

On the face of it, the other planets should be ruled out without question (Mercury too hot and devoid of atmosphere, the others too cold) but we may be taking too parochial an outlook. Although, for example, the temperature at the cloud tops of Jupiter is about −140°C, Jupiter is very hot internally, and so an equable temperature may be possible at some depth in its atmosphere. The presence of ammonia and methane in large quantities on Jupiter has lead to speculation as to the possibility of ammonia-based life existing there. As things stand at present, however, the Earth remains the only known abode of life in the Solar System.

Current popular theories of the origin of planetary systems suggest that a large proportion (possibly as high as 50 per cent) of all stars will have planetary systems ($\Diamond$ PLANETS OF OTHER STARS) and that such systems, if they exist, are likely to be similar in general nature to the Solar System. Since there are some 10^{11} stars in the GALAXY (2) the number of planetary systems is likely to be very large, and the number of stars with planets inside their ecospheres should be substantial. Not all stars would be suitable for having life-bearing planets; the very hot and highly luminous stars of spectral type ($\Diamond$ SPECTRAL CLASSIFICATION) O, B and A are probably too short-lived ($\Diamond$ STELLAR EVOLUTION) and too luminous (particularly in the ultra-violet) for life to exist in their vicinities, while the cool red main-sequence stars of type M and later will have narrow ecospheres close to their surfaces. The most likely stars to have life-bearing planets are main-sequence stars of spectral types F, G and K (the Sun is of type G), and such stars account for some 10 per cent of all the stars in the Galaxy. If may be that the number of potentially suitable planetary systems could be as high as 10^{10}. If one system in ten had a suitable planet, then, assuming that, once life originates, it persists for thousands of millions of years (as in the case of life on Earth), then it may be that there are as many as *a thousand million* life-bearing planets in the Galaxy at this time. Even taking a pessimistic view, it is hard to avoid the conclusion that life is likely to be commonplace in the Galaxy.

The possibility that advanced intelligent forms of life exist in the Galaxy cannot be ignored ($\Diamond$ INTELLIGENT LIFE IN THE UNIVERSE).

In summary, although there is as yet no direct evidence, it does seem most probable that life exists elsewhere in the universe. All our observations suggest that there is nothing special or unique about the Earth, the Solar System or the Sun, and it seems unreasonable to suppose that life itself should be a phenomenon unique to the Earth.

Life, Origin of. How life originated on Earth is not known with any certainty, but the sequence of events is thought to have been as follows.

The early atmosphere is assumed to have been hot, and water vapour, ammonia, hydrogen cyanide, nitrogen, carbon dioxide, etc., were present in clouds. Ultra-violet radiation from the Sun, it is supposed, caused the synthesis of basic amino acids and sugars, which then fell in rain, collecting in the oceans, and in pools. In these pools long-chain molecules may have been built up, leading eventually to the production of self-replicating systems. Thereafter, the process of evolution led, by trial and error and a wide range of mutations, to the present variety of living creatures and material. There is still very considerable argument over the nature of this chain of events.

The oldest fossil remains found on Earth date back over 3000 million years.

Light. ELECTROMAGNETIC RADIATION of those wavelengths to which the human eye responds; i.e. from just below 400 nanometres (4×10^{-7} m, 0·4 micron, or 4000 angstroms) to just over 700 nm. Different wavelengths within this range correspond to different colours as perceived by the eye; in order of decreasing wavelength we have red, orange, yellow, green, blue, indigo and violet. Wavelengths shorter than visible are referred to as ultra-violet, while wavelengths longer than red are infra-red. Light may also be regarded as particles, or photons, the longer wavelength radiation corresponding to lower energy photons.

In common with other types of electromagnetic radiation, light travels in a vacuum at a speed of about 300 000 km per second (◊VELOCITY OF LIGHT).

Light-gathering power. ◊TELESCOPE.

Light year (l.y.). A unit of distance measurement equal to the distance travelled by a ray of light *in vacuo* in one year. Since light travels at a speed of 299 792 km per second, this distance is equivalent to 9·46 $\times 10^{12}$ km (i.e. 9·46 million million km) or 63 240 ASTRONOMICAL UNITS. The unit is commonly used to express large distances in the universe and represents the time taken for a ray of light to cross these distances.

Limb darkening. ◊PHOTOSPHERE.

Line of nodes. ◊NODE.

Lines of force. ◊MAGNETIC FIELD.

Limb. The edge of the visible disc of an astronomical body such as the Sun, Moon or a planet.

Local Group of Galaxies. The local cluster of galaxies of which our galaxy is a member. The galaxies in the Local Group do not share in the general expansion of the universe (all other galaxies appear to be receding from us). There are over twenty galaxies in the group, although there are a few whose membership is in doubt; of these the majority are small or dwarf elliptical or irregular galaxies. The more massive members are our galaxy, the ANDROMEDA GALAXY – a spiral similar to our own – and a massive elliptical galaxy, Maffei I, which was discovered in 1971 by infra-red techniques (it lies in a direction near to the galactic centre, and is heavily obscured by interstellar dust). Maffei II, a spiral galaxy, may not be a member of the Group. There is a further spiral, M33, which has a mass of less than one-tenth that of our galaxy. Our galaxy has two irregular satellite galaxies, the MAGELLANIC

CLOUDS, while the Andromeda galaxy has two elliptical satellites. The radius of the Group is about one megaparsec. ($\diamond$ CLUSTERS OF GALAXIES.)

Long-period variables. Stars whose brightness varies in a fairly regular way over periods of between 100 and 700 days. They are generally highly luminous RED GIANTS and SUPERGIANTS – giant cool stars, emitting most of their radiation in the infra-red part of the spectrum – and they show large changes in brightness throughout their cycles; typical variations range between 3 and 7 magnitudes. They are pulsating stars, i.e. they expand and contract through their cycles of variation. A well-known example is the star Mira Ceti which ranges in brightness from magnitude 3 (a naked-eye star) to below magnitude 9 (too faint to be seen without optical aid); its effective temperature varies between about 2600 K and 1900 K during the cycle.

Longitude of ascending node. $\diamond$ ELEMENTS OF AN ORBIT.

Longitude of perihelion. $\diamond$ ELEMENTS OF AN ORBIT.

Luminosity. The total amount of energy per unit time emitted from a star; i.e., the power output of a star. The luminosity, L, of a star of radius R and EFFECTIVE TEMPERATURE T_e is given by

$$L = 4\pi R^2 \sigma T_e{}^4$$

where σ is a constant known as Stefan's constant.

The luminosity of a star, in other words, is proportional to the surface area of the star ($4\pi R^2$) multiplied by the rate of emission of radiation from unit area of its surface ($\sigma T_e{}^4$). It follows that if two stars have different luminosities but the same value of effective temperature, then the more luminous star must be the larger of the two.

The luminosity of the Sun is $3 \cdot 8 \times 10^{26}$ watts. Most stars have values of luminosity in the range 10^6 to 10^{-4} times that of the Sun; the greater proportion of stars in the GALAXY (2) is less luminous than the Sun. ($\diamond$ ABSOLUTE MAGNITUDE; BLACK BODY; HERTZSPRUNG–RUSSELL DIAGRAM, Figure 24.)

Luna Series. The series of Soviet unmanned lunar probes (sometimes referred to as Luniks). The first of the series, Luna 1, was launched on 2 January 1959 and, after passing the Moon at a range of some 6000 km on 4 January, entered orbit round the Sun. The series has achieved an impressive range of firsts. Luna 2 crashed onto the Moon (at longitude 0°, latitude 30°N) on 14 September 1959, so becoming the first man-made object to reach another world, while Luna 3, on 6 October of that year, passed behind the Moon and photographed the far side for the first time.

Luna 9 soft-landed on the lunar surface on 3 February 1966, transmitted photographs, and conclusively demonstrated that the Moon's surface was sufficiently rigid to support a spacecraft, and was not – as had been supposed by some astronomers – deeply covered in dust. Luna 10 became the first orbiting lunar satellite on 3 April 1966. Luna 16, which landed in the Mare Foecunditatis on 20 September 1970, drilled a core sample of about 0·1 kg of lunar material and automatically returned it to Earth. Two months later, on 17 November 1970, Luna 17 deposited on the surface a remote-controlled roving vehicle, Lunokhod 1 (◇LUNOKHOD).

The series of launchings is continuing.

Lunar orbiter. Series of US lunar orbiting space probes, five of which were launched successfully between 10 August 1966 and August 1967. Their primary objective was to photograph the lunar surface in detail and to assist in the selection of the Apollo landing sites (◇APOLLO PROJECT). In addition, studies of the motion of these spacecraft improved our knowledge of the gravitational field of the Moon and led to the discovery of MASCONS.

Lunar rover. ◇APOLLO PROJECT.

Lunation. One complete cycle of lunar phases, from new moon to new moon. This takes place in a period of time equal to the SYNODIC PERIOD of the Moon (the lunar month), which on average is 29·53 days.

Luni-solar precession. ◇PRECESSION.

Lunokhod. A Soviet remote-controlled lunar roving vehicle, the first of which, Lunokhod 1, was placed on the Moon by the unmanned probe Luna 17 on 17 November 1970. The vehicle could be steered and operated by a 'driver' in the control room on 'Earth. It proved to be outstandingly successful, operating during the lunar day and remaining stationary throughout the night, and continued to function for more than ten months. In that time it covered a total distance of 10·5 km, surveyed an area of some 80000 square metres, analysed the mechanical and chemical properties of the lunar soil, and sent back a total of about 20000 photographs.

Lyman series. A series of lines in the SPECTRUM of the hydrogen atom corresponding to transitions between the first energy level (i.e. the ground state, or closest orbit for an electron relative to the nucleus) and other energy levels (see Figure 41b). These lines, denoted by Lα, Lβ, Lγ, and so on, occur in the ultra-violet part of the spectrum. Lα has a wavelength of 121·6 nm and the wavelengths of lines in this series converge to the series limit at 91·15 nm. (◇BALMER SERIES; PASCHEN SERIES; ◇ATOM.)

M

Mach number. The velocity of an object compared to the velocity of sound in the medium through which it is moving. Thus Mach 1 equals the speed of sound, Mach 2 is twice the speed of sound, and so on.

Mach's principle. The concept, formulated in 1872 by Ernst Mach, that the property of INERTIA is due to some (unspecified) interaction between a mass and all the distant matter in the universe. The implication is that if a particle existed in isolation, i.e. if the rest of the matter in the universe did not exist, then a massive particle would not possess inertia. Discussion of Mach's principle lies at the heart of many cosmological debates.

Magellanic clouds. Two, relatively small, satellite galaxies of our own system which are visible to the unaided eye (for observers in the southern hemisphere), looking like detached portions of the MILKY WAY. The Large Magellanic Cloud (LMC) is an irregular galaxy with a mass of about 10^{10} solar masses, lying at a distance of some 170000 light years (52 kiloparsecs), and contains a wealth of Population I objects ($\Diamond$STELLAR POPULATIONS), including the largest known emission NEBULA, the Tarantula nebula. The Small Magellanic Cloud (SMC) is about one-fifth of this mass, irregular in structure, and located at a distance of 206000 light years (63 kiloparsecs). Although the LMC is described as irregular, there is some evidence of a barred spiral structure. (See Plate 22.)

The clouds were first recorded in 1519 by the navigator, Ferdinand Magellan, during his circumnavigation of the world.

Magnetic field. The region around a magnet in which its effects are apparent. The lines of force indicate the direction in which the magnetic force acts, and these converge at the magnetic poles. The magnetic field of the Earth is a dipole field, i.e. it is like the field of a bar magnet, having a north and a south magnetic pole. Magnetic field strengths are measured in units of gauss or tesla, the latter being the SI unit. The term gauss tends to be met in astronomical literature.

Magnetic fields, Celestial. Magnetic fields are in evidence in a wide variety of celestial bodies. The GALAXY (2) has a weak general field of less than 0·00001 gauss (10^{-9} tesla); stars have magnetic field strengths of up to 30000 gauss (3 tesla) in extreme cases, but the Sun is more typical with a field of about 1 or 2 gauss (10^{-4} to 2×10^{-4} tesla); SUNSPOT fields are much stronger, up to 4000 gauss (0·4 tesla). The Earth, Mercury and Jupiter have measurable magnetic fields – about 0·6 gauss (6×10^{-5} tesla) in the case of the Earth.

Magnetopause. ⟩MAGNETOSPHERE.

Magnetosphere.   The region around a planet within which its magnetic field is dominant (compared to the interplanetary magnetic field). In the case of the Earth, the magnetosphere is essentially a 'tear-drop' shape, extending on the sunward side of the planet for about 10 Earth radii, and much further outwards on the side away from the Sun. This shape arises as a result of the interaction between the SOLAR WIND and the Earth's magnetic field. The boundary of the magnetosphere is called the magnetopause, beyond which lies the shock front (rather like the bow wave of a ship) where the solar wind meets the magnetic field. The VAN ALLEN BELTS lie within the magnetosphere.

Magnification. ⟩TELESCOPE.

Magnitude. ⟩ABSOLUTE MAGNITUDE; APPARENT MAGNITUDE; BOLOMETRIC MAGNITUDE.

Main sequence. ⟩HERTZSPRUNG–RUSSELL DIAGRAM; STELLAR EVOLUTION.

Major axis. ⟩ELLIPSE.

Mare (pl: maria).   Term applied to the dark, relatively smooth, lunar plains; the name derives from the Latin for 'sea', since the early observers of the Moon imagined that the dark patches on its disc were indeed seas filled with water.

The maria are roughly circular, basin-like structures, usually surrounded in whole or in part by mountain chains. They range in size from about 300 km in diameter (e.g. the Mare Crisium) to larger, less regular plains such as the Oceanus Procellarum (Ocean of Storms) which occupies a large fraction of the Moon's western hemisphere. Of considerable interest is the Mare Imbrium (Sea of Rains) near the centre of the northern hemisphere, bounded on the east by the lunar Alps, and to the south by the impressive mountain chain known as the Apennines, which runs for a total length of some 800 km and in the foothills of which Apollo 15 landed (⟩APOLLO PROJECT).

Analysis of lunar samples reveals that the surface rocks in the maria are of a volcanic, basaltic nature, and there is little doubt that they represent areas of tremendous lava-flow in the past. Dating of these rocks fixes the era of the formation of the maria at between three and four thousand million years ago. The most popular view is that they were formed by the impact of large rocky masses in the early history of the Solar System (the rocky masses must have been comparable with small ASTEROIDS). The fracturing of the surface layer by such impacts allowed the later intrusion into the basins of large amounts of sub-surface magma and the flow of lava to give rise to the present appearance. The mare material is relatively denser than the material making up the highland regions, and it may be that the concentration of dense material in the maria is responsible for the MASCONS.

A curious feature of the distribution of the maria – which has not yet adequately been explained – is that by far the majority of them lie on the hemisphere of the Moon which faces the Earth.

Mariner Series. A series of US planetary space probes which have been used so far to investigate the planets Mercury, Venus and Mars. The first successful mission was Mariner 2, launched on 27 August 1962, which by-passed Venus at a range of 35000 km and transmitted back to Earth the first detailed information on the surface temperature and atmospheric composition of that planet. The results obtained were rather unexpected; Mariner 2 revealed a surface temperature of the order of 400°C, a retrograde rotation period of the order of 250 days (⟡RETROGRADE MOTION (3)), and the lack of a magnetic field. These results have in essence been confirmed by more recent Soviet and American space probes such as Mariner 5 which flew by the planet on 19 October 1967 (⟡VENERA SERIES).

Mars has been investigated by Mariners 4 (launched 28 November 1964), 6 and 7 (launched 24 February and 27 March 1969) and 9 (launched 30 May 1971). Mariner 9 became the first successful Mars-orbiting vehicle when it entered orbit round the planet on 14 November 1971; it obtained detailed photographs, 7329 in all, of most of the surface.

Mariner 10, launched on 3 November 1973, became the first space probe successfully to fly-by two planets, Venus and Mercury. As Mariner 10 flew by Venus on 5 February 1974, it was deflected by the gravitational field of that planet (⟡GRAND TOUR) towards the orbit of Mercury, by-passing that planet on 29 March 1974 and sending back the first photographs of the surface features. It then entered an elliptical orbit round the Sun which resulted in two further useful encounters with Mercury.

Future Mariner missions are to include a Jupiter–Saturn fly-by (scheduled launch 1977) and a Uranus fly-by (launch 1979).

Mars. The fourth planet in order of distance from the Sun, and the outermost of the TERRESTRIAL PLANETS. When near OPPOSITION it can approach to within 56 million km of the Earth, closer than any other planet with the exception of VENUS. It can be studied in fair detail with Earth-based telescopes, and the existence of well-defined surface features, polar caps (analogous to the Earth's polar ice caps) and a thin atmosphere was well established before the advent of space exploration. The first successful Mars probe was Mariner 4 which revealed in 1965 that the surface of Mars is cratered. Since that time a number of US and Soviet space probes have investigated the planet and Mariner 9, the first successful orbiter, has produced detailed maps of most of the surface.

In general terms, Mars is half as far again from the Sun as is the Earth, is just over half the Earth's diameter, and has about one-tenth of the Earth's mass. Its mean density is lower, suggesting the absence of a large massive core, and the absence of a magnetic field confirms this view. Temperatures at the equator can exceed 240 K (about $-30°C$) but the mean temperature is lower than this; at night the equatorial temperature can drop below 150 K (about $-120°C$) (VIKING measurements). The atmosphere is composed very largely of carbon dioxide (95 per cent) with nitrogen and argon being the other principal components; oxygen makes up only about 0·15 per cent of the total. Water vapour has been detected by the Viking spacecraft and although the quantity is small (if all the water vapour were precipitated from the planet's atmosphere it would form a layer less than 0·1 millimetres thick), it is more than had previously been expected.

In the light of the Viking missions it now seems almost certain that the polar caps consist largely of frozen water, possibly overlaid by a layer of frozen carbon dioxide (the freezing points of water and carbon dioxide on Mars are, respectively, about 200 K and approximately 145 K). There may, too, be substantial amounts of water trapped below the planetary surface. The seasons on Mars are similar to, but longer than, those on Earth; this is because the axial tilt of Mars is almost the same as that of the Earth but the Martian 'year' is nearly twice as long as ours. The polar caps show seasonal changes – enlarging in winter and contracting in summer – and it seems likely that the atmospheric composition has a seasonal cycle too. About one third of the Martian atmosphere is thought to freeze out each year at one or other of the poles.

The surface features include craters, mountain ranges, valleys (notably the Coprates Canyon which runs for about 3000 km, reaching a maximum width of 400 km, and having an average depth of 5 km), and giant volcanic features such as Olympus Mons, a conical formation with a summit crater 65 km across. Many features give the impression of having been caused by water erosion (e.g. features which look like dried-up river beds), and it may be that the Martian climate goes through some sort of cyclic pattern involving periods when surface water can exist.

Whether or not life exists, or has existed, on the surface of Mars is uncertain; certainly the present conditions are rather hostile, but the possibility remains. One of the objectives of the Viking Project is to look for evidence of life, but the results so far are inconclusive.

Mars has two moons, Phobos and Deimos. They are both small, irregular cratered lumps of rock, with maximum diameters of 22 and 12 km respectively, and moving round the planet at mean distances of 9000 km and 23000 km. (See Plates 10, 11 and 12.)

Mars data

		(Earth = 1)
Mean distance from Sun	227900000 km	1·52
Orbital eccentricity	0·093	—
Orbital inclination	1° 51′ 00″	—
Sidereal orbital period	686·98 days	1·88
Mean synodic period	779·94 days	—
Axial rotation period	24h 37m 23s	1·02
Mass	$6·4 \times 10^{23}$ kg	0·11
Radius	3395 km	0·53
Mean density	$3·95 \times 10^3$ kg m^{-3}	0·71
Surface gravity	3·74 m s^{-2}	0·38

Mascons – MASs CONcentrationS. Small perturbations noted in the orbits of the LUNAR ORBITERS and Apollo spacecraft (⬦APOLLO PROJECT) suggest that there are regions over the Moon's surface where the gravitational attraction is slightly higher than the mean value. This suggests that there are regions of higher density (i.e. concentrations of mass) in localized areas of the Moon's surface. Mascons are located in some of the lunar MARE regions, and may be due to the flooding by heavier basaltic material of the craters formed by the impact of exceptionally massive bodies in the early history of the Solar System.

Mass–luminosity relation. The luminosity, L, of a star is proportional to its mass, M, raised to a power, p, where p lies between 2·8 and 4. This relationship has been established on the basis of observations of stars, and can also be shown to have a reasonable basis in theory. As an approximate 'rule of thumb', we can say,

$$L \propto M^3.$$

Thus, a star ten times the Sun's mass is likely to be at least a thousand times more luminous. It follows that, since luminosity is a measure of the rate at which a star is consuming fuel, the more massive the star, the shorter its lifetime. (⬦STELLAR EVOLUTION, Figure 42.)

Mass ratio (1). The ratio of the masses of two associated celestial bodies, for example, the two stars making up a binary. For two such bodies, of masses M and m, respectively, the mass ratio $M:m = r:R$, where R and r are the respective distances at any instant of M and m from their common centre of mass ($\diamondsuit$ BARYCENTRE).

Mass ratio (2). In astronautics, the ratio of the initial mass of a rocket plus fuel at lift-off to the mass of the rocket when all the fuel has been expended. If this ratio is $2 \cdot 72 : 1$ then the rocket will, under ideal conditions, attain a final velocity (when all fuel is expended) exactly equal to the exhaust velocity of the rocket motor (i.e. the speed at which gas emerges from the nozzle). Because existing chemical rockets do not have high exhaust velocities, rockets must have large mass ratios, and the PAYLOADS must be correspondingly small.

Mean anomaly. For a body moving round a massive body in an elliptical orbit, the mean anomaly at a particular instant is the angle through which a particle moving at uniform angular speed on a circle of area equal to the ellipse (and with an orbital period equal to that of the real body in its elliptical orbit) will have moved in the time which has elapsed since the real body last passed its closest approach to the massive body. For an ellipse, mean anomaly equals TRUE ANOMALY at opposite ends of the major axis; for a circular orbit, mean and true anomaly are identical at all times. The concept of mean anomaly is useful in the calculation of the time taken for a body to move along a segment of its orbit (see Figure 47).

Mean time. The time system in use for most civil and many astronomical purposes and based on the motion of a hypothetic object called the mean Sun, the RIGHT ASCENSION of which increases from day to day at a uniform rate. The local mean time is defined to be the local hour angle of the mean Sun plus twelve hours. Greenwich mean time is taken as the standard for reference; the term universal time (UT) is synonymous with Greenwich mean time (GMT). ($\diamondsuit$ EQUATION OF TIME and Figure 19.)

Mercury. The nearest planet to the Sun, and the smallest of the TERRESTRIAL PLANETS. It is a small body, virtually devoid of atmosphere, and, because of its proximity to the Sun, is rather difficult to observe from the Earth. It was not until the fly-by missions of the US space probe Mariner 10 ($\diamondsuit$ MARINER SERIES) in 1974 that detailed information about the planet and its surface features was obtained. The planet has a cratered surface, similar to that of the Moon, but the planet has a mean density almost the same as that of the Earth (i.e. 60 per cent greater than the Moon's density and greater than that of Mars or Venus). Since the surface rocks appear to be of low density it seems fairly certain that Mercury has a dense (metallic) core like that of the Earth. The existence of a magnetic field confirms this view and suggests the possibility that the core may be liquid. An extremely tenuous atmosphere, made up of hydrogen and helium streaming from the Sun, has been confirmed, but its density is less than one million millionth that of air at sea level on the Earth.

Being so close to the Sun, the temperature on the Sun-facing hemisphere reaches 500 K, while on the night side it falls below 100 K. Mercury rotates on its axis in fifty-nine days, a fact which was discovered as recently as 1965 by the techniques of RADAR ASTRONOMY; previously it had been thought that the planet rotated on its axis in the same period of time required for it to complete one orbit of the Sun – eighty-eight days. When the angular rotation rate is combined with the angular rate of the planet's motion round the Sun, it is found that an observer standing on Mercury's surface would see the Sun move slowly across the sky from east to west at a rate of just under 2 degrees per day. Consequently, the mean length of a solar day (the interval between two successive noons) on Mercury is 176 days.

Mercury data

		(Earth = 1)
Mean distance from Sun	57 900 000 km	0·39
Orbital eccentricity	0·206	—
Orbital inclination	7° 00′ 15″	—
Sidereal orbital period	87·97 days	0·24
Axial rotation period	59 days	59
Mass	$3·3 \times 10^{23}$ kg	0·055
Radius	2430 km	0·38
Mean density	$5·5 \times 10^3$ kg m^{-3}	1
Surface gravity	3·63 m s^{-2}	0·36

The orbital eccentricity of Mercury is the greatest of all the planets apart from Pluto: the perihelion and aphelion distances of its orbit are 46 000 000 km and 69 800 000 km respectively. (See Plate 6.)

Meridian. (a) A GREAT CIRCLE on the Earth's surface, running perpendicular to the equator and passing through the north and south poles. To an observer located at a particular position on the Earth, the meridian represents his north–south line. The Greenwich meridian (i.e. the meridian passing through the Old Greenwich Observatory) is taken as the zero of longitude measurement; thus the longitude of a point on the Earth's surface is the angle (measured parallel to the equator) between the Greenwich meridian and the meridian passing through that point.

(b) For purposes of astronomical position and time measurement, the meridian is taken to be a great circle on the CELESTIAL SPHERE passing through the north and south celestial poles and the observer's ZENITH; i.e. for an observer on the Earth's surface, the celestial meridian is the projection of his terrestrial meridian onto the celestial sphere.

Messier number. In the eighteenth century the French astronomer, Charles Messier, drew up a catalogue of 109 of the brighter nebulae and star clusters. Objects in this catalogue are denoted by the letter M followed by a number; e.g. M31 is the ANDROMEDA GALAXY.

Meteor. A visible streak of light in the sky, which lasts for at most a few seconds, due to the burning up of a fast-moving particle as it enters the Earth's atmosphere. The term *shooting star* is sometimes used to describe this phenomenon, but it is misleading, since there is no similarity between a star and a meteor.

The particles which give rise to meteors are tiny, few are larger than the size of a pin head, and enter the atmosphere at speeds typically in the range 20 to 40 km per second; maximum speeds are about 70 km per second for meteors approaching the Earth 'head on' (i.e. in the opposite direction to the Earth's motion round the Sun). Although millions of meteors per hour are entering the atmosphere, most are too faint to be seen without optical aid, and an average observer can expect to see only about ten per hour on a clear, dark night. The ionized trails of meteors may be studied by radar. A promising new technique for observing faint meteors involves the use of low-light-level television cameras.

In addition to sporadic meteors (which appear at random), there are also meteor showers during which many meteors may be observed apparently emanating from the direction of a particular point in the sky (the radiant). Such showers are due to streams of particles (METEOROIDS) following particular elliptical orbits round the Sun; when the Earth crosses such a stream, many meteors are seen, and because they are following parallel paths, they appear to diverge from the radiant. It is quite widely accepted that meteor showers represent the debris of old comets.

Meteorite. A solid lump of matter in interplanetary space which can survive passage through the atmosphere and reach ground level, despite entering the atmosphere at speeds of several tens of kilometres per second. While passing through the atmosphere the outer layer of a meteorite becomes intensely heated and ablates (i.e. melts and streams away); the passage of a meteorite may be marked by a brilliant trail of light, and fragments may be seen breaking away from the main body. Sometimes a meteorite will break into small fragments which are scattered over a wide area, while at other times it may land in one piece.

There are three principal types of meteorites, the irons (almost entirely nickel–iron), the stones (composed primarily of silicates) and the stony-irons (a mixture of both). The mean masses of meteorites found on the Earth's surface are of the order of 15 kg (for irons) and 3 kg (for stones). Exceptionally massive meteorites, say in excess of 100 tonnes – and these are extremely rare – will reach ground level at more or less the same speed at which they entered the atmosphere, and the resultant explosive impact gives rise to craters. The best known example of a meteorite crater is in Arizona; it has a diameter of over 1200 metres, a depth of some 180 metres and is thought to have been caused by the prehistoric impact of a mass of the order of 10^4 to 10^5 tonnes.

The ages of meteorites, obtained by radioactive dating methods, have been estimated at up to $4 \cdot 7 \times 10^9$ years, indicating that meteorites probably originated about the time of the formation of the solar system. The orbits followed by meteorites before entering the atmosphere suggest that they may represent material from fragmented ASTEROIDS. Certain meteorites, carbonaceous chondrites, appear to contain quantities of organic matter.

Meteroid. Collective term applied to meteoritic material in space. ▷METEOR; METEORITE; MICROMETEORITE.

Michelson–Morley experiment. A celebrated experiment carried out by Michelson in 1881 and by Michelson and Morley in 1887 which attempted and failed to detect the motion of the Earth through the ETHER. The basis of the experiment was that if a beam of light travelled a known distance in the direction in which the Earth was supposed to be moving through the ether, and another beam travelled the same distance at right angles to this direction then, if light moved at a constant velocity through the ether, the two beams should take different times to cover the distance. The failure of the experiment is accounted for by the SPECIAL THEORY OF RELATIVITY.

Michelson stellar interferometer. ▷INTERFEROMETER.

Micrometeorites. Microscopic particles, less than 100 microns (0·1 millimetres) in diameter, which enter the Earth's atmosphere, but are too tiny to give rise to the phenomenon of METEORS. It has been estimated that about 400 tonnes of material per day are added to the Earth in this way. Micrometeorites have been studied extensively by means of satellites.

Micron. A millionth part of a metre. Strictly speaking, in SI units the term micro-metre (μm) should be used; however, the term micron is still widely encountered in astronomical literature, particularly in the field of INFRA-RED ASTRONOMY.

Microwave background radiation (cosmic). Weak isotropic (i.e. approaching uniformly from all directions) microwave radiation from space, first discovered in 1965 by Penzias and Wilson of Bell Telephone Laboratories. In the same edition of *Astrophysical Journal* which published the results was a paper suggesting that such radiation should exist if the universe had originated as a hot fireball as predicted by the BIG-BANG THEORY.

Subsequent observations have shown that the microwave radiation has a black-body spectrum ($\Diamond$ BLACK BODY) corresponding to a temperature of 2·7 K (i.e. it is as if the universe had a background temperature of 2·7 K) and this is exactly what is expected according to the Big-Bang theory. The discovery of the cosmic microwave background is the most important piece of evidence favouring that theory, and has helped to establish it as the most reasonable current cosmological theory.

Microwave radiation. $\Diamond$ ELECTROMAGNETIC SPECTRUM.

Milky Way. The faint band of starlight which may be seen stretching across the sky on a clear moonless night; it is made up of the combined light of millions of stars too faint to be seen individually with the unaided eye.

The Milky Way arises because the region of the GALAXY (2) in which the Sun is located is the flattened disc-shaped part of the system (see Figure 23b). Consequently, if we observe in a direction close to the plane of the galactic disc we see large numbers of stars (the Milky Way), while if we look in a direction perpendicular to the relatively thin disc, we see comparatively few stars. The centre of the Galaxy lies in the plane of the Milky Way in the direction of the constellation Sagittarius, but is heavily obscured by interstellar dust ($\Diamond$ INTERSTELLAR MATTER).

Minor axis. $\Diamond$ ELLIPSE.

Minor planets. $\Diamond$ ASTEROIDS.

Mira Ceti. $\Diamond$ LONG-PERIOD VARIABLES.

Molecule. $\Diamond$ ATOM.

Moon (1). A popular term for a natural SATELLITE.

Moon (2). The Earth's natural satellite, and our nearest celestial neighbour. It is of importance to the Earth both in the sense that it provides light at night and is the principal cause of the TIDES, and in the sense that it represents the only other world on which men have set foot.

The Moon is devoid of atmosphere (apart from the occasional leakage of gas from within its surface; the mean atmospheric pressure is less than 10^{-12} of a terrestrial atmosphere) and in consequence is subject to a large temperature range from a maximum of 390 K on the sunlit side to a minimum of about 100 K at night. The length of the solar day on the Moon is equal to the Moon's synodic period (the period of its cycle of phases). The Moon exhibits the phenomenon of captured rotation, its axial rotation period being the same length as its orbital period, so that it keeps the same hemisphere permanently turned to the Earth (⟡LIBRATIONS). It does *not* keep the same hemisphere turned towards the Sun.

The main surface features are the craters, roughly circular walled depressions, ranging in diameter from nearly 300 km to microscopic pits, mountain ranges, and relatively flat plains of darker material known as maria or MARE regions. There are, too, a host of minor features: valleys, ridges, etc. For a long time there has been controversy over the question of the origin of the craters (⟡RAYS, LUNAR) and, even after the Apollo landings, this is not completely resolved. The consensus of opinion is that some of the craters were formed by internal volcanic activity and others (including the major ones) were caused by the pre-historic impacts of very large METEORITES. In the case of the maria, both processes may have contributed to their formation.

The lunar surface rocks turn out to have densities of between $2 \cdot 4$ and 3×10^3 kg m^{-3} (similar to terrestrial rocks), which is a value quite close to the mean density of the Moon as a whole; this implies that the Moon is fairly homogeneous, and does not have a massive central core composed of heavier elements like that of the Earth. Surprisingly, the Moon does have a very weak magnetic field. Seismic results indicate that mild 'moonquakes' occur from time to time, and appear to show that the sub-surface layer of the Moon consists of rocky fragments rather than solid layers of rock.

The oldest surface rocks have been dated at about 4×10^9 years (the oldest terrestrial rocks are about $3 \cdot 5 \times 10^9$ years of age) indicating that the Moon must have formed and reached its present structure about the same time as the Earth itself was formed. This implies that the Moon originated as a separate body, and not, as some theories have suggested, from material ejected from the Earth at some time after the formation of the Earth itself.

The ratio of the mass of the Moon to the mass of the Earth $(1:81\cdot3)$ is much greater than the satellite:planet ratio for any other planet in the Solar System. (See Plate 5.)

Lunar data

Mass	$7 \cdot 35 \times 10^{22}$ kg
Radius	1738 km
Mean density	$3 \cdot 34 \times 10^3$ kg m^{-3}
Mean distance from Earth	384 400 km
Orbital eccentricity	0·0549

Orbital inclination (to ecliptic)	5° 8′ (mean value)
Sidereal orbital period	27·32 days
Mean synodic period	29·53 days
Surface gravity	1·62 m s^{-2}

Morning star. Term applied to describe a planet when it is visible in the morning sky before sunrise, and reaches culmination (⟡TRANSIT) after midnight. The term is used particularly in connection with the planet Venus. It is thought that in ancient times the planet Venus may have been regarded as two separate bodies, the 'morning star' (corresponding to Venus in the morning sky) and the 'evening star' (corresponding to Venus in the evening sky).

Moving cluster. An open or GALACTIC CLUSTER of stars, the members of which share a common motion in space; i.e. the member stars appear to be converging towards a point on the celestial sphere. Analysis of the motion of such clusters can lead to the determination of their distances. (⟡HYADES.)

N

NASA – National Aeronautics and Space Administration. The space agency responsible for all aspects (other than military) of the American space programme came into being on 1 October 1958. Its fields of interest include scientific satellites, applications satellites, interplanetary space probes, the manned space programme, and the application of space technology to terrestrial problems. It offers a launcher service to other nations. (◊APOLLO PROJECT; GEMINI PROJECT; MARINER SERIES; PIONEER; VIKING PROJECT; SKYLAB; SPACE SHUTTLE.)

Nebula (pl: nebulae). A cloud of gas and dust visible either as a luminous region or a dark patch against the star background. There are three principal types of nebulae, emission, reflection and dark (or absorption).

Emission nebulae are clouds which shine because the gas absorbs short wavelength (ultra-violet) radiation emitted by very hot and highly luminous stars (of spectral types O and early B; ◊SPECTRAL CLASSIFICATION), and re-emits visible light. The spectrum of such a nebula is an emission-line spectrum, quite unlike the spectrum of a star. Emission nebulae are often referred to as H II regions as they contain a high proportion of ionized hydrogen (◊IONIZATION). Generally the emission nebula is only part of a much larger hydrogen cloud, for it is only that part of the cloud sufficiently close to hot stars which will actually emit visible light; for example, the Orion Nebula (M42) has a visible diameter of some sixteen light years, but is part of a cloud which may be 300 light years across. (See Plate 17.)

Reflection nebulae may be detected around hot stars of spectral type later than B1; these are clouds of INTERSTELLAR MATTER where light from the central stars is reflected from the dust particles contained in such clouds. The spectrum of a reflection nebula is essentially the same (but characteristically 'bluer') as that of the illuminating star. Reflection nebulae are much less conspicuous than emission nebulae. The best-known example of such nebulae is the nebulosity surrounding the brighter stars in the PLEIADES.

Dark nebulae are relatively dense clouds of interstellar matter in which the effect of the dust particles is to attenuate light approaching from stars beyond (✧INTERSTELLAR EXTINCTION). As a result, they appear as dark patches against a starry background (William Herschel regarded these as 'holes in the heavens'). A good example, visible to the unaided eye, is the 'Coal Sack', a dark nebula some twenty-five light years in diameter in the southern part of the MILKY WAY.

Nebular hypothesis. A theory of the origin of the Solar System proposed in 1796 by the French mathematician P. S. de Laplace. According to Laplace, the Sun formed from a large cloud of gas which was initially rotating very slowly (essentially the same view is held today). As this cloud contracted it began to rotate more rapidly, becoming flattened into a lens-shape. Eventually a stage was reached where the CENTRIFUGAL FORCE at the outside edge of the disc was sufficiently great for a ring of matter to be thrown off. This ring was considered then to form into a planet. As the contraction proceeded, successive rings of matter were thought to have been ejected, so giving rise to all the planets.

There were (and still are) many objections to this theory, although it remained popular throughout the nineteenth century; for example, it is not clear how such a ring could form into a planet. The strongest objection concerns ANGULAR MOMENTUM: if the planets had been formed as Laplace suggested, then the Sun ought to be rotating hundreds of times faster than it does. It was largely on account of this objection that different types of theories were proposed in the early twentieth century. However, current theory suggests ways round this difficulty, and the present view of the origin of the Solar System bears some similarity to the theory of Laplace. (✧SOLAR SYSTEM, ORIGIN OF.)

Neptune. The eighth planet in order of distance from the Sun, and the outermost of the JOVIAN PLANETS. The discovery of Neptune was a triumph for Newton's theory of gravitation. Observations of the planet URANUS indicated that its orbit was being disturbed by some influence, presumably the gravitational attraction of another planet lying beyond the orbit of Uranus. Independently, U. J. J. Leverrier in France and J. C. Adams in England calculated the probable position of the unknown massive body, and their results were in good agreement. Although Adams completed his calculation a little earlier than Leverrier, it was from the latter's prediction that the planet Neptune was discovered in 1846 by Galle and d'Arrest, working at the Berlin observatory.

Neptune is primarily a gaseous body made up largely of hydrogen, hydrogen compounds and helium. However, the mean density of the planet (2·3 times that of water) is the highest of all the Jovian planets, and it is likely that Neptune contains a higher proportion of heavier elements than Jupiter; it may have an appreciable core. The atmosphere

145

is thought to contain cloud belts rather like those on Jupiter, and contains hydrogen and methane in large quantities. It has a rapid rotation period, 22h (approx.), and therefore the equatorial radius exceeds the polar radius by about 2 per cent.

It has two known satellites, one of which, Nereid, is very small, while the other, Triton, is one of the most massive moons in the Solar System. The mass ratio Triton:Neptune is 1:750, a much higher ratio of satellite:planet than for any planet other than the Earth.

Neptune data

		(Earth = 1)
Mean distance from Sun	4 497 000 000 km	30·06
Orbital eccentricity	0·0086	—
Orbital inclination	1° 46′ 22″	—
Sidereal orbital period	164·79 years	164·79
Axial rotation period	22h (approx.)	0·92
Mass	$1·03 \times 10^{26}$ kg	17·2
Radius	25 000 km	3·9
Mean density	$2·3 \times 10^{3}$ kg m^{-3}	0·41
Surface gravity	14 m s^{-2}	1·4

Neutral point. That point on a line joining the centres of mass of two celestial bodies (e.g. the Earth and the Moon) at which their gravitational attractions are equal and opposite, and so cancel out.

Neutrino. A sub-atomic 'particle' having zero charge and, apparently, zero mass, but which carries away energy from certain types of nuclear reactions. Neutrinos are extremely hard to detect, as they interact only very weakly with matter (thus most neutrinos from space will pass straight through the Earth), but some experiments have been carried out ($\diamond$ SOLAR NEUTRINO PROBLEM). Neutrino emission may be an important means of energy loss from stars with extremely hot cores (well in excess of 10^9 K), and this loss may contribute to the formation of SUPERNOVAE.

Neutron. A nuclear particle having zero charge, and a rest mass of $1·675 \times 10^{-27}$ kg (i.e. 1·009 atomic mass units). The hydrogen nucleus contains no neutrons, the helium nucleus two, and the uranium (U^{235}) nucleus 143. A free neutron (i.e. not bound in the nucleus of an ATOM) decays into a PROTON and an ELECTRON with the release of energy by the process of beta decay; the HALF-LIFE of this process is 12·8 minutes. The reverse process takes place in the formation of NEUTRON STARS.

Neutron star. A star which has been so severely compressed that most of the positively charged PROTONS and negatively charged ELECTRONS within it have combined to form neutral NEUTRONS. The radius of such a star would be of the order of 10 km and the mean density of the order of 10^{15} to in excess of 10^{18} kg m^{-3} (i.e. up to and beyond a thousand million million tonnes per cubic metre). It is thought that neutron stars may be formed in the following way: towards the end of its life cycle as a massive star exhausts the nuclear fuel in its core, the core collapses under the weight of stellar matter on top of it; the outer layers fall in on the collapsed core, and are so severely heated that they explode, giving rise to a SUPERNOVA explosion. In this explosion the central core is compressed to neutron star densities. If this view is correct, a neutron star represents the collapsed core of a massive star, and the formation of neutron stars is likely to be associated with supernovae. There may, of course, be other ways in which neutron stars can be formed.

The possible existence of such objects was suggested as long ago as 1932 by the Russian physicist Landau, while in the USA, in 1934, Fritz Zwicky had suggested that highly compressed bodies of this kind might be formed in supernova explosions. For a long time neutron stars remained a theoretical concept only, but the discovery of PULSARS, announced in 1968, suggested that it was possible to detect such bodies; for the best way to account for pulsars is to assume that their radiation sources are rapidly rotating neutron stars. Neutron stars can in theory rotate in periods as short as a millisecond; the period of the pulsar in the CRAB NEBULA is 33 milliseconds (0·033 seconds), which is consistent with the possible rotation period of a neutron star.

The maximum possible mass for a neutron star is thought to lie between 2 and 3 solar masses. A dying star whose final mass exceeds this limit may end up as a BLACK HOLE. ($\Diamond$STELLAR EVOLUTION.)

Newton. $\Diamond$NEWTON'S LAWS OF MOTION; GRAVITATION.

Newton's laws of motion. Laws governing the motion of all bodies which were set out by Isaac Newton in 1687. They form the basis of Newtonian mechanics. The three laws are as follows:

1. Every body continues in a state of rest or uniform motion in a straight line unless acted upon by a force.

2. If a body is acted upon by an external force, it accelerates, the acceleration being directly proportional to the force and inversely proportional to the mass of the body; the acceleration takes place in the direction of the force. This may be expressed as the rate of change of *momentum* of a body is proportional to the applied force. We can write the law as

$$F = ma$$

where F is the applied force, m is the mass of the body and a the acceleration.

3. To every action there is an equal and opposite reaction; in other words, if a force acts on one body an equal and opposite force must act on another body. For example, a person standing on the Earth is pressing down on its surface with a force equal to his weight; the Earth's surface in resisting this force (so preventing the person from falling towards the centre of the Earth) exerts a reaction, an upward force equal to that person's weight.

The essence of some of these laws was appreciated by other workers prior to and contemporary with Newton (e.g. Galileo), but he was the first fully to appreciate and to formalize them. Newton's laws of motion express a completely different point of view to the earlier belief that force is necessary to maintain motion; in Newtonian theory force is only required to *change* the state of motion of the body.

Newtonian mechanics.   ♢NEWTON'S LAWS OF MOTION.

Newtonian reflector.   The type of reflecting telescope first constructed in 1671 by Sir Isaac Newton, and presented by him to the Royal Society in 1672. Although designs for a different type of reflector had been produced earlier (♢GREGORIAN REFLECTOR), Newton's instrument was the first such telescope to be constructed. The Newtonian reflector (♢TELESCOPE, Figure 44b) utilizes a concave (paraboloid) primary mirror which collects light and brings it to a focus; a small, flat, secondary mirror, set at 45° to the axis of the telescope, reflects the converging beam of light through a right angle, so that the focus is at the side of the telescope tube. This type of instrument, which is relatively easy to construct, is still widely used today, particularly by amateur astronomers.

NGC – New General Catalogue of Nebulae and Clusters of Stars published by Dreyer in 1888.   Objects in this catalogue (which include galaxies) are denoted by the letters NGC followed by a number; for example, the ANDROMEDA GALAXY is NGC 224.

Nitrogen.   The element which is the principal constituent of the Earth's atmosphere (making up, at ground level, 78·08 per cent by volume). By volume, it is the fifth most abundant element in the universe (by mass, it is seventh). The chemical symbol for nitrogen is N, and its normal molecular form, N_2 (i.e. a molecule made up of two nitrogen atoms). Its atomic mass is 14 and its atomic number, 7 (♢ATOM). Although nitrogen makes up the major part of the Earth's atmosphere, it is almost entirely absent from the atmospheres of Venus and Mars.

Nix Olympica.   Former name of Olympus Mons (♢MARS).

Node. A point of intersection of an orbit and some reference plane, or a point of intersection of two great circles on the CELESTIAL SPHERE. For example, the orbit of the Moon is inclined to the plane of the Earth's orbit (the ECLIPTIC) by an angle of about 5 degrees; the point of intersection where the Moon passes from south of the ecliptic to north of the ecliptic is called the ascending node, and the point at which the Moon's orbit re-crosses the ecliptic, going south, is the descending node. The line joining two nodes, and representing the intersection of the orbit plane and the reference plane, is known as the line of node. (⊘ORBITAL ELEMENTS and Figure 29b.)

Nova (pl: novae). A star which flares up in brightness, typically by a factor of 10000 to 100000 (i.e. 10 to 13 magnitudes) within a few hours, or at most a few days. Thereafter such stars decline in brightness to values usually close to their 'pre-nova' magnitudes. In the eruption, a shell of gas, containing perhaps one hundred thousandth of the star's mass, is ejected into space. It has been shown that most if not all novae are members of close BINARY systems in which one member star is a hot compact body such as a white dwarf; material deposited from the second star onto the surface of the hot compact star would be expected to undergo violent, explosive burning, so giving rise to the observed nova outburst.

A given star may suffer a series of such outbursts. Stars which flare up in this way at intervals of from twenty-five to fifty years are known as recurrent novae. Dwarf novae are rather faint blue-white stars which suffer a nova-like outburst (brightening by from 2 to 5 magnitudes) every few weeks.

Because of the unpredictability of novae, many are discovered by amateur astronomers. The most recent bright naked-eye nova occurred in the constellation Cygnus, and was discovered in August 1975 by the Japanese amateur astronomer Honda.

Nubeculae. Latin name for the MAGELLANIC CLOUDS, the Large Magellanic Cloud being the Nubecula Major, and the Small Magellanic Cloud the Nubecula Minor.

Nucleus, Atomic. ⊘ATOM.

Null-geodesic. ⊘GEODESIC.

O

Object glass (OG). The principal lens of the refracting telescope (◊TELESCOPE), which gathers light from a distant object and forms an image of the object at the focal plane of the lens. It is also known as the objective.

Objective. ◊OBJECT GLASS.

Oblate spheroid. The solid body obtained by rotating an ELLIPSE about its minor axis. The shape of the Earth (◊GEOID) is approximately an oblate spheroid, for the equatorial diameter is slightly greater than the polar diameter. Jupiter and Saturn are considerably more oblate than the Earth.

Oblateness. The degree of flattening of an oblate spheroid; it is the ratio of the difference between the equatorial and polar radii to the equatorial radius. For example, if a (hypothetical) planet had a polar radius of 10 000 km and an equatorial radius of 20 000 km, the oblateness (or flattening) would be

$$\frac{20\,000 - 10\,000}{20\,000} = 0\cdot5.$$

Obliquity of the ecliptic. ◊ECLIPTIC.

Occultation. The temporary disappearance of an astronomical object of small angular size when another of larger apparent size passes in front of it; e.g. the passage of the Moon in front of a star, or of the moons of Jupiter behind that planet.

Olbers' paradox. A paradox discussed in 1826 by the German mathematician, H. Olbers (although it had been raised earlier, by Halley for example). Essentially the problem is that if one assumes the universe to be infinite in extent and uniformly populated with stars then 'Why is the sky dark at night?' Olbers argued that if all the stars were about the same brightness as the Sun and if the universe were infinite then, no matter in which direction one looked, eventually one would be looking at the surface of a star; the entire sky, therefore, should appear as bright as the surface of the Sun. Since this is obviously not so, Olbers argued that the universe of stars could not be infinite in extent.

It was suggested that the paradox might be resolved by assuming that space is filled with dust which absorbs starlight; however, given a sufficiently long period of time dust would heat up and re-emit as much radiation as it was receiving (i.e. it would reach a state of radiative equilibrium) so that the sky should still be bright.

Since Olbers' time it has been realized that stars are not uniformly distributed but are contained in galaxies. Nevertheless, a similar paradox would be posed if it were assumed that galaxies are uniformly distributed throughout an infinite universe. However, the observed recession of the galaxies (♢COSMOLOGY) with velocities proportional to their distances provides a neat solution in that beyond a certain range the radiation emitted by galaxies would be so weakened by the RED-SHIFT that it could not be detected; i.e. even if the universe were infinite (which is not a popular view at present) and uniformly populated with galaxies, we should only receive radiation from those within a range of ten to twenty thousand million light years.

The value of Olbers' paradox is that by means of a simple observation which we can all make (i.e. that the sky *is* dark at night) we can place quite strong restrictions on theories of COSMOLOGY.

Olympus Mons. ♢MARS.

Open clusters. ♢GALACTIC CLUSTERS.

Opposition. The position of an astronomical object (in particular, a SUPERIOR PLANET) when it is opposite the Sun in the sky and so reaches culmination (♢TRANSIT) at midnight. When an outer planet is at opposition, the Sun, Earth and planet lie in a straight line, with the Earth between Sun and planet; the planet is then at its closest to the Earth, and best placed for observation. (♢PLANETARY CONFIGURATIONS, Figure 32.)

Optical double. ♢DOUBLE STAR.

Orbit. The path pursued by a body moving in a field of force. In most astronomical contexts we consider motion in a gravitational field, but the term applies equally well to motion under the action of other types of forces, e.g. to charged particles moving in a magnetic field. Bodies moving freely (♢FREE FALL) in the gravitational field of a massive body (e.g. the planets moving round the Sun or an artificial satellite moving round the Earth) follow conic orbits (♢CONIC SECTION), which may be elliptical, circular, parabolic or hyperbolic. The precise orbit which such a body will pursue depends upon the strength of the gravitational field and the velocity of the body (see Figure 28).

Orbital elements. The parameters required to define the shape and orientation in space of an orbit and to fix the position in that orbit at any time of the planet or satellite moving in that orbit. For a planet

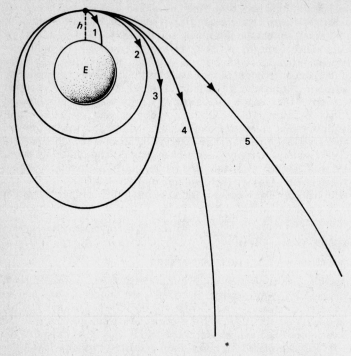

Figure 28. Orbits. The orbits pursued by bodies moving under the influence of a gravitational field are conic in nature ($\diamond$ CONIC SECTIONS). For example, if we imagine launching space vehicles from a given height, *h*, above the Earth (and in a direction parallel to the Earth's surface), there are five possibilities.

(1) If the velocity is less than circular velocity, the craft will strike the Earth's surface.

(2) If the velocity is precisely equal to the circular velocity, a circular orbit will result.

(3) If the velocity is greater than circular velocity but less than escape velocity, the craft will follow an elliptical orbit.

(4) If the velocity is precisely equal to escape velocity, a parabolic trajectory will be pursued.

(5) A velocity in excess of escape velocity results in a hyperbolic trajectory.

moving round the Sun, six elements are required and these would be as follows:

a the semi-major axis of the ellipse;

e the eccentricity of the ellipse;

i the inclination of the orbit plane to the ECLIPTIC;

Ω the longitude of the ascending NODE, i.e. the angle measured anti-clockwise in the ecliptic from the VERNAL EQUINOX to the point of intersection of the orbit with the ecliptic at which the planet passes from south to north of this plane;

ω the longitude of perihelion (sometimes called 'argument of peri-helion'), i.e. the angle, measured anticlockwise in the orbit plane, from the ascending node to perihelion;

T the time at which the planet passed perihelion.

For a satellite in orbit round the Earth, the ascending node and inclination would be referred to the plane of the celestial equator. In addition, the orbital period, P, or the mean motion, n $(=2\pi/P)$, may be quoted. (See Figure 29.)

Orbiting Astronomical Observatory (OAO).   Series of US astronomical satellites. After initial failures, OAO 2 was launched on 7 December 1968 carrying a payload of telescopes and ultra-violet detection equipment. Although designed for one year of operation it continued to function until 13 February 1973. Its achievements include the detection of a huge hydrogen cloud round comet Tago-Sato-Kosaka, and the first ultra-violet observation made from above the atmosphere of a SUPERNOVA.

The last of the series, OAO 3 (actually the fourth OAO, but the second successful one) was launched on 21 August 1972, and named Copernicus in honour of the Polish astronomer, the 500th anniversary of whose birth was in 1973. It carried ultra-violet and X-ray detectors, and its achievements include the detection of molecular hydrogen and deuterium in interstellar clouds, and the increasing period of the binary X-ray source, Cygnus X-3. The pointing accuracy of the instrumentation turned out to be 0·03 second of arc, three times better than specification.

Orbiting Geophysical Observatory (OGO).   Series of US geophysical satellites employed to study, for example, the IONOSPHERE, the inter-planetary magnetic field, the solar wind, Van Allen Belts, etc. The first of the series, OGO 1 was launched on 5 September 1964 into a highly elliptical orbit (perigee altitude 281 km and apogee altitude 149 385 km) typical of the series.

153

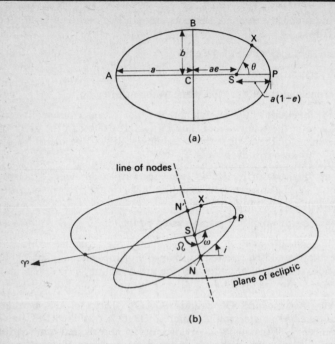

Figure 29. Orbital Elements. The orbit of one body relative to another, and the position of that body in its orbit, are described in terms of orbital elements. The diagram illustrates the elements of an elliptical orbit relative to the Sun, S, the fundamental reference plane in this case being the ecliptic. In the case of a satellite in orbit round the Earth, the reference plane would be the celestial equator.

(a) The dimensional elements of the orbit itself are the semi-major axis, a ($=$ AC) and the eccentricity, e. C is the centre of the ellipse AP, the major axis; A is aphelion and P is perihelion. The angle PSX is the true anomaly, θ, of a body, X, at a particular instant.

(b) The orientation elements are: inclination, i, the angle between the plane of the ecliptic and the orbital plane; the longitude of the ascending node, Ω ($=$ angle ΥSN, where Υ is the vernal equinox and N the ascending node, the point at which the orbit crosses from south to north of the ecliptic); and the longitude of perihelion, ω ($=$ angle NSP).

The elements a, e, i, Ω, ω, together with the time at which the body last passed perihelion, T, fully specify the orbit of the body.

Orbiting Solar Observatory (OSO). Series of US scientific satellites designed to study the Sun from orbit round the Earth. The first of the series was OSO 1, launched on 7 March 1962 into a near-circular orbit of altitude 570 km. To date seven successful launchings have taken place and more are anticipated. A considerable success was achieved with OSO 5; launched on 22 January 1969, it continued to function until 'closed down' three years later. In July 1974, after more than two years' inactivity, it was reactivated and brought back into service.

Instrumentation carried by these satellites includes a coronagraph, a SPECTROHELIOGRAPH, and an ultra-violet spectrometer (♢SPEC-TROGRAPH). One of the principal objectives is to study SOLAR FLARES.

Orrery. A mechanical model which illustrates the relative positions and motions of bodies in the Solar System. The name derives from the fourth Earl of Orrery, for whom such a device was constructed in about 1725.

Oscillating universe theory. A theory which suggests that the entire universe expands and contracts in a cyclic way, reaching a hyper-dense state between each cycle. According to this theory we are at present living in an expansion phase. (♢COSMOLOGY and Figure 13.)

Outer planets. Planets whose orbits lie further from the Sun than does the orbit of the Earth (♢SUPERIOR PLANETS).

Oxidizer (or oxidant). A substance which provides the oxygen required for the combustion of the fuel (or propellant) in a rocket motor. In common use is liquid oxygen (often denoted by LOX), employed, for example, in the US Saturn 5 and the Russian Vostok launcher. Other oxidizers in use include hydrogen peroxide and nitrogen tetroxide.

Oxygen. A gas which makes up 20.95 per cent by volume of the Earth's atmosphere at ground level. It appears to be the third most abundant element in the universe (after hydrogen and helium), but its abundance – in terms of numbers of atoms – is only about $1/1500$ that of hydrogen). The chemical symbol is O, and it normally occurs in the atmosphere in molecular form (two atoms linked), O_2. Its atomic mass is 16 and its atomic number 8 (♢ATOM). It is essential to the sustenance of human and animal life on Earth. Oxygen combines with most other elements and, when this reaction occurs rapidly with the release of heat and light, we describe the reaction as combustion, or burning. Oxygen liquefies under normal pressure at about $90 K$ ($-183°C$) and liquid oxygen (LOX) is commonly used as the oxidizer in the propellant of chemical rockets.

Free oxygen is almost entirely absent from the atmospheres of Venus and Mars.

Ozma Project. The first serious attempt to try to detect signals from other technological civilizations (if any such exist) in the Galaxy. The experiment, conducted by Frank Drake at the US National Radio

Astronomy Observatory, employed a 27-metre radio dish operating at a wavelength of 21 cm (i.e. a frequency of 1420 MHz) to search for possible signals from two neighbouring stars, Epsilon Eridani and Tau Ceti. This particular wavelength was selected because it is the wavelength at which neutral hydrogen in space emits radiation, the argument being that any other civilizations with radio astronomy technology would be aware of this and would choose this wavelength as the logical one on which to transmit and receive. This argument has been challenged (◊INTERSTELLAR COMMUNICATION and CYCLOPS PROJECT). No success was reported.

Ozone. A highly reactive variety of OXYGEN in which the molecule contains three atoms; it is denoted O_3. (◊OZONOSPHERE.)

Ozonosphere. A layer in the Earth's atmosphere which lies between altitudes of 12 to 50 kilometres, and which is notable for having a relatively high concentration of OZONE. The ozone is formed by the action of solar ultra-violet radiation on molecular oxygen (O_2). The layer is of the utmost importance to life on the Earth for, although the maximum concentration of ozone is only about one part in 30000000, this layer very strongly absorbs solar ultra-violet radiation of wavelengths shorter than 0·3 MICRON and shields the surface from the harmful effects of this radiation (for example, excessive exposure to ultra-violet radiation is instrumental in causing skin cancer). As any reduction in the concentration of ozone implies that an increased quantity of ultra-violet radiation would reach ground level, concern has recently been expressed as to the possible effects on the ozonosphere of some of man's activities. It has been suggested that the chlorine content of the gas Freon which is used in aerosol spray cans may be breaking down ozone in this layer; this possibility is currently under investigation both theoretically and observationally with the aid of satellites such as Copernicus (◊ORBITING ASTRONOMICAL OBSERVATORY) and Atmosphere Explorer-E.

P

Parabola. A CONIC SECTION obtained by cutting a right circular cone by a plane parallel to the side of the cone. Such a curve is open (i.e. it does not form a closed shape such as an ellipse or circle), with eccentricity = 1, and stretches to an infinite distance with the two arms tending to become parallel (see Figure 12). The parabola forms the boundary between closed ellipses and open hyperbolas.

Parabolic trajectory. The orbit pursued by a body moving at precisely the ESCAPE VELOCITY; it takes the form of a PARABOLA (⬦ORBIT, Figure 28). In practice an escaping space probe moving away from the Earth will follow a HYPERBOLIC TRAJECTORY; a true parabola cannot be attained in practice. Many comets move on orbits which are very nearly parabolic and, since the calculations are easier for parabolas, orbital computations for newly discovered comets tend to be made on the initial assumption that they are following parabolic trajectories.

Parabolic velocity. The velocity of an object following a PARABOLIC TRAJECTORY relative to a massive body. The value of parabolic velocity at a given distance from the massive body is equal to the ESCAPE VELOCITY at that point.

Parallax, Trigonometrical. The displacement in the apparent position of an object when viewed from two different positions. Parallax provides the fundamental means of determining distance in the universe (Figure 30): in principle the distance to a star may be determined by making observations of its apparent position on two occasions separated by an interval of six months. The two observations are made from positions in space separated by the diameter of the Earth's orbit (300 million km) and they yield the value of the angle Sun–star–Earth which is known as the parallax of the star. If the observations of the star are made at a time when the angle Earth–Sun–star is a right angle, then the displacement of the star from its mean position is a maximum; the value of parallax so obtained is the annual parallax. Knowing the value of parallax, the triangle Sun–star–Earth may be solved to yield the distance of the star. In practice, observations made over the course of a year reveal that the star traces out a small ellipse on the sky, the

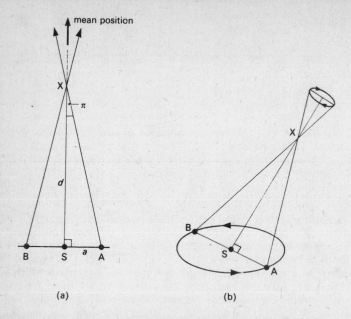

Figure 30. Parallax. (a) The annual parallax, Π, of the star X is the angle SXA where A is the position of the Earth when the angle ASX is a right angle. In principle the value of Π may be obtained by measuring the apparent change in position of the star when measured at intervals of six months (the Earth reaches B six months after A) so that the measurements are made from points separated by the diameter of the Earth's orbit. Once the value of Π is known, and knowing a, the radius of the Earth's orbit, simple trigonometry allows us to calculate d, the distance to the star.

(b) As the Earth moves round the Sun, the star appears to trace out a small ellipse in the sky. The semi-major axis (i.e. half of the maximum diameter) of this ellipse is equal (in angular measure) to the value of annual parallax.

semi-major axis of which equals the annual parallax ($\diamondsuit$ ABERRATION OF LIGHT).

Values of annual parallax are extremely small; even for the nearest star (PROXIMA CENTAURI) the value is only 0·76 seconds of arc, corresponding to a distance of 4·2 light years, or just under 1·3 parsecs. Beyond about 100 parsecs the method is unreliable as the errors of observation become greater than the values of parallax to be measured.

Note that for a star with annual parallax π (arcsecs), its distance, d (in parsecs), is given by

$$d = 1/\pi.$$

Within the Solar System, the parallax of the nearer planets may be obtained by making observations from opposite sides of the Earth (planetary parallax), but such measurements have been superseded by the techniques of RADAR ASTRONOMY.

For distances in excess of 100 parsecs, alternative methods are available for distance measurement: ◊ DISTANCE DETERMINATION IN THE UNIVERSE; DISTANCE MODULUS; MOVING CLUSTERS.

Parking orbit. An orbit into which a satellite or spacecraft is placed prior to being injected into its planned orbit. A spacecraft might be placed into such an orbit in order that its various systems be tested prior to undertaking an interplanetary flight. For example, the manned spacecraft of the Apollo series (◊ APOLLO PROJECT) were placed into a circular parking orbit round the Earth prior to firing the motor for the translunar trajectory. In the case of Apollo 17, the altitude of this orbit was 173 km and the spacecraft remained in the orbit for two revolutions round the Earth.

Parsec (pc). A unit of distance commonly used by astronomers. It is the distance at which a star would have an annual PARALLAX of exactly one second of arc; from this distance, the Earth's orbit would have an apparent radius of one second of arc. One parsec is equivalent to 3·26 light years ($3·09 \times 10^{13}$ km) or 206265 ASTRONOMICAL UNITS. Multiples of this unit are kiloparsecs (kpc) = 1000 parsecs and megaparsec (Mpc) = 1000000 parsecs.

The distance of a star expressed in parsecs = 1/annual parallax (in seconds of arc); thus a star whose annual parallax is 0·1 seconds of arc lies at a distance of 1/0·1 = 10 parsecs. (◊ PARALLAX, Figure 30.)

Partial eclipse. ◊ ECLIPSE.

Paschen series. A series of lines in the SPECTRUM of the hydrogen atom corresponding to transitions between the third energy level (i.e. the third permitted orbit for an electron in order of distance from the nucleus) and higher levels (see Figure 41b). These lines, denoted by Pα, Pβ, Pγ, and so on, occur in the infra-red part of the spectrum. Pα has a wavelength of 1·875 microns, and the wavelengths of spectral lines converge to the series limit at 0·819 micron. (◊ BALMER SERIES; LYMAN SERIES; ATOM.)

Payload. The mass, excluding the mass of the rocket vehicle itself and its propellant, which can be transported into a specified orbit by means of a rocket; i.e. the mass of the artificial satellite, spacecraft, etc., which can be carried by a rocket vehicle. This usually represents a very small fraction of the launch weight of the rocket. For example, the Atlas–Centaur vehicle used to launch the spacecraft Pioneer 11 towards Jupiter had an initial weight of 146 500 kilogrammes, while the spacecraft itself had a mass of only 260 kg; in this case the ratio payload : launch weight was about 1 : 500. On the other hand, the Saturn 1B, with a launch weight of 600 tonnes, can place a payload of over 15 tonnes into near-Earth orbit; the ratio in this case is better than 1 : 40. Generally, the largest fraction of the weight of a launch vehicle is made up by propellant.

Penumbra. The outer, lighter, part of a shadow, observable when a shadow is cast by an extended object illuminated by a light source of finite angular size. The penumbra represents the region within which the light source would be seen to be partly obscured. Thus, when the Moon casts its shadow on the Earth during an eclipse, observers located in the central umbra will observe a total eclipse of the Sun, while observers in the penumbra will see a partial eclipse (◊ECLIPSE, Figure 15).

The term is also applied to the lighter outer part of a SUNSPOT.

Penumbral eclipse. ◊ECLIPSE.

Periastron. The point in its orbit at which a body makes its closest approach to a star. The term is usually applied to the point in their relative orbit at which the two members of a BINARY system are closest together.

Perigee. The point in its orbit at which a satellite makes its closest approach to the Earth. (◊◊APOGEE.)

Perihelion. The point of closest approach to the Sun in the orbit of a body, e.g. one of the planets (◊ORBITAL ELEMENTS, Figure 29a). In the case of the Earth, this point is reached on 1 January each YEAR, when the distance to the Sun is 147 000 000 km, some 5 million kilometres less than the distance six months later when the Earth is at aphelion.

Period–luminosity relation. ◊CEPHEID VARIABLE.

Phase angle. The angle between the Sun, a planet and the Earth (measured at the planet) (see Figure 31). For a SUPERIOR PLANET this angle is greatest when the planet is near QUADRATURE while for an INFERIOR PLANET it is greatest at INFERIOR CONJUNCTION. The value of this angle, divided by 180°, gives the proportion of the unilluminated side of the planet which may be seen; thus when a planet is at SUPERIOR CONJUNCTION, the phase angle is 0° and the planet's disc is completely illuminated, whereas at inferior conjunction the phase angle is 180° and the unilluminated hemisphere is presented to

14. *Above:* Aerial view of the Cambridge 5-kilometre radio telescope; the four rail-mounted aerials are just visible in the distance (→ RADIO TELESCOPE).

15. *Right:* One of the rail-mounted aerials of the 5-kilometre radio telescope. The similarity to the Cassegrain reflector is apparent (→TELESCOPE) The complete instrument comprises eight aerials, four of which are mounted on rails.

16. The Pleiades. This conspicuous galactic star cluster shows evidence of reflection nebulosity (→ NEBULA) round the brighter stars. It is a relatively young cluster.

17. *Opposite:* The Great Nebula in Orion, M42, photographed by the 100-inch (2.5-metre) Hooker reflector. This emission nebula is about 20 light years across and at a distance of 1600 light years ; nevertheless it may be seen without optical aid. Within it, star formation is taking place.

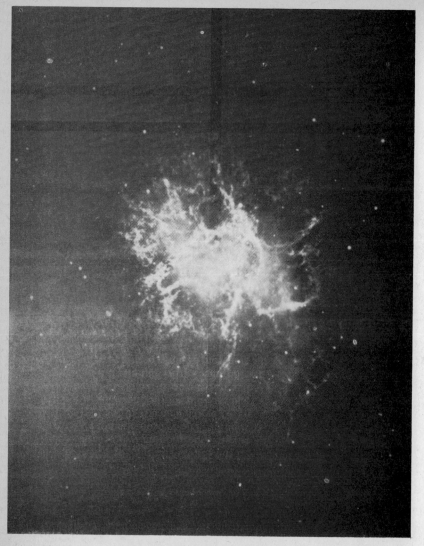

18. The Crab Nebula, M1, photographed in red light. This is the remnant of the supernova of 1054, and its turbulent structure is evident.

19. *Opposite:* The Pulsar NP 0532 in the Crab Nebula. Stroboscopic photographs taken with a television camera on 3 February 1969 show four different phases of the pulsar, the only pulsar to show obvious optical variations. In the upper left frame the pulsar is invisible.

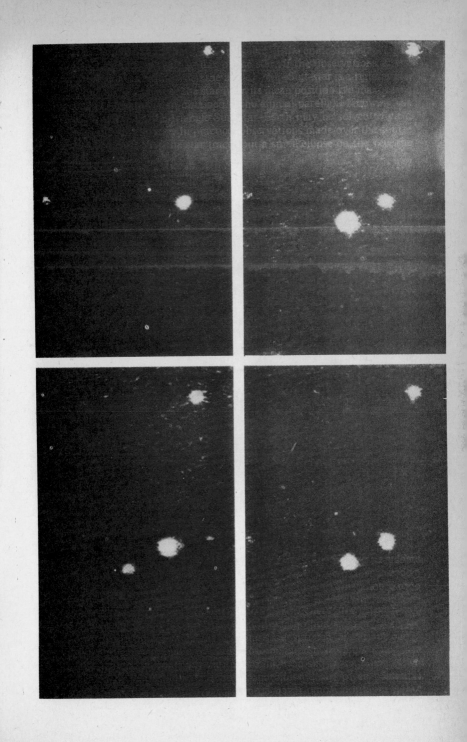

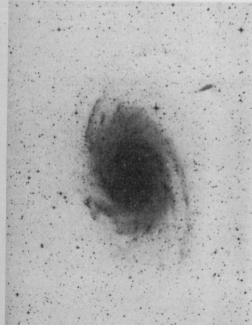

20. *Above:* The
Andromeda Galaxy, M31.
This is the nearest spiral
galaxy similar to our own.
Its two satellite elliptical
galaxies NGC 205 and
NGC 221 are also shown.

21. *Left:* Large spiral
galaxy NGC 6744. The
spiral structure is clearly
seen in this negative pint.

23. *Right:* The Seyfert Galaxy, NGC 4151, showing the conspicuous nucleus typical of these objects.

22. *Below:* The Small Magellanic Cloud, a satellite of our Galaxy. The globular cluster on the left of the picture is 47 Tucanae, a foreground object in our own Galaxy.

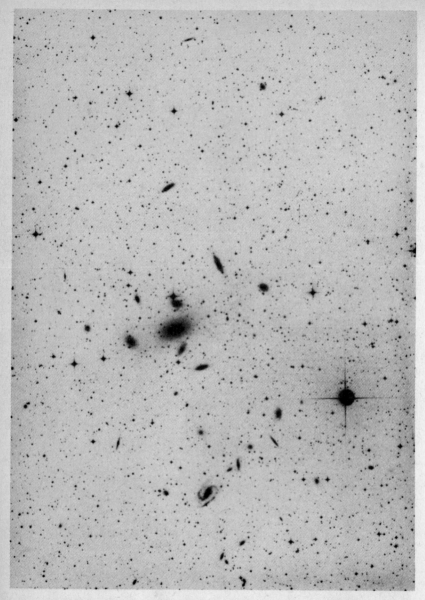

24. Cluster of galaxies in the constellation Pavo. In this negative photograph small round dots are foreground stars in our Galaxy, the other objects are galaxies.

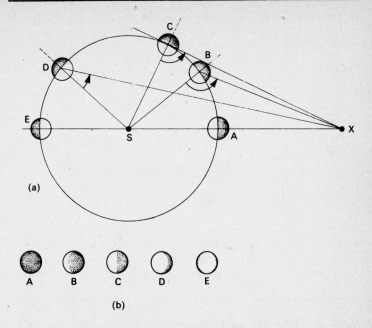

(a)

(b)

Figure 31. Phase angle. The phase angle is the angle Sun–planet–Earth measured at the planet. (In the case of the phases of the Moon, it is the angle Sun–Moon–Earth). (a) As an example, the case of an inferior planet is illustrated here. S represents the Sun and X the Earth. At A, the phase angle is angle SAX which is 180°. The proportion of the unilluminated side of the planet seen from the Earth is given by: phase angle/180° = 180/180 = 1 (i.e. 100 per cent), and only the dark side is presented to Earth. The observed appearance is shown in (b). The phase angles and corresponding appearance are shown for various positions – A, B, C, D, E – of the planet.

the Earth. In the case of the Moon, the phase angle is 180° at new moon, 90° at first and last quarter, and 0° at full moon.

Phobos. ◊MARS.

Photometry. The measurement of the apparent brightness of sources of radiation. The brightness of visible objects is usually quoted in terms of APPARENT MAGNITUDE but, at wavelengths longer and shorter than optical, it is normal to describe brightness in terms of the amount of energy reaching unit area of the telescope in unit time (e.g. ◊FLUX DENSITY).

The earliest form of photometry consisted of making estimates by eye of the brightness of an unknown source compared to known comparison stars (and a practised observer can achieve an accuracy of ± 0.1 magnitudes in this way). In modern optical astronomy, the two most common methods are photographic and photoelectric. The photographic method relies on the fact that the density of an image, or the size of a star image on a photographic plate, is proportional to the magnitude of the source. This method allows a large number of stars to be measured simultaneously, but is limited in accuracy where a wide range of magnitudes or colours is involved. The photoelectric method examines one star at a time: starlight is allowed to fall on a device (such as the PHOTOMULTIPLIER) which converts the incoming radiation into a measurable electric current, which can be calibrated to give high accuracy.

The eye responds to the whole of the visible spectrum, so that an eye estimate of brightness gives the integrated magnitude of the source; a device which responds to all wavelengths of electromagnetic radiation is a bolometer ($\lozenge$ BOLOMETRIC MAGNITUDE). In many cases, however, it is convenient to be able to measure brightness at particular wavelengths, or at particular wavebands, as, for example, in the determination of the COLOUR INDEX of a star. This may be achieved by placing suitable colour FILTERS in front of the detector. In order to facilitate the comparison of results, the following standard filter wavebands have been adopted by astronomers:

Filter										
	U	B	V	R	I	J	K	L	M	N
Central wavelength (micron)	0·36	0·44	0·55	0·7	0·9	1·25	2·2	3·4	5	10·2

Photomultiplier. A device consisting of a sensitive surface which emits electrons when light falls upon it; the electrons are accelerated in an electric field and strike a further series of surfaces, releasing many more electrons at each encounter. In this way, the original electrons are amplified millions of times to give a measurable current proportional to the intensity of incoming radiation. The photomultiplier has wide application in astronomy, particularly in the measurement of the intensity of starlight ($\lozenge$ PHOTOMETRY).

Photon. $\lozenge$ ELECTROMAGNETIC RADIATION; LIGHT.

Photosphere. The visible surface of the SUN (see Figure 43), literally, 'sphere of light'. It is the layer from which almost all of the Sun's radiation is emitted, and has an EFFECTIVE TEMPERATURE of 5800 K. The general texture of the photosphere is mottled ($\lozenge$ SOLAR GRANU-

LATION), this being evidence of convection in the outer regions of the Sun. The most obvious features of the photosphere are SUNSPOTS. Although the edge or limb of the Sun appears quite sharp and clear-cut, it must be remembered that the Sun is gaseous and does not have a hard surface at all. The edge of the visible disc is less bright than the centre, a phenomenon known as limb darkening. Due to the gaseous nature of the Sun it is possible to see into the photosphere to a depth of the order of 200 km; looking at the centre of the disc we are receiving radiation from hotter inner layers of the Sun, while at the limb we are looking tangentially into the cooler outermost region of the photosphere. Consequently the limb appears less luminous than the centre.

Pioneer. Continuing series of US interplanetary space probes. The early launchings were either unsuccessful or only partially successful; thus Pioneer 1, launched on 11 October 1958, reached a height of 117000 km before falling back to Earth. Pioneer 3, in December of that year, established the existence of the outer VAN ALLEN BELT.

Pioneers 4 to 9 inclusive entered orbits round the Sun, studying the interplanetary medium (magnetic fields, SOLAR WIND, etc.), and setting new standards for longevity; thus Pioneer 6 was still operating after eight years in space.

The most spectacular successes of the series have been the Jupiter fly-bys of Pioneer 10 and Pioneer 11. Pioneer 10 was launched on 2 March 1972 on a trajectory which encountered Jupiter on 5 December 1973 after a flight of some 1000 million km which included the first passage through the ASTEROID belt by a man-made object. The closest approach to Jupiter was at a range of 130000 km above the cloud tops and, as a result of the encounter, Pioneer 10 was accelerated to a speed in excess of solar ESCAPE VELOCITY. It is expected to pass beyond the orbit of Pluto in 1987 and will then enter interstellar space (◊GRAND TOUR).

Pioneer 11 made a closer approach on 3 December 1974, flying by at a minimum range of 41000 km on a trajectory which took it below Jupiter's south pole and over the north pole; this minimized the time spent in the intense equatorial radiation belt. As a result of the encounter Pioneer 11 entered an orbit taking it well above the plane of the ECLIPTIC which should lead to a fly-by of Saturn in 1979. At these large distances, SOLAR PANELS do not provide sufficient electrical power, so these spacecraft are equipped with nuclear generators.

Future Pioneer missions are likely to include a pair of Venus probes in 1978.

Plages. Bright regions of the PHOTOSPHERE of the Sun visible over the entire solar disc, particularly at wavelengths corresponding to emission lines (◊KIRCHHOFF'S LAWS) of hydrogen and calcium. They are regions of gas hotter by several hundred degrees than their sur-

163

roundings and associated with active areas on the Sun. They are usually associated with sunspots and tend to cover a wider area than the related spots (typically, the plage area would be about ten times that of the sunspots area). Plages usually appear before the sunpots, and persist for longer periods. The term bright flocculi is sometimes applied to these areas. ($\Diamond$ FACULAE.)

Planet. A relatively small body which revolves round a star and which does not emit light produced by internal nuclear reactions in the way that a star does. The Earth is one of a system of nine planets revolving round the Sun ($\Diamond$ SOLAR SYSTEM) and it is thought that a large proportion of stars may have such planetary systems ($\Diamond$ PLANETS OF OTHER STARS).

The one characteristic common to planets is that their masses are low compared to their parent stars (say 0·01 solar masses or less); for example, the Earth has a mass of only 1/329000, and the giant planet JUPITER has a mass of only 1/1047 that of the Sun. The planets in the Solar System shine by reflected sunlight; however, it is worth noting that Jupiter in particular has so much internal heat that it emits more INFRA-RED RADIATION than it receives from the Sun.

The term 'planet' derives from the concept of a 'wandering star' since the planets are seen to move relative to the apparent fixed background stars.

Planetary configurations. See Figure 32.

Planetary nebula. Compact round or oval regions of nebulosity which when seen through a telescope under low magnification look not unlike the visible discs of planets; it is because of this appearance that they are referred to as planetary nebulae. Such a nebula represents a roughly spherical or ellipsoidal shell of gas round a central star, usually of spectral type O or W ($\Diamond$ SPECTRAL CLASSIFICATION) with a temperature of between 30000 K and over 100000 K. Such a star emits most of its radiation in the short-wave ultra-violet part of the spectrum, and the gas in the shell shines as a result of absorbing this radiation and re-emitting it as visible light. The nebula probably represents a shell of gas expelled from the central star which is itself approaching the end of its life cycle, and spectroscopic evidence suggests that planetary nebulae are expanding while their central stars are contracting. Although the formation of planetary nebulae is not well understood at present, it does seem likely that the central stars are in the process of evolving into WHITE DWARFS.

The best-known example of a planetary nebula, visible in small telescopes, is the Ring Nebula in the constellation Lyra.

Planetary parallax. $\Diamond$ PARALLAX.

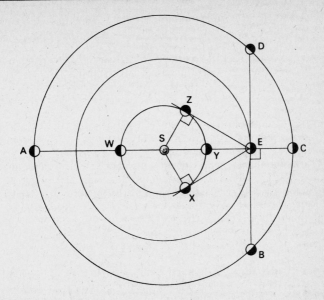

Figure 32. Planetary configurations. In the figure S represents the Sun and E the Earth. When the inner (or interior) planet is at W it is said to be at superior conjunction; position Y represents inferior conjunction; position X, greatest elongation east (i.e. the angle between the Sun and the planet, as seen from Earth, is a maximum, with the planet apparently on the east side of the Sun and visible in the evening sky); and position Z, greatest elongation west.

For the outer (or superior) planet, position A denotes that the planet is at superior conjunction; position C represents opposition; and positions B and D denote quadrature (at these positions the angle Sun–Earth–planet is a right angle and the apparent phase of the planet is most obvious).

Planetology. The study of the structure and surface features of planets; the extension of the science of geology to include planets other than the Earth. However, the term 'geology' is now considered to be applicable to other bodies apart from the Earth (e.g. 'the geology of Mars').

Planets of other stars. At present it is not possible to 'see' planets of other stars directly; the distances even to the nearest stars are so great that planets would in general be too faint to be detected with existing telescopes (for example, if JUPITER were observed from the distance of the nearest star, it would have an APPARENT MAGNITUDE of +22, barely within the detectable range of the largest telescopes) and, in any case, any light from planets would be lost in the glare of their parent stars.

It is possible to infer the existence of massive planets (comparable with Jupiter) from the perturbing effects they exert on their parent stars. A star and a massive planet will revolve round their common centre of mass (◊BARYCENTRE); this point will lie much nearer to the star than the planet (in the case of the Sun and Jupiter, this point would lie one thousandth of the way from the Sun to Jupiter). In a few cases, with nearby stars, it has proved possible to observe such motion of these stars which seems to indicate the presence of planetary bodies; stars for which there is some evidence of planetary companions include BARNARD'S STAR, 61 CYGNI, Epsilon Eridani, and Lalande 21185, and of these the best attested case appears to be the first.

Current theory (◊SOLAR SYSTEM, ORIGIN OF) suggests that the formation of planetary systems may be a natural process in the early life of a large proportion of stars. If this is so, then it is likely that there are many thousands of millions of planetary systems in our GALAXY (2).

Plasma. The state of matter in which ATOMS are wholly ionized (◊IONIZATION); i.e. a plasma is made up of positively and negatively charged particles (protons or atomic nuclei and electrons) moving freely. Much of the material in the universe is in the form of plasma; for example, the material inside stars is almost wholly ionized. The study of plasma physics is of considerable importance in connection with attempts to produce energy by FUSION (i.e. to duplicate the energy process operating in the Sun). Such an energy source could use cheap fuel (DEUTERIUM from the oceans) and would be relatively pollution-free. However, the problem which has not yet been overcome is the containment of the extremely hot plasma for long enough periods to produce usable energy.

Pleiades. The best-known open or GALACTIC CLUSTER of stars. At least six stars in the cluster are visible to the unaided eye (on a clear, dark night) in this compact group which lies in the constellation Taurus; altogether there are some 200 stars in the cluster. The diameter of the cluster is some fourteen light years, and the distance 410 light years. Some of the hotter and more luminous stars in the cluster are seen to be surrounded by faint nebulosity (reflection nebula) due to the reflection of starlight from dust clouds around these stars (◊NEBULA). It appears to be a young cluster, with an age of at most a few tens of millions of years.

The name originates from seven sisters of Greek mythology; one can only speculate on the possible misdemeanours which led to the seventh sister being fainter than her six companions. (See Plate 16.)

Pluto. The outermost known planet in the Solar System, Pluto was discovered in 1930 after an extensive photographic programme by Clyde Tombaugh of the Lowell Observatory, Flagstaff, Arizona. Slight suspected irregularities in the orbits of Uranus and NEPTUNE led Percival Lowell to carry out a computation – similar to the Adams–Leverrier calculation which led to the discovery of Neptune – to determine the possible mass and position of the then unknown planet thought to be responsible for these effects. His prediction was made in 1915.

Pluto is a curious planet in a number of ways and little is known with certainty about its physical nature. Its mass appears to be less than a fifth of the Earth's mass, and it is therefore rather too small to exert a significant perturbation on the orbits of Uranus and Neptune. It moves in an orbit which is the most eccentric (eccentricity 0·25) of all the planets, and which has the greatest inclination (17°) to the ECLIPTIC. Its mean distance from the Sun is 39·4 astronomical units (a.u.), but at PERIHELION it approaches to within 29·6 a.u., while at aphelion it recedes to 49·2 a.u. At its closest, Pluto is nearer to the Sun than Neptune (⇨ SOLAR SYSTEM, Figure 38b). Pluto next reaches perihelion in 1989 and is at present closer in than Neptune; it will remain closer for the remainder of the twentieth century. Because of its small mass and size (radius about 3000 km, but this value is very uncertain) and its curious orbit, it has been suggested that Pluto is a former satellite of Neptune which may have escaped as a result of some perturbation, such as a close encounter with Neptune's massive satellite, Triton.

Pluto data
(Values denoted (?) are extremely uncertain)

		(Earth = 1)
Mean distance from Sun	5 900 000 000 km	39·4
Orbital eccentricity	0·25	—
Orbital inclination	17° 10′	—
Sidereal orbital period	247·7 years	247·7
Axial rotation period	6·3 days	6·3
Mass	10^{24} kg (approx)	0·17
Radius	3000 km (approx)	0·5
Mean density	7×10^3 kg m^{-3} (?)	1·3 (?)
Surface gravity	7 m s^{-2} (?)	0·7 (?)

Polarimeter. A device which enables the state of polarization of electromagnetic radiation (⇨ POLARIZATION OF LIGHT). It can take a wide variety of forms. In the simplest case a rotatable sheet of polaroid may be used; this material transmits light vibrating in one plane and does not transmit light vibrating at right angles to that plane. If plane-polarized light is entering the polaroid, rotation of the sheet until the source is extinguished will reveal the plane of polarization. The same principle is used in polaroid sunglasses; reflected light is polarized, and the polaroid lenses are orientated to cut out such polarized light and so eliminate glare.

Polaris. The Pole Star. It is a second magnitude star in the constellation of Ursa Minor which happens to lie about one degree distant from the north CELESTIAL POLE. As the celestial sphere rotates, Polaris traces out a small circle of about one degree radius round the pole, but to a casual eye it maintains a more or less fixed position above the horizon throughout the night. Due to the phenomenon of PRECESSION, the position of the celestial pole changes with time so that Polaris will not remain close to the celestial pole over a long period of time.

Polarization of light. Light is regarded as a transverse wave motion, i.e. a wave which vibrates perpendicularly to its direction of propagation (like a wave on the sea). A plane-polarized beam of light contains waves vibrating in one plane only, while an unpolarized beam contains waves vibrating in all planes perpendicular to the direction of motion of the beam (see Figure 33). There is a wide variety of possible states of polarization between these two extremes. The most general case is elliptical polarization where, as the waves advance, the plane of polarization rotates and the amplitude varies. In the case of circular polarization, the plane rotates but the amplitude remains constant.

The state of polarization of a beam of light provides information on the mechanism responsible for producing the light and/or what has happened to the light between the source and the observer. For example, light is polarized by reflection and studies of the state of polarization of light reflected from the lunar or planetary surfaces yield information about these surfaces.

The property of polarization may be associated with any form of ELECTROMAGNETIC RADIATION.

Positron. The antiparticle (⟡ ANTIMATTER) of the ELECTRON. It has the same mass, but opposite charge and spin.

Potential energy. The energy which a body possesses by virtue of its position. For example, if a mass, m, is held at a height, h, above the ground, its potential energy is given by mgh (where g is the acceleration due to gravity); if it is then released, it accelerates until it hits the ground at some velocity. At this instant, its potential energy has been converted into KINETIC ENERGY.

More generally, the sum of the kinetic and potential energy of a system is a constant. The potential energy of a mass, m, located at a distance, r, from the centre of a massive body is given by $-Gm/r$, where G is the gravitational constant.

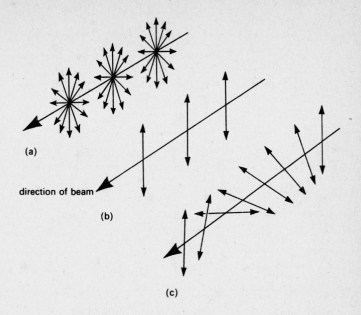

Figure 33. Polarized light. (a) An unpolarized beam of light is made up of waves vibrating in all planes perpendicular to the direction of propagation of the beam.

(b) A plane-polarized beam contains waves vibrating in one plane only.

(c) A circularly polarized beam comprises waves for which, as the wave advances, the plane of polarization rotates.

In the case of elliptical polarization, the amplitude (i.e. the height) of the wave varies also.

If a gas cloud contracts under its mutual gravitational attraction (e.g. in the formation of a star) about half of the potential energy lost as the cloud contracts goes to heating the cloud, and the other half is released as radiation.

Power. The rate of doing work (or the rate of expenditure or emission of energy). Power is measured in units of watts (1 watt = 1 joule per second); thus, the Sun radiates 3.8×10^{26} joules per second and its power output, therefore, is 3.8×10^{26} watts.

Precession. The slow periodic change in the orientation of the Earth's axis of rotation due to the gravitational attractions of the Sun and

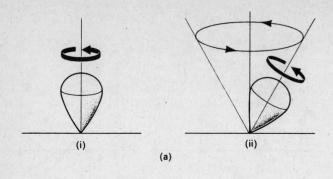

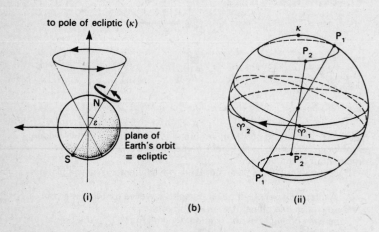

Figure 34. Precession. (a) (i) A spinning top, if maintained on a vertical axis, will continue to spin steadily round this vertical axis. However, (ii) if its axis is tilted to the vertical, then the gravitational attraction of the Earth on the top will cause its spin axis to rotate slowly about the vertical direction. This phenomenon is called precession.

(b) (i) The axis of the Earth is tilted by an angle ϵ. The effect, primarily of the attractions of Sun and Moon, is to cause the axis of the Earth to precess in a similar way, over a period of 25 800 years. (ii) This precession causes the celestial pole to trace out a circle of radius ϵ round the pole of the ecliptic. Likewise, the celestial equator moves relative to the ecliptic, so that as the pole moves from P_1 to P_2, the vernal equinox moves from Υ_1 to Υ_2 (the precession of the equinoxes).

Moon on the non-spherical globe of the Earth ($\Diamond$ GEOID); the effect is often referred to as luni-solar precession. The term is also applied to the periodic change in the rotation axis of any spinning body, e.g. an artificial satellite (see Figure 34a).

The axis of the Earth is inclined to the perpendicular to the ECLIPTIC by an angle ϵ (approximately $23\frac{1}{2}°$), and precession results in the celestial pole tracing out a circle of radius ϵ round the pole of the ecliptic in a period of some 25800 years (see Figure 34b). Thus the north celestial pole is at present located close to the fairly conspicuous star POLARIS, which we call the Pole Star; 4500 years ago, it lay close to the star Thuban in the constellation Draco, while in 12000 years' time, it will be near the bright star Vega.

As the celestial pole moves, so the celestial equator moves relative to the ecliptic (see Figure 34b). Thus the points of intersection of these two circles, i.e. the equinoxes ($\Diamond$ EQUINOX) move along the ecliptic in a clockwise direction at a mean rate of about 50 seconds of arc per annum (i.e. 360° in 25800 years). Since the celestial longitude of a star is measured from the VERNAL EQUINOX, it follows that this must increase at a rate of 50 arcsecs per annum due to precession.

Because of precession, star catalogues and charts must be drawn up for a particular instant, or epoch (e.g. 00 hrs on 1 January for the years 1900, 1950, 2000, etc.); if a precise position for a star is required at some other time, the effects of precession must be calculated to determine by how much the star will have moved from its tabulated position.

The effects of precession were first noted by Hipparchus in the second century B.C.

Principle of equivalence. $\Diamond$ GENERAL THEORY OF RELATIVITY.

Project Apollo. $\Diamond$ APOLLO PROJECT.

Project Daedalus. $\Diamond$ DAEDALUS PROJECT.

Projectile. $\Diamond$ BALLISTIC TRAJECTORY.

Prominences. Flame-like projections from the edge of the Sun's disc, these are regions of hot hydrogen gas, characteristically reddish in colour, and normally visible only at total solar eclipses unless specialized equipment is employed, such as the SPECTROHELIOSCOPE or a very narrow band filter tuned to a wavelength at which hydrogen emits radiation (the H-α emission line at a wavelength of 6563 angstroms is normally selected for this purpose).

The bases of prominences lie in, or just above, the CHROMOSPHERE and they usually originate in the vicinity of sunspots or general active solar regions ($\Diamond$ SUN, Figure 43). The hydrogen gas in prominences flows under the influence of magnetic fields, flow taking place upwards from the surface or downwards from the CORONA. Typical dimensions

171

of prominences are: height 30000 km; length 200000 km. However, heights of 100000 km are not uncommon and over 400000 km has been recorded, while lengths exceptionally may attain 2000000 km.

There is a number of different prominence types: a surge prominence takes the form of a column of gas which shoots up from the surface and falls back along more or less the same path; a loop prominence, generally associated with sunspots, where gas appears to condense from the corona at the top of the loop and flows down both sides of it; an arch prominence is propelled upwards from the solar surface; quiescent prominences may retain their form with little change for months on end.

By observing at hydrogen wavelengths, prominences may be seen against the bright disc of the Sun as dark filaments due to the absorption of light from the photosphere by the hydrogen gas contained in those prominences.

Proper motion. The angular motion per annum of a star on the celestial sphere (i.e. perpendicular to the radial direction) due to its physical motion through space relative to the Sun. It is usually denoted by the symbol μ. If the distance of the star is known, the proper motion can be converted into a value of transverse velocity (velocity across the line of sight).

The distances of stars are so great that, over periods of hundreds of years, their proper motions are usually imperceptible to the unaided eye. The star with the largest known value of proper motion, 10·3 arcsecs per annum, is BARNARD'S STAR; it is one of the nearest stars.

Proton. One of the basic nuclear particles, having one unit of atomic charge (positive, and equal to $1·602 \times 10^{19}$ coulomb), and one unit of atomic mass (strictly speaking the mass of a proton is $1·672 \times 10^{-27}$ kg $= 1·007$ atomic mass units). The nucleus of the hydrogen atom is made up of one proton ($\Diamond$SPECTRUM, Figure 41a), while the uranium nucleus contains ninety-two. ($\Diamond$ATOM.)

Proton–proton reaction. The nuclear-fusion chain reaction which is thought to be responsible for most of the energy production in the Sun, and to be the dominant energy-producing reaction in stars of spectral type later than A ($\Diamond$SPECTRAL CLASSIFICATION). Essentially, the reaction builds up helium nuclei from hydrogen nuclei (i.e. PROTONS), with the release of energy. In the reaction, about 0·7 per cent of the reacting mass of hydrogen is converted into energy.

The first stage of the reaction involves the combination of two hydrogen nuclei, denoted by $_1H^1$, where the subscript denotes atomic charge ($\Diamond$ATOM) and the superscript atomic mass, as follows:

$$_1H^1 + {_1H^1} \rightarrow {_1H^2} + e^+ + \nu + \gamma,$$

where $_1H^2$ is a nucleus of 'heavy hydrogen', a deuteron; e^+ is a positively charged equivalent of the electron, i.e. a positron; γ is a quantum of very short wavelength gamma radiation; and ν a NEUTRINO.

The next step is

$$_1H^1 + {}_1H^2 \rightarrow {}_2He^3 + \gamma,$$

where $_2He^3$ is a nucleus of 'lightweight' helium. The final step (usually) is

$$_2He^3 + {}_2He^3 \rightarrow {}_2He^4 + {}_1H^1 + {}_1H^1.$$

Thus in the final stage a normal helium nucleus is produced, having two units of charge and four units of mass, and two protons are released at the end of the chain.

These reactions begin to take place at significant rates in the interiors of stars when temperatures exceed 10 million K.

Protostar. ⟡STELLAR EVOLUTION.

Proxima Centauri. The nearest known star (apart from the Sun itself). It is a member of the triple star system Alpha Centauri, and with an annual PARALLAX of 0·76 seconds of arc, lies at a distance of 1·31 parsecs, i.e. 4·26 light years. It is a faint, cool red main-sequence (⟡HERTZSPRUNG–RUSSELL DIAGRAM) star of a type known as a red dwarf (it has spectral type M5 (⟡SPECTRAL CLASSIFICATION), and an ABSOLUTE MAGNITUDE of $+15\cdot4$ which implies that its luminosity is only about one ten thousandth that of the Sun). Although nearer to us than any other star, it is too faint to be seen with the unaided eye, having an APPARENT MAGNITUDE of $+11$.

It is, too, a FLARE STAR.

Ptolemaic system. The geocentric view of the universe as expounded by Ptolemy (Claudius Ptolemaus, *c.* A.D. 100–170, librarian at Alexandria) in the second century A.D. According to this view, the Earth lay at the centre of the universe and around it, in order of distance, moved the Moon, the planets Mercury and Venus, the Sun, the planets Mars, Jupiter, and Saturn. Beyond the outermost planet lay the sphere of the stars. The Sun and Moon were envisaged as moving round the Earth in circular paths while, in order to account for their observed motions, each planet was considered to move round a circle or epicycle, the centre of which moved round a larger circle, the deferent, which was itself centred on the Earth (⟡EPICYCLE, Figure 18). The system required additional complex devices in order to account fully for planetary motions and was never entirely satisfactory (although surprisingly successful predictions of planetary positions were achieved). At that time it was felt that the circle was the perfect geometrical form, and that only perfect motion was possible in the heavens; it was not until the work of Kepler (⟡KEPLER'S LAWS) that it was appreciated that the planets move round the Sun in elliptical orbits.

Ptolemy. ⟡PTOLEMAIC SYSTEM.

Pulsar. A radio source which emits brief pulses of signal at very regular short intervals, typically one second or less (see Figure 35a). The first pulsar was discovered in 1967 by Jocelyn Bell (now Burnell) and Antony Hewish at the Mullard Radio Astronomy Observatory, Cambridge, U K. At first the discovery of such regular sources, 'ticking'

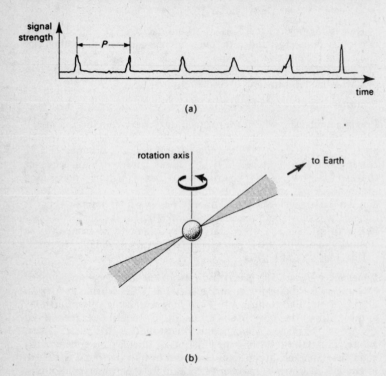

(a)

(b)

Figure 35. Pulsars. (a) The principal characteristic of a pulsar is its radio emission which takes the form of pulses of signal having a very precise period, *P*. The individual successive pulses may differ appreciably, but the period remains constant (apart from a slow long-term increase).

(b) The widely accepted model of a pulsar is that it is a highly compact, rapidly rotating neutron star having an intense magnetic field. By some mechanism (and the mechanism is not fully understood as yet, although it involves the motion of particles in the strong field) radiation is emitted in a quite narrow beam. As the star rotates, this beam sweeps round like the beam of a lighthouse. Each time the beam is directed towards the Earth, a pulse of signal is received.

with the precision of a clock, made some astronomers regard pulsars as evidence of transmissions by extra-terrestrial technologies (◊ INTER-STELLAR COMMUNICATION), but several possible natural explanations were soon proposed, and it is now generally accepted that pulsars are due to rapidly spinning NEUTRON STARS.

These represent the collapsed central remnants of massive stars which may well be rotating several times per second, and which are likely to have strong magnetic fields (possibly of the order of 10^{12} gauss) near their surfaces. It seems likely that the motion of charged particles (electrons) in these strong fields (◊ SYNCHROTRON RADIATION) will give rise to the emission of a fairly narrow beam of radiation which sweeps round like a lighthouse beam with the rotation of the neutron star (see Figure 35b). If the beam is radiated in a plane which allows it to reach the Earth, then each time the beam sweeps round, we receive a pulse of signal (if the beam is fairly narrow, as is thought to be the case for most pulsars, then there must be many pulsars which we cannot see because their radiation is not directed towards the Earth).

Theory suggests that neutron stars are likely to be formed from the central remnants of a SUPERNOVA. The discovery, in late 1968, of a pulsar in the CRAB NEBULA (a known supernova remnant) added credence to the association between pulsars and neutron stars. The Crab pulsar is the fastest known, having a period of 0·033 seconds (each pulse has a duration, or pulse width, of only 0·002 seconds); denoted by the catalogue number NP0532, it is also known to pulse at optical and X-ray wavelengths.

Pulsar periods are known to increase slowly with time, and this is thought to be due to the slowing down of the central neutron stars (these are losing energy by accelerating the charged particles responsible for the radiation emission). Thus, the younger the pulsar, the shorter is its period expected to be; the Crab pulsar is known to be of recent origin and this is consistent with its very short period. Sudden decreases in period are sometimes observed. These are thought to be due to 'starquakes'; shrinkage of the solid crust of a neutron star reduces its radius and, in order to conserve its ANGULAR MOMENTUM, it must increase its rate of spin, so reducing the period between pulses.

The study of pulsars remains one of the major areas of interest in astronomy today. (See Plate 19.)

Q

Quadrature. The configuration of two celestial bodies when they differ in CELESTIAL LONGITUDE by 90 degrees. For example, a SUPERIOR PLANET is said to be at quadrature when it is 90° east or west of the Sun on the celestial sphere (i.e. the angle Sun–Earth–planet = 90°). (◊PLANETARY CONFIGURATIONS, Figure 32.)

Quantum. ◊ATOM; SPECTRUM.

Quark. A 'particle' which, in the view of many physicists, may form the building block from which the more familiar massive sub-atomic particles (e.g. the PROTON and the NEUTRON) are built up. At present it is envisaged that there are three, or possibly four (the fourth being known as the 'charmed quark'), types of quarks, and that massive sub-atomic particles are made up of combinations of three quarks. Thus, the proton consists of two quarks of one type plus one of another.

It is possible that even the quark (if it 'exists') is not the ultimate 'fundamental' particle; the degree of complexity that already exists in the world of sub-atomic physics is overwhelming, but all the evidence suggests that the picture may become even more involved.

Quasar (or QSO) – Quasi-Stellar Radio Source. The curious nature of quasars was discovered by M. Schmidt of the Mount Wilson and Palomar Observatories in 1963. Quasars need not necessarily be radio sources (the term QSO is short for Quasi-Stellar Object) but share the following common characteristics:

compactness – they are usually almost star-like in appearance, and most quasars are extremely blue in colour (they were previously assumed to be blue stars);

large RED-SHIFTS – quasars show strong red-shifts in their spectral lines; the largest value of red-shift so far recorded is 3·5 (this is greater than for any known galaxy).

In addition, many of them show large random variations in brightness over periods of months or even days in some cases.

If the red-shifts of quasars are solely due to their velocities, and if it is assumed that the quasars share in the general expansion of the universe, then some of the quasars are the most distant objects known to us. For example, a quasar with a red-shift of 3·5 would be moving in excess of 90 per cent of the speed of light and would be at a distance (according to Hubble's law; ⊳HUBBLE'S CONSTANT) of something over fifteen thousand million light years. If quasars are at cosmological distances, then their apparent brightnesses are such that they must be emitting about a hundred times as much energy as a normal galaxy like our own. Yet they seem to be extremely compact objects.

The rapid brightness variation tells us that the regions from which most of their energy is emitted must be small, less than a light year in radius, and even as small as a few light-days in some cases. How can an object which may be less than a hundred thousandth of the radius of a galaxy emit a hundred times more energy? As yet, there is no satisfactory explanation: suggestions abound, e.g. their energy sources may be massive black holes, the annihilation of matter and anti-matter, chain reactions of supernovae, etc., but there is no general agreement. It has even been suggested that they may be local, fast-moving objects, and not at vast distances, but the general view is that they *are* as distant and as luminous as they seem to be.

It may be that quasars are galaxies with extremely compact and luminous nuclei, and that objects such as SEYFERT GALAXIES represent some sort of intermediate stage between quasars and normal galaxies such as our own. They remain among the most enigmatic objects in the universe.

R

Radar astronomy. That branch of astronomy which uses radar techniques to determine the distances to and/or surface properties of nearby celestial bodies. In principle, the distance of an object may be determined in the following way: a pulse of microwave ($\diamond$ ELECTRO-MAGNETIC SPECTRUM) signal is transmitted by means of a radio telescope towards a target (a planet, for example). The part of the signal which is reflected from the target may be detected by a radio telescope, and the total distance travelled (out and back) by the signal is equal to the time interval between transmission and return multiplied by the speed of the signal (i.e. the speed of light). The distance to the planet is half this total distance.

The nature of the returning signal depends upon the surface roughness of the target, and provides the astronomer with information about this. Furthermore, since planets are more or less spherical in shape, the edge of the visible disc of a planet is further away than the centre of the disc (in the case of Venus, for example, this difference amounts to 6000 km); therefore, the returning pulse of signal is spread out a little in time (the signal from the edge having travelled further than the signal from the centre). Analysis of the signal can yield a map of the surface of a planet, and in the case of Venus has revealed that that planet has a cratered surface.

The earliest astronomical application of radar was to the analyses of ionized ($\diamond$ IONIZATION) trails of METEORS in the upper atmosphere, but improved techniques have allowed measurements of the planets to be made. One result of these measurements has been a much more precise determination of the ASTRONOMICAL UNIT. The rings of Saturn represent the most distant target so far reached by radar techniques; the 64-metre radio dish at Goldstone, California, successfully reflected a 400-kilowatt beam from the rings in January 1973.

Radial velocity. The velocity of a celestial body directly towards or away from the observer. Generally speaking, the velocity of a star relative to the Sun (or to the Earth) can be split into two components, radial velocity and transverse velocity ($\diamond$ PROPER MOTION). Radial velocity may be determined from the DOPPLER EFFECT on the lines in the SPECTRUM of a moving light source.

Radiation pressure. Electromagnetic radiation exerts a small but finite pressure on any surface which it strikes. For massive, dense bodies, the effects of radiation pressure are negligibly small, but for tiny particles (or objects of large surface area but small mass) the effects can become appreciable. For example, the small dusty particles in the tails of COMETS are driven away from the head of the comet by solar radiation pressure.

Radio astronomy. That branch of astronomy which studies radio waves arriving from cosmic sources. Microwave and radio radiation having wavelengths of between a few millimetres and about 20 metres can penetrate the Earth's atmosphere and so may be studied by means of ground-based radio telescopes; this range of wavelengths is referred to as the radio window.

The accidental discovery that radio waves are reaching the Earth from astronomical sources was made in 1932 by Karl Jansky, an American physicist working for Bell Telephone Laboratories on problems of atmospheric static. Although an American engineer, Grote Reber, did build a radio telescope in 1937, little attention was devoted to radio astronomy until after the Second World War; since that time it has developed into a major and vital branch of observational astronomy. Among the wide range of cosmic radio sources are the Sun, the planet Jupiter, certain types of stars, PULSARS, interstellar gas clouds, the galactic centre, RADIO GALAXIES and QUASARS. There are two important aspects of radio astronomy: first, radio observations provide additional data concerning sources which were already known (as optical sources); secondly, observations have revealed the existence of new categories of sources whose existence was previously unknown, e.g. pulsars and quasars.

Radio galaxy. A galaxy which is emitting significantly large amounts of radio radiation. A strong radio galaxy may be emitting a radio power of up to 10^{40} watts, i.e. up to a hundred times as much total power as an ordinary galaxy such as our own. In most cases the apparent size of the radio source is very much greater than the apparent size of the associated visible galaxy, and the radiation appears to be generated by the synchrotron process ($\lozenge$SYNCHROTRON RADIATION). It seems likely that this radiation is produced as a result of charged particles being hurled outwards from the galaxy at relativistic speeds due to some unknown violent process ($\lozenge$SPECIAL THEORY OF RELATIVITY).

Because radio galaxies are so luminous, they can be detected to large distances, and so observations of these objects have been used to try to test theories of COSMOLOGY.

Radio source. A cosmic source of radio or microwave radiation ($\lozenge$ELECTROMAGNETIC RADIATION). In general, sources are either discrete (compact and point-like) or extended (covering a measurable area). Within the Solar System, the Sun and the planet Jupiter are radio sources, the radiation in the latter case being thought to come from charged particles moving in the strong magnetic field of the planet. Within the GALAXY (2) sources include emission nebulae (H II REGIONS), PLANETARY NEBULAE and SUPERNOVA remnants; extragalactic sources include peculiar galaxies (e.g. those having unusual compact nuclei) and QUASARS (◊RADIO GALAXIES).

In addition, radiation emitted by neutral hydrogen gas (◊21-CENTIMETRE RADIATION) can be detected from wide areas of the galactic disc, and weak emission of this type may also be detected from some of the nearer galaxies. The strongest discrete source is a supernova remnant known as Cassiopeia A which lies at a distance of nearly 10000 light years.

Radio star. An outmoded term, originally applied to what is now known as a discrete RADIO SOURCE. Generally speaking, such sources are not stars at all.

Radio telescope. An instrument used to collect and detect radio waves from cosmic sources. Radio telescopes take a number of different forms. The simplest radio telescope consists of a fixed array of aerials, but the most familiar form is the steerable dish, the best-known example of which is the 76-metre (250-foot) dish of the Mark I radio telescope at Jodrell Bank, Cheshire, UK. Radio telescopes of this type are analogous to optical reflectors (◊TELESCOPE) in that the incoming radiation is reflected by a parabolic dish and brought to a focus; the signal is then amplified and displayed as a trace on a chart recorder, or stored directly on magnetic tape in a computer. In order to produce a contour map of the strength of signal from an extended source of radiation (◊RADIO SOURCE), the telescope must be made to scan a pattern across the desired area of sky.

Because the wavelengths studied by radio telescopes may be a million times longer than those of visible light, the resolving power of a radio telescope is typically a million times poorer than that of an optical telescope of the same aperture. For example, the resolving power of a 1-metre aperture, optical telescope (i.e. the closest points of light which can be seen as separate sources) is about 0·1 seconds of arc; a radio telescope operating at a wavelength of about 0·5 metres would, in order to achieve the same resolution, have to be 1000 km in diameter. Clearly this cannot be achieved for a single dish. The problem can to a large extent be overcome by the techniques of interferometry (◊INTERFEROMETER) and APERTURE SYNTHESIS. (See Plates 14 and 15.)

The largest single radio dish is the 300-metre (1000-foot) instrument at Arecibo, Puerto Rico; it cannot be steered as it is built into a natural hollow in the ground.

Radio window. The band of wavelengths in the microwave and radio region of the ELECTROMAGNETIC SPECTRUM to which the Earth's atmosphere is transparent. It covers the waveband stretching approximately from wavelengths of a few millimetres to the order of 20 metres (i.e. a FREQUENCY range of the order of 10000 MHz to about 10 MHz). Shorter wavelengths are absorbed by the atmosphere, while longer wavelengths are reflected back into space by the IONOSPHERE.

Radioactivity. The process whereby atoms of certain heavy elements (such as radium, thorium, or uranium) spontaneously emit atomic particles and/or electromagnetic radiation (in the form of short-wave GAMMA RAYS). The atomic particles commonly emitted in this process are referred to as alpha rays and beta rays, the former being positively charged helium nuclei (made up of two PROTONS and two NEUTRONS), and the latter being negatively charged ELECTRONS. Although the term 'rays' is commonly applied to these emissions, it is important to note that both alpha and beta rays are streams of particles.

As a result of this process, i.e. of radioactive decay, elements are slowly converted into different elements. Thus, for example, an element X, having an atomic number (equal to the number of positive charges on the nucleus) Z and an atomic mass number (equal to the number of protons plus neutrons in the nucleus) A, and which is denoted by $_ZX^A$, would decay by the emission of an alpha particle into some other element $_{(Z-2)}Y^{A-4}$. An alpha particle, which is the nucleus of a helium atom, may be denoted as $_2He^4$. A natural example is afforded by the isotope ($\diamond$ ATOM) of uranium $_{92}U^{238}$ which decays over a long period of time to form lead, $_{82}Pb^{206}$, which is not radioactive and remains stable thereafter. The time taken for half of a quantity of radioactive material to decay is known as the HALF-LIFE; in the case of $_{92}U^{238}$, this period is 4500 million years.

Radioactive decay can be utilized to calculate the ages of rock samples, etc. For example, if a sample of lead, formed by the decay of uranium, is analysed and the proportion of uranium remaining is determined, then, knowing the half-life of uranium, it is possible to determine when the rock in which the sample was found was itself formed. The age of the Earth has been estimated by such means. More recently formed materials, up to a few tens of thousands of years old, can be dated by analysis of the decay of the radioactive isotope of carbon, $_6C^{14}$.

Ranger. A series of US space probes intended to crash onto the lunar surface while transmitting photographs up to the moment of impact. The first attempted launching was on 23 August 1961, but the series was dogged by failure. Successful completion of mission was achieved with Rangers 7, 8 and 9 (the last of the series, Ranger 9, being launched on 17 February 1965) which, between them, returned over

17000 photographs with resolution better than 10 centimetres in some cases.

Rays, Lunar. Light-coloured streaks on the MOON's surface which appear to radiate like the spokes of a wheel from certain lunar craters such as Copernicus, Tycho and Kepler. They represent surface material which reflects more strongly than the general surface layer and are normally most prominent about the time of full moon (when they are subject to near vertical illumination from the Sun). The longest rays extend for some 2000 km. Although there is still some dispute as to their origin, it is quite widely accepted that they represent material ejected during the massive impacts which gave rise to some of the craters.

Reaction (1). An opposing force. According to Newton's third law (◇NEWTON'S LAWS OF MOTION), every action is opposed by an equal and opposite reaction. Thus, for example, when a shell is fired from a gun, the reaction causes the gun barrel to recoil. The principle of reaction applies to the rocket motor: as hot gas is expelled from the rocket, the vehicle is accelerated in the opposite direction.

Reaction (2). A general term, applied, for example, to the process of change which takes place when chemicals are brought together. Such chemical reactions may be exothermic (releasing heat) or endothermic (heat-absorbing). It is clearly desirable that rocket propellants react exothermically.

Recession of the galaxies. ◇COSMOLOGY.

Red giant. A star which has a relatively low effective temperature (typically around 4000 K to 3000 K) and a large radius (say 100 times that of the Sun). The low temperature gives the star its red colour, and with its large radius it is a 'giant' compared to a normal main-sequence (◇HERTZSPRUNG–RUSSELL DIAGRAM and Figure 24) star of the same spectral type (◇SPECTRAL CLASSIFICATION). Such stars are highly luminous, and may have values of luminosity between about 100 and over 10000 times that of the Sun. Densities, too, are extremely low, ranging between 10^{-4} and 10^{-7} times the Sun's mean density (i.e. the mean density of a typical red giant is less than that of air at sea level).

Typical stars of this type, visible to the unaided eye, are Aldebaran (in Taurus) and Betelgeuse (in Orion), the latter being highly luminous and, strictly speaking, a SUPERGIANT. If Betelgeuse were placed where the Sun is, all the planets out to and including Mars would be contained within it.

Red giants are stars in the late stage of evolution (many are LONG-PERIOD VARIABLES) and it is estimated that in between five and six thousand million years the Sun will expand to become one. ($\diamondsuit$ STELLAR EVOLUTION and Figure 42.)

Red-shift. The displacement of spectral lines from their normal positions (as observed in a stationary laboratory) towards the long wavelength (i.e. red) end of the SPECTRUM, which is observed in the spectra of galaxies, QUASARS and certain other celestial bodies ($\diamondsuit$ GALAXY (1)).

The observed red-shifts in the spectra of these bodies is usually interpreted in terms of the DOPPLER EFFECT, i.e. it is taken to imply that these sources are receding from us and sharing in the expansion of the universe ($\diamondsuit$ COSMOLOGY). This seems by far the most plausible explanation. However, red-shifts may also be produced in strong gravitational fields; according to the GENERAL THEORY OF RELATIVITY, light loses energy and therefore becomes red-shifted in moving outwards through a powerful gravitational field. This type of gravitational red-shift has been observed in, for example, the spectra of WHITE DWARFS, and it has been suggested that part of the red-shifts observed in quasar spectra may be due to this effect.

The value of red-shift is usually denoted by z, and is equal to the change in wavelength $\Delta\lambda$ divided by the original wavelength λ (the wavelength emitted by a stationary source).

Red spot. $\diamondsuit$ GREAT RED SPOT.

Reflection nebula. $\diamondsuit$ NEBULA.

Reflector. $\diamondsuit$ TELESCOPE.

Refractor. $\diamondsuit$ TELESCOPE.

Relativity. $\diamondsuit$ GENERAL THEORY OF RELATIVITY; SPECIAL THEORY OF RELATIVITY.

Resolving power. The ability of an instrument to distinguish fine detail in a source of radiation. Resolving power (or resolution) for an optical TELESCOPE is usually expressed in terms of the minimum separation of two equal stars which can *just* be seen to be separate points of light, and is given approximately by the formula, resolution $(R) = 12/D$ seconds of arc, where D is the aperture of the instrument in centimetres.

In general terms, R is proportional to the wavelength of radiation; $R = 1 \cdot 22\lambda/D$ where λ is wavelength. The longer the wavelength, the poorer the resolving power.

Retrograde motion (1). The 'backwards' (i.e. east to west) apparent motion of a planet against the background stars ($\diamondsuit$ DIRECT AND RETROGRADE MOTION, Figure 14); when a planet is moving retrograde, its RIGHT ASCENSION is decreasing. A superior planet, which, being further from the Sun than is the Earth, moves more slowly than the Earth, will exhibit retrograde motion during the period around OPPOSITION when the Earth is overtaking it; the planet appears to be moving backwards only because it is dropping behind the Earth. Conversely an INFERIOR PLANET is seen to move in a retrograde direction while it is overtaking the Earth.

Retrograde motion (2).   The motion of a body round the Sun, or a satellite round a planet, in an east-to-west or clockwise direction.

Retrograde motion (3).   The rotation of a planet on its axis such that – if the planet were viewed from a position north of its orbit plane – it would be seen to rotate in a clockwise (east to west) direction. The planet Venus exhibits retrograde rotation.

Retro-rocket.   A rocket motor used to decelerate a space vehicle, in order to change its orbit or to achieve a soft-landing. Such a motor ejects gas ahead of the space vehicle so that the THRUST produced opposes the motion of the vehicle. Manned spacecraft of the Soviet space programme (such as the SOYUZ craft) use parachutes and retro-rockets to achieve soft-landing on land.

Reversing layer.   The region in the Sun's atmosphere in which the dark absorption lines in the solar SPECTRUM are produced. It is a region of relatively cool, rarefied gas (temperature around 4500 K) in the CHROMOSPHERE, the layer immediately above the visible surface, or PHOTOSPHERE, which itself has an effective temperature of about 5800 K. ATOMS in the reversing layer absorb radiation at particular wavelengths from the continuous spectrum emitted from the lower, denser regions of the Sun, so producing the observed dark lines.

Revolution.   The motion of one celestial body about another, e.g. the motion of a satellite round a planet or of a planet around the Sun. The Earth completes one revolution of the Sun in a year.

Right ascension (RA).   The angle between the HOUR CIRCLES passing through the VERNAL EQUINOX and a celestial body, measured east-wards (i.e. anticlockwise) from the vernal equinox and expressed in time units (hours, minutes and seconds) where twenty-four hours is equivalent to 360 degrees. In other words, it is the angle between the vernal equinox and a point on the celestial equator such that the angle between the vernal equinox, this point and a star is a right angle (see Figure 36). The position of a star is normally expressed in terms of right ascension and DECLINATION. (⟡CELESTIAL COORDINATES.)

Roche limit.   The critical distance from the centre of a planet (or other celestial body) within which the tidal forces would be sufficiently great to disrupt and tear apart a satellite (⟡TIDES). The basic principle may

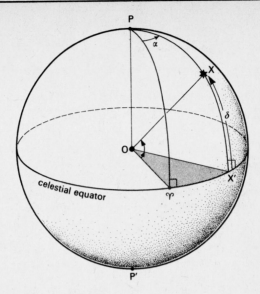

Figure 36. Right ascension and declination. A star X is located on the celestial sphere and an observer, O, at the centre. The declination, δ, of X is the angle X'OX, where X' is the point on the celestial equator vertically below X (angle X'OX is equal to the length of the arc X'X).

The right ascension of X, α, is the angle ♈OX' = angle ♈PX (and is equal to the length of the arc ♈X'). ♈ denotes the vernal equinox (the point of intersection of the ecliptic and the celestial equator).

be understood by considering two particles, adjacent to each other and moving round the planet. The particle closer to the planet will be subject to a slightly stronger gravitational attraction by the planet than that experienced by the more distant particle; if this difference in attraction exceeds the mutual gravitational attraction between the two particles, then the particles will be drawn apart. The limit is normally given in terms of a satellite which has no tensile strength (i.e. made up of particles held together only by mutual gravitational attraction); but a real satellite, such as the Moon, has a more rigid structure and could, therefore, resist disruption until some distance inside the limit. For a satellite having the same density as its parent planet, the limit is 2·4 times the radius of the planet. The rings of SATURN lie within this limit, and this fact has led to the speculation that they represent the fragments of a small satellite disrupted by tidal forces.

The limit is named after the French mathematician, Edouarde Roche, who derived it in 1850.

Rocket. A vehicle propelled by reaction thrust. The term is often applied to the rocket motor rather than the complete vehicle. The principle of the rocket is straightforward and depends upon Newton's third law (◊NEWTON'S LAWS OF MOTION); if hot gas is expelled from a chamber (the combustion chamber) in one direction, then there is a reaction on the chamber which accelerates it in the opposite direction. A good analogy is given by considering a person standing with a load of bricks upon a sledge on an icy surface. Each time he throws a brick in one direction the sledge is given an impulse in the opposite direction, and the faster he throws bricks off the sledge, the more rapidly it accelerates.

In a rocket motor, the hotter the gas produced in the combustion chamber the faster it moves (◊EXHAUST VELOCITY), and the faster the rocket accelerates. A rocket will continue to accelerate until all its fuel is exhausted and clearly the greater the quantity of fuel which can be expelled the greater the final velocity of the rocket (◊MASS RATIO (2)). In order to propel useful PAYLOADS into space, rockets are constructed in a number of stages; this improves the mass ratio. (◊THRUST.)

The rocket performs at its best in a vacuum as it does not require an external medium to act upon in order to function (unlike, for example, the airscrew), and it is the only known method of propulsion suitable for use in space. Present-day rockets use either liquid or solid fuel (the latter tends to be restricted to smaller vehicles), but other fuels are being developed (◊ION ROCKET).

It is uncertain when the rocket was first invented, but crude rockets were employed by the Chinese for military purposes at least as long ago as the thirteenth century. The basic concept of the liquid-fuelled rocket was first seriously discussed at the end of the nineteenth century by the Russian, Konstantin Tsiolkovskii, while the first such rocket to fly was developed independently by Robert Goddard in the USA, and made its flight on 16 March 1926.

Rotation. The motion of a body about an axis; for example, the Earth rotates on its axis in a period of 23 hours 56 minutes. All celestial bodies, e.g. planets, stars and galaxies, exhibit some degree of rotation.

S

Salyut. Series of Soviet orbiting space laboratories, visited and operated in orbit by a number of SOYUZ crews. The first Salyut was launched on 19 April 1971 into a close Earth orbit (PERIGEE altitude 200 km) and the first docking with a Soyuz craft took place five days later (but with no transfer of crew to the Salyut). On 7 June 1971, the Soyuz 11 crew (Dobrovolsky, Volkov and Patsayev) docked and spent twenty-three days in the space station. Tragically, due to a pressure leak in the Soyuz craft, the crew died during the re-entry of the Earth's atmosphere. Subsequent Salyut stations have been visited for extended periods by two-man Soyuz crews.

The Salyut, when docked with a Soyuz craft (which makes up an integral part of the working laboratory), has an overall length of 23 metres, a mass of 25 tonnes, and provides a habitable volume of about 100 cubic metres. Scientific studies carried out on board include Earth observations, biological studies and astronomical observations.

Saros. The eclipse cycle of 18 years 11·3 days, after which the pattern of eclipses which occurred at the beginning of the cycle is quite closely repeated. The cycle was known in ancient Greek times and was used for eclipse prediction. The repetition is not perfect, however, changes in the pattern increasing with time. The cycle is almost exactly equal to the time taken for the NODES of the Moon's orbit to make a complete circle of the Earth. After one cycle, the Sun, Moon and nodes return almost to the same relative positions and it is the alignment of these which determines the occurrence of eclipses.

Satellite. A body which travels round a planet.

Saturn. The sixth planet in order of distance from the Sun and the most distant planet which can normally be seen with the unaided eye. It is one of the JOVIAN PLANETS and, with a mass over ninety-five times that of the Earth, is the second most massive planet in the SOLAR SYSTEM. However, it has a very low density (one-eighth that of the Earth) and appears, like JUPITER, to be made up largely of hydrogen, hydrogen compounds and helium, with no solid surface other than a possible small rocky central core. It is in rapid rotation (axial rotation period 10h 14m) and is markedly flattened in appearance, the ratio of equatorial to polar radii being 1·098:1.

The unique feature of Saturn is its ring system. Galileo was the first to observe this but was unable to discern the nature of the rings; this was first achieved by Christian Huyghens in 1655. The ring system has an overall diameter of 270 000 km, yet is no more than a few kilometres thick (probably 2 or 3 km). There are three principal rings: the outer ring, ring A, is moderately bright and is separated from the brighter ring B by a gap (known as the Cassini Division) some 2800 km wide and having a radius (measured from the centre of the planet) of 117 000 km. The least conspicuous ring, ring C (sometimes called the Crepe ring), is the innermost one and is separated from the planet by some 13 000 km. Evidence is mounting for the existence of a very faint ring, D, within and separate from ring C.

The rings are made up of millions of individual particles orbiting the planet; any solid structure of these dimensions would be broken up by tidal forces (◇ROCHE LIMIT). Spectroscopic evidence indicates the presence of various kinds of ice, while radar measurements indicate the presence of some large rocky masses within the rings. The appearance of the rings as seen from the Earth varies in a periodic way from edge-on to quite wide open (when they are seen inclined to the line of sight by 29 degrees). This situation arises because the rings of Saturn lie in the plane of that planet's equator, and this is inclined to the plane of its orbit by nearly 27 degrees; thus, as Saturn moves round its orbit, the aspect of the rings as seen from the Earth continually changes. The inclination of Saturn's orbit to the ecliptic (just over 2 degrees) also affects the angle of presentation of the ring system. The cycle of ring phenomena follows a period more or less equal to Saturn's orbital period (29½ years).

Saturn has ten known satellites, the largest of which, Titan, has a radius of 2400 km and is known to possess a methane atmosphere. The divisions in the rings are due to the gravitational perturbations exerted on the ring particles by the satellites.

The planet is expected to be examined from close range in 1979 by the US probe Pioneer 11, and again, two years later, by a Mariner-type spacecraft (◇MARINER SERIES). (See Plate 9.)

Saturn data

		(Earth = 1)
Mean distance from Sun	1 427 000 000 km	9·54
Orbital eccentricity	0·056	—
Orbital inclination	2° 29′ 22″	—
Sidereal orbital period	29·46 years	29·46
Axial rotation period	10h 14m	0·42
Mass	$5·69 \times 10^{26}$ kg	95·15

Radius (equatorial)	60 100 km	9·42
Mean density	$0·70 \times 10^3 \text{ kg m}^{-3}$	0·127
Surface gravity	$11·3 \text{ m s}^{-2}$	1·15

Schmidt camera. A compound reflecting telescope used to photograph wider areas of sky at faster speeds than can be achieved with ordinary telescopes. The instrument, which was invented in 1930 by Bernhard Schmidt, uses a spherical mirror of short focal length to form an image; such a mirror introduces distortions (SPHERICAL ABERRATION) into the image and, to compensate for this, a specially-shaped correcting plate is placed at the opposite end of the telescope tube, ahead of the mirror (◊TELESCOPE, Figure 44b). Light passes through this plate before reflection from the mirror. This type of telescope can photograph areas of the sky several degrees in diameter and has been used for photographic surveys of the entire sky. (See Plate 2.)

Schwarzschild radius. The critical radius (R_s) around a collapsed mass (M) at which an emitted ray of light would be unable to escape and would remain stationary (loosely speaking, one could say that, at this radius, the escape velocity equals the velocity of light). No signal emitted within this radius can move outwards. The value for this radius was calculated by Schwarzschild, using the general theory of relativity, in 1916, and is given by

$$R_s = 2GM/\text{c}^2,$$

where G is the GRAVITATIONAL CONSTANT and c the velocity of light. (◊BLACK HOLE.)

Scintillation. Rapid fluctuations in the radiation from stars due to its passage through the atmosphere; the more familiar term for the effect on visible light is 'twinkling'. The effect is most marked for a point source of light, such as a star; an extended source (covering a finite area) does not exhibit the effect so appreciably (thus a planet tends to twinkle less obviously than a star). Scintillation is caused by turbulence in layers of the atmosphere (which may have differing temperatures, refractive indices, velocities, etc.). Seen from space, stars would not appear to twinkle.

At radio frequencies it is possible to detect scintillation due to the passage of radiation through the SOLAR WIND.

Selenography. The science concerned with the mapping of the surface of the Moon.

Semi-major axis. ◊ELLIPSE.

Sextant (1). Term occasionally applied to an arc of 60 degrees, being one sixth of a circle.

Sextant (2).   An instrument having a graduated arc of 60 degrees, two mirrors, a small telescope and a movable arm to which one of the mirrors is fixed. The observer looks through the telescope directly at the horizon and adjustment of the movable arm allows the reflected image of a celestial body to be seen in the field of view. Fine adjustment of the arm brings the reflected image into coincidence with the horizon in the field of view, at which stage the ALTITUDE (1) of the celestial

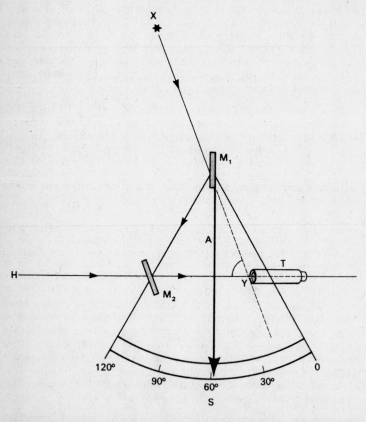

Figure 37.   The Sextant. The observer looks at the horizon, H, through the telescope, T. Light from a star, X, is reflected from the mirror, M_1 (attached to the movable arm, A) to the part-silvered mirror, M_2, and thence to the telescope. When the rays of light from the star and the horizon exactly coincide, the altitude of the star (angle HYX) is indicated on the scale, S.

body is indicated on the graduated arc. The instrument is used primarily at sea, to determine the altitudes above the horizon of known celestial bodies, so permitting the position of the observer to be determined.

Since the image, reflected from a mirror, is deflected through an angle *twice* the magnitude of the angle through which the mirror itself is moved, the graduated scale allows angles of up to 120 degrees to be measured. (See Figure 37.)

Seyfert galaxy. A type of galaxy first investigated by Carl Seyfert in 1942. Seyfert galaxies are peculiar in having very bright compact nuclei within which gas appears to be moving at high speed as if some violent event had occurred or was taking place there. They are also quite strong infra-red and radio sources. About 1 per cent of all galaxies appear to be Seyferts, and it is not at all clear whether this implies that 1 per cent of galaxies are Seyferts for all of their lives, *or* that all galaxies become Seyferts for 1 per cent of their lifetimes as part of an evolutionary process. Possibly the truth lies between these extremes.

Considerable attention is being devoted to Seyfert galaxies at the present time as there does appear to be some evidence of a possible evolutionary progression between Seyferts, RADIO GALAXIES, QUASARS and normal galaxies. Even our own Galaxy has strong radio and infra-red sources located in its nucleus. (See Plate 23.)

Shadow transit. ⬦TRANSIT.

Shooting star. A visible streak of light in the sky caused by the burning up of a tiny particle entering the Earth's atmosphere at high speed (⬦METEOR). It is *not* a star.

Shuttle. ⬦SPACE SHUTTLE.

Sidereal period. A period of time measured relative to the 'fixed' stars. In normal usage the term refers to the time taken by a planet to complete one orbit of the Sun, returning to its original position relative to the positions of the stars, or the time taken for a satellite to complete one orbit of its parent planet, again measured relative to the background stars. In the case of the Earth, this period of time is referred to as the sidereal year (⬦YEAR) and is equal to 365·2564 mean solar days.

Sidereal time. A time system based on the rotation of the Earth measured relative to the background stars, which for this purpose are regarded as fixed in position. Relative to the stars, the Earth rotates on its axis in a period of 23 hours 56 minutes 04·1 seconds of mean time (i.e. ordinary civil time), and this period is called the sidereal day, which is, in turn, divided into twenty-four sidereal hours.

For an observer located at a particular longitude on the Earth, the sidereal day is equivalent to the apparent rotation period of the CELESTIAL SPHERE. This period may be determined by measuring the interval between two successive upper transits of a given star across his MERIDIAN. The value of sidereal time at any instant is defined to be the HOUR ANGLE (see Figure 25), i.e. the angle measured clockwise from the meridian, of the VERNAL EQUINOX (a fixed point on the celestial sphere). Thus, when the vernal equinox is on the meridian, its hour angle is zero, and the sidereal time is zero hours; by the time that the rotation of the celestial sphere has increased this angle to 90 degrees, six hours have elapsed, and the sidereal time is six hours, and so on. After twenty-four hours, the vernal equinox returns to the meridian.

The hour angle measured by this observer relative to his meridian is the local hour angle, and the sidereal time so obtained, the local sidereal time (LST). Greenwich sidereal time (GST) is the hour angle of the vernal equinox measured from the Greenwich meridian. The difference between LST and GST corresponds to the longitude of the observer expressed in time units (where one hour is equivalent to 15 degrees, since the Earth rotates through 15 degrees per hour). If the observer is east of Greenwich, LST is greater than GST, while if he is west of Greenwich his LST is less than GST.

Sidereal year. ⟡YEAR.

Siderite. Term sometimes used to describe a METEORITE of metallic composition. On average, such meteorites contain about 90 per cent iron and 8 per cent nickel.

Siderolite. Term sometimes used to describe a METEORITE of stony-iron composition.

Signs of the Zodiac. ⟡ZODIAC.

Single-line binary. ⟡SPECTROSCOPIC BINARY.

Singularity. ⟡BLACK HOLE.

Sirius. The brightest star in the sky, i.e. the star with the greatest apparent brightness (and, therefore, the lowest value of APPARENT MAGNITUDE). Its apparent magnitude is −1·45; only the Sun, Moon, and the planets Venus, Jupiter and Mars (when near opposition) are brighter. It is one of the nearest stars, lying at a distance of 8·6 light years; it is a white main-sequence star of spectral type (⟡SPECTRAL CLASSIFICATION) A1 V, and luminosity twenty-six times greater than that of the Sun.

61 Cygni. A fifth-magnitude BINARY star in the constellation Cygnus, this was the first star whose distance was successfully measured by the method of PARALLAX. Although faint, it is one of the nearest stars, and was selected for measurement by Friedrich Bessel because of its large

PROPER MOTION (which suggested that it was relatively near by). In 1838 he obtained a value of distance close to the currently accepted value of 11·1 light years (corresponding to a parallax of 0·294 arcsec). Observations appear to indicate that the stars have a dark companion a few times more massive than Jupiter; such a low mass implies that the body must be a planet rather than a star.

Skylab. US manned orbiting space station constructed from components adapted from the APOLLO PROJECT, and which was placed into a 435 km altitude orbit on 14 May 1973. Crews were ferried to and from the laboratory by means of Apollo-type spacecraft. With the Apollo craft (the command service module) attached, Skylab had an overall length of 36 metres, and a mass of 90·6 tonnes, and the major component, the orbital workshop, provided a total of 292 cubic metres of laboratory and crew accommodation.

In all, three crews, each of three astronauts, spent a total of 513 man-days in space, carrying out a wide variety of experiments and observations. The areas which received most of the time allocation were solar astronomy (31 per cent of total), Earth observations (19 per cent), astrophysics (9 per cent) and life sciences (27 per cent); other areas of interest where work was undertaken included engineering technology and materials science. The final Skylab mission devoted much time to the study of comet Kohoutek.

Skylab proved to be an outstanding success, all the more so as the first crew had to carry out quite extensive repairs to damage incurred during its launching.

Small circle. ◇GREAT CIRCLE.

Solar antapex. ◇APEX OF THE SUN'S WAY.

Solar apex. ◇APEX OF THE SUN'S WAY.

Solar constant. The amount of energy in the form of solar radiation received normally on unit area at the top of the Earth's atmosphere; it is approximately equal to the amount of energy reaching ground level on a clear day. The value of the solar constant is 1360 joules per second per square metre, corresponding to 1·36 kilowatts of power per square metre. The constant is sometimes expressed as 1·95 calories per square centimetre per minute.

It has been suggested that relatively small changes in the value of the solar constant may have been responsible for major climatic changes on the Earth in the past, but this suggestion is as yet unconfirmed.

Solar cycle. The variation in the level of surface activity on the Sun which takes place over a period of, on average, 11·1 years. The most obvious evidence of this is the variation in the numbers of SUNSPOTS, the sunspot cycle which was first pointed out by H. Schwabe in 1851;

furthermore, in 1861 F. Spoerer showed that the mean latitudes at which spots appeared also varied throughout the cycle.

A new cycle begins at sunspot minimum when the solar disc may be devoid of spots for weeks at a time. Thereafter spots begin to appear at relatively high latitudes (30° north or south of the solar equator), the mean latitude declining throughout the cycle. The number of spots build up to a maximum about four or five years after minimum, and thereafter numbers decline over the succeeding six or seven years to the next minimum. As the next cycle begins, there is a period during which spots of the new cycle may be seen at high latitudes at the same time as spots of the old cycle are seen near the equator (◊BUTTERFLY DIAGRAM and Figure 7).

A further feature associated with the cycle is the reversal of spot pair polarity; thus if, for example, all leading spots in pairs in the northern hemisphere had north magnetic polarity during one cycle (and all pairs in the southern hemisphere had leading spots of south polarity), the situation would be reversed (south poles in leading spots in the northern hemisphere) in the next cycle. The entire magnetic field of the Sun reverses at the end of each cycle; consequently, it may be argued that the full solar cycle lasts twenty-two years.

The solar cycle affects all aspects of solar activity, e.g. the frequency of SOLAR FLARES, the flow of charged particles from the surface, the shape and structure of the CORONA, the frequency of PROMINENCES, etc., and it does appear that the solar cycle has detectable effects here on Earth. For example, the frequency of the AURORA is closely linked to the solar cycle.

Solar energy. The basic source of solar energy is the nuclear fusion reactions taking place in its central core (◊SUN). These reactions release $3\cdot8 \times 10^{26}$ joules of energy per second, corresponding to a power output from the solar surface of $3\cdot8 \times 10^{26}$ watts (i.e. 380 million million million million watts). The Earth, which is located at a mean distance from the Sun of 150 million km, intercepts only about four ten-thousand millionths of this total, i.e. $1\cdot7 \times 10^{16}$ watts; nevertheless, this quantity of energy exceeds the human energy demand by many orders of magnitude. (◊SOLAR CONSTANT.)

Solar flares. Sudden short-lived (typically a few minutes) outbursts of light sometimes seen in the vicinity of SUNSPOT groups. They are thought to originate from a build up, at a point between a pair of spots, of gas flowing out along the lines of force of the magnetic field associated with sunspots. When the hot gas builds up such a pressure that it cannot be contained by the magnetic field, it erupts outwards as a bright filament accompanied by a shock wave spreading over the solar surface.

Flares are classified according to their brightness, and the brightest

Class 3 flares cause appreciable effects on the Earth's atmosphere. Charged particles released from flares reach the Earth after about two days, disturbing the ionosphere (and so disrupting long-range radio communication) and giving rise to auroral displays. Flares are also responsible for the emission of a variety of radiations, from X-rays to radio waves, and were at one time regarded as a possible major hazard for space travellers.

Similar phenomena are thought to be responsible for the behaviour of FLARE STARS.

Solar granulation. The mottled structure exhibited by the visible surface of the Sun, i.e. the PHOTOSPHERE, when it is observed under good conditions. Due to convection hot gas is rising and cooler gas descending in the outer layers of the Sun, and this gives rise to the visible granules, typically 1200 km in diameter, which are about 100 K hotter than the duller regions which separate them.

Solar nebula. ⟡SOLAR SYSTEM, ORIGIN OF.

Solar neutrino problem. The apparent scarcity of NEUTRINOS emitted by the Sun. The nuclear reactions thought to be producing energy in the solar core (⟡PROTON–PROTON REACTION) are expected to release neutrinos, and the number of expected neutrinos can be calculated on the basis of the expected conditions in the core. An experiment to detect solar neutrinos, begun in the mid 1960s, has so far failed to detect the expected flux of neutrinos, and has cast some doubts on our precise understanding of the interior of the Sun. (The experiment used a 100000 gallon tank of dry-cleaning fluid, located a mile underground in a mineshaft in South Dakota, to trap neutrinos; it is still possible that some kind of experimental error is responsible for the shortage of observed neutrinos.)

Solar panels. Arrays of cells which convert sunlight into electrical energy used to provide power for satellites and spacecraft, and which are finding terrestrial applications.

Solar System. The system consisting of the Sun, the planets and their satellites, the asteroids, comets, meteoroids and interplanetary material. (See Figure 38.)

Solar System, Origin of. There is now a fair measure of agreement that the Solar System formed as a natural by-product of the formation of the Sun itself (⟡STELLAR EVOLUTION), but many difficulties remain to be solved, and no one theory can claim to account for all of these.

Any theory has to explain a number of features of the system, including the following:

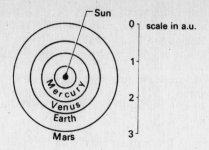

(a) Inner Solar System

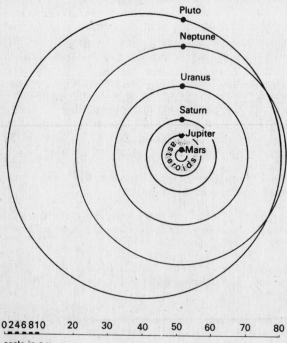

(b) Outer Solar System

1. The planets move in nearly coplanar orbits;

2. The planets revolve round the Sun in the same direction, which is also the direction of rotation of the Sun itself;

3. BODE'S LAW;

4. Although the combined mass of all the planets is less than 0·2 per cent of the Sun's mass, the planets contain in their motions 98 per cent of the angular momentum of the system;

5. The TERRESTRIAL PLANETS are made up largely of silicates and heavier elements, while the JOVIAN PLANETS are made up mostly of hydrogen and helium and are therefore similar to the Sun in composition.

The earliest theory of note was the NEBULAR HYPOTHESIS proposed by Laplace in the eighteenth century. This theory basically suggested that the material which formed the planets was hurled out from the young Sun as it was contracting and spinning rapidly. Item 4 above proved to be the real stumbling block for this hypothesis; it appeared that the Sun ought to be rotating hundreds of times faster than it is seen to do if such a theory were to work.

The early twentieth century saw a series of 'catastrophic' theories which suggested that the planets were formed by some cosmic accident. For example, it was suggested by Jeans (modifying an earlier proposal by Moulton and Chamberlain) that a close encounter between the young Sun and a passing star drew out filaments of material from the Sun, part of which remained in orbit, giving rise to the planets. This, the tidal theory, appeared to overcome the problem of item 4 above, since the speeds of the planets would have been independent of the rotation of the Sun. If such a theory were correct, then planetary systems would be very rare; present evidence suggests that this is not so (◊PLANETS OF OTHER STARS).

The present majority view is that the formation of planetary systems is a natural stage in the early evolution of a large proportion of stars (it may be that star formation results in binary or multiple stars, or in

---

Figure 38. The Solar System. (a) The inner Solar System is shown to scale (in astronomical units). Although the orbits of the planets are represented by circles, it should be borne in mind that they are, in fact, ellipses (in the case of Mercury the eccentricity is about 0·2).

(b) The outer Solar System, again to scale (the scale in this case differs from that of the inner Solar System by a factor of 10). The considerable eccentricity of Pluto's orbit is evident from the fact that it passes within the orbit of Neptune for a time. The asteroids are spread out between the orbits of Mars and Jupiter.

single stars plus planetary systems). The young Sun as it approached the main sequence ($\diamondsuit$ STELLAR EVOLUTION) was probably surrounded by a flattened disc of interstellar material, rotating with it, and within this disc the condensation of material took place, first into small particles, and later the particles began to collide to build up planet-sized bodies.

The slow rotation of the Sun is accounted for by assuming that the interaction between the solar magnetic field and the surrounding ionized ($\diamondsuit$ IONIZATION) gas accelerated the gas (much of which was lost into space) while slowing down the rotation of the Sun. The difference in composition between terrestrial and Jovian planets may be explained by the higher temperature which prevailed in the inner Solar System during planetary formation (at that time the Sun was probably more luminous than it is now) preventing the retention of these light elements by the low-mass inner planets. The composition of the Jovian planets is probably similar to that of the original solar nebula, out of which the planets formed. (See Figure 38.)

Solar wind. The stream of atomic particles (protons and electrons) which flows outwards from the Sun through the Solar System (see Figure 43). Particles emitted from the Sun take several days to reach the vicinity of the Earth, and stream past the Earth at a speed of about 600 km per second. At this distance from the Sun, the mean density of particles is low (about five million protons per cubic metre), but they nevertheless interact with the Earth's MAGNETOSPHERE. The level of particles is enhanced during periods of solar activity, and it is thought that particles ejected from SOLAR FLARES entering the VAN ALLEN BELTS, and then the Earth's upper atmosphere, are responsible for the AURORAE.

The effects of the solar wind are apparent on the tails of comets, for it is the interaction between the solar wind and the ionized particles in the comet which causes the gas tail to be driven in a direction away from the Sun.

Solstice. The point on the ECLIPTIC at which the Sun reaches its maximum DECLINATION north or south of the CELESTIAL EQUATOR. The greatest northerly declination corresponds to the summer solstice, the greatest southerly declination to the winter solstice.

Source counts. $\diamondsuit$ COSMOLOGY.

Soyuz. A continuing series of Soviet manned spacecraft, the first of which, Soyuz 1, was launched on 23 April 1967. The term 'Soyuz' means 'union'. The spacecraft itself consists of three principal sections, an orbital module, a re-entry module (the only part which returns to Earth) and a propulsion/instrumentation section. With the aid of the propulsion unit a maximum orbital altitude of 1300 km can be attained.

The orbital module is used as an experiment, rest and sleeping area for the crew while in orbit. The re-entry module provides accommodation for up to three crew members during flight into and descent from orbit. The total habitable volume is about 9 cubic metres.

Loss of control of the spacecraft resulted in the death of the pilot of Soyuz 1 (V. Komarov) during re-entry. Highlights of the programme to date include the first docking of two manned spacecraft (Soyuz 4 and 5 in January 1969), and the first docking and transfer of crew to a space laboratory (Soyuz 11 and SALYUT).

Space. Term applied to the near-vacuum beyond the atmosphere within which all the bodies in the known universe exist. At one time space was considered to be completely empty between the stars and galaxies, but it is now well established that very rarefied matter, gas and solid particles (interstellar dust), exists in the space between the stars. The terms interplanetary space, interstellar space, and intergalactic space are sometimes applied to the space between the planets, the stars and the galaxies respectively. It is known that interplanetary and interstellar matter exists (the latter having a mean density in our galaxy of 10^{-21} kg m^{-3}, i.e. one thousand million million millionth of the density of air at ground level), but it is not yet at all certain how much intergalactic matter exists. The mean density of matter in the universe is still unknown.

It is not yet known for certain whether space is finite or infinite; this is a problem in COSMOLOGY.

Space medicine. The study of human physiology in a space environment. One of the areas of interest has been in the effects of prolonged periods of weightlessness. A substantial proportion of SKYLAB time was devoted to such studies. In the long term the possibility exists of using the space environment as a medical laboratory, or even to assist in certain forms of treatment.

Space platform. ▷SPACE STATION.

Space probe. An unmanned vehicle designed to investigate the interplanetary medium or conditions upon or in the vicinity of another celestial body. To date space probes have flown by or landed on the Moon and the planets, Mercury, Venus, Mars and Jupiter. Saturn is the next target, the US probe Pioneer 11 being due to reach the vicinity of the planet in 1979.

Space Shuttle. Re-usable space vehicle under development in the USA for use in the 1980s and beyond. It is intended to be able to perform a wide variety of space missions in near-Earth orbit, each having a typical duration of seven days, with a maximum of thirty days. It was originally intended that there would be some sixty to seventy launchings per year in the 1980s, but this number is likely to be seriously reduced due to financial considerations. Each shuttle vehicle is designed to undertake 100 flights.

The Shuttle will take the form of a re-usable orbiter vehicle mounted 'piggy-back' on a large expendable liquid-propellant tank together with two strap-on re-usable solid fuel boosters. The orbiter will be like a delta-wing aircraft (comparable in size with a DC-9) in appearance. The overall length is 37 metres and the wingspan 24 metres. It is designed to have a cargo bay 18 metres long and 4·5 metres in diameter with a payload capacity of 29·5 tonnes. Piloted by a crew of two, there will be space for two passengers in the crew compartment, and with modules in the cargo bay, the number of passengers could be increased by up to twelve.

When operational the Shuttle is expected to be used in roughly equal proportions for science (astronomy, physics, etc.), applications (Earth resources, communications, etc.) and military purposes. The Shuttle will allow large payloads (e.g. the LARGE SPACE TELESCOPE) or a number of separate satellites to be placed in orbit at one time; satellites may be serviced in orbit or retrieved from orbit for maintenance. Non-astronaut-trained scientists, engineers, etc., may be taken into orbit together with a complete laboratory (◊SPACELAB). It is envisaged that a space tug will be available to move satellites from the Shuttle altitude to their required orbits. The advent of the Shuttle is expected to reduce the cost per kilogramme of placing a payload in orbit by a factor of about ten compared to present costs.

Space sickness. A feeling of dizziness experienced by some astronauts and cosmonauts in a weightless environment due to disturbance of the balance mechanism in the ears. These effects generally wear off after the first few hours in space.

Space station. An orbiting space laboratory containing substantial living accommodation, and which is expected to have an extended working life. Thus, a space station would remain in orbit while crews were ferried up to it for stays of varying duration. In the long term it is likely that large, permanent space stations will be established, possibly continuously manned (on a rota basis) and serving multiple roles as astronomical observatories, Earth-monitoring platforms, etc., and as bases for the launching and return of interplanetary space missions. The term space platform is sometimes applied to such a concept.

The first orbiting laboratories which might be considered as space stations were the Soviet SALYUT and the US SKYLAB.

Space tug. ◊SPACE SHUTTLE.

Spacecraft. Any vehicle, manned or unmanned, which is capable of travelling in space.

Spacelab. A laboratory facility under development by the European Space Agency (ESA) for use in conjunction with the NASA SPACE SHUTTLE in the 1980s. It consists of two basic elements: a pressurized manned laboratory (in which up to four scientists can work in a 'shirt-sleeves' environment), and an external unpressurized platform or pallet which carries instruments that require direct exposure to space. Other possible configurations include a full-sized pressurized laboratory and a full-sized pallet operated from within the Shuttle orbiter's crew compartment.

In a typical mission, Spacelab will be carried into orbit in the Shuttle cargo bay, the cargo-bay hatches will be opened to expose it to space (the laboratory remains attached to the Shuttle) for the duration of the working period (one to four weeks) and, finally, the hatches will be closed for re-entry and landing. Spacelab will thus be a re-usable facility which can be modified and equipped specially for each mission. It will therefore be cheaper and more effective than SKYLAB.

Spacetime. ⟡ GENERAL THEORY OF RELATIVITY.

Special theory of relativity. The theory, developed by Albert Einstein (1879–1955) and published in 1905, which relates the observations of events made by observers who are in uniform relative motion (i.e. observations made in INERTIAL FRAMES of reference). This theory must be used to describe the behaviour of particles moving at velocities close to that of light, such particles being called relativistic particles.

There are two basic postulates: (a) all inertial frames are totally equivalent for the performance of all physical experiments, and (b) light travels through a vacuum at a constant velocity, c, in all inertial frames. The former postulate implies that the speed at which a laboratory may be moving through space (provided it is uniform speed) has no effect on the results of any experiments carried on inside it; while the latter implies that regardless of the relative velocity of a source of light and an observer (again assuming uniform motion), the speed at which a ray of light passes the observer is still precisely equal to the velocity of light (some 300000 km per second). This is contrary to our common-sense notion of the addition of velocities. For example, we would imagine that if a source of light were receding at a velocity of $0.5c$, then the light we received would reach us at a speed of $c - 0.5c = 0.5c$; this is not so, and according to special relativity, the light would arrive at velocity c.

From this, it follows that we cannot detect the absolute motion of the Earth through space, and it is therefore meaningless to talk about 'absolute space' or the ETHER as providing some fundamental frame of reference for the measurement of velocity (⟡ MICHELSON–MORLEY EXPERIMENT).

Among the consequences of the theory are the phenomena of length contraction, TIME DILATION and variation of mass. The length of a moving object is contracted (in the direction of its motion) by a factor of $\sqrt{(1 - v^2/c^2)}$, but an observer on such an object would be unaware of this as both he and any measuring devices would be contracted in the same proportion. Time dilation is a similar effect whereby the rate of passage of time is slower on a moving object than the rate measured by a stationary observer; there is no 'absolute time'. The mass of a moving object varies in proportion to the factor $1/\sqrt{(1 - v^2/c^2)}$, so that the faster the body, the more massive it becomes. In principle, a body which reached the speed of light would have infinite mass; this implies that no material object can travel at the speed of light (but ◊TACH-YONS). A further consequence of the theory is the equivalence of mass and energy; if a mass, m, is converted into energy, the energy released, E, is given by $E = mc^2$. This provides the clue to the production of energy in stars.

The predictions of the special theory of relativity have been well tested and the theory verified.

Spectral classification. Stars may be classified according to the visible features in their spectra (◊SPECTRUM), in particular, the dark absorption lines. The first attempts to classify stars in this way were made by Secchi between 1863 and 1867; this was followed by the Harvard system, introduced in 1890. The current system is the MKK (after Morgan, Keenan and Kellman), or Yerkes system.

On this system, stars are divided into ten principal classes, or *spectral types*, each denoted by a capital letter:

O, B, A, F, G, K, M, R, N, S,

for which a useful, and widely quoted, mnemonic is 'Oh Be A Fine Girl, Kiss Me Right Now, Smack!' Each class is further subdivided into ten subclasses, denoted by a numeral, 0, 1, 2, . . . 9; thus, for example, a G5 star is mid-way between types G0 and K0.

The precise classification of a given star is a complicated process, but the main absorption-line features of the principal classes are as follows:

O: ionized and neutral helium, ionized metals, hydrogen lines weak.
B: neutral helium, ionized metals, hydrogen stronger.
A: hydrogen dominant, ionized metals.
F: hydrogen weaker, neutral and singly ionized metals (notably calcium).
G: singly ionized calcium prominent, hydrogen weaker, neutral metals.
K: strong metallic lines, some molecular bands.
M: neutral metals, strong titanium oxide bands.
R and N: strong molecular carbon and cyanide bands (these are the 'carbon stars').
S: zirconium oxide bands.

The most important factor governing the strength and appearance of spectral lines is temperature; thus the sequence of classes goes from high temperature ($\diamond$EFFECTIVE TEMPERATURE), typically about 35000 K at type O, to lower temperature (3000 K or less) at types M, R, N, S. The Sun, with an effective temperature of 5800 K, is of type G2. Colour and temperature are related ($\diamond$COLOUR INDEX); thus the hottest (O, B-type) stars are bluish, A-type stars are white, G-type stars yellow, K-type orange, and M-type red. The hot stars (O, B, A) are sometimes referred to as early-type, the cooler stars (K, M, R, N, S) as late-type.

Each class may be further subdivided on the basis of a star's LUMINOSITY. In a given subclass a highly luminous star will be larger, and its outer layers more rarefied, than a fainter star; since one of the most important mechanisms responsible for broadening spectral lines is pressure, by and large, the spectral lines in the larger, more rarefied star will be narrower than those in the smaller, denser star. Thus in general, the more luminous a star, the narrower will be its spectral lines.

There are seven luminosity classes, as follows:

I: supergiants (highly luminous)
II: bright giants
III: giants
IV: sub-giants
V: main sequence (dwarfs)
VI: sub-dwarfs
VII: white dwarfs.

Additional information may be included by the addition to the classification of one of the following:

e: emission lines
n: nebulous lines
s: sharp lines
k: interstellar lines present
m: metallic lines
p: peculiar spectrum
v: variable.

Examples of the classification system are:

Sun G2 V; Betelgeuse (red supergiant) M2 I; Ross 986 (red dwarf) M5e; Algol B8 V.

($\diamond$HERTZSPRUNG–RUSSELL DIAGRAM and Figure 24.)

Spectral line. $\diamond$SPECTRUM.

Spectral type. $\diamond$SPECTRAL CLASSIFICATION.

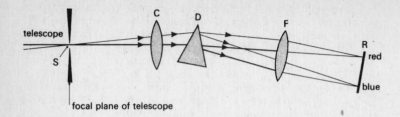

telescope

S

focal plane of telescope

C

D

F

R
red

blue

Figure 39. Spectrograph. In essence a spectrograph consists of the principal elements shown. At the focal plane of a telescope is the narrow slit, S. Light from, say, a star passes through the slit to a collimator, C, and thence to a dispersing element, D, which may be a prism or a diffraction grating. This spreads out the light according to its wavelength. Finally, the focusing system, F, produces an image of the spectrum on the recording element, R, which may be a photographic plate, image tube etc.

Spectrograph. A device which allows the SPECTRUM of a light source to be recorded, usually on a photographic plate, or on an IMAGE TUBE or similar device.

Essentially, a spectrograph consists of a narrow slit, a collimating system, a dispersing element, an imaging system and a recording system (see Figure 39). Light from, say, a star falls on the slit which is placed at the focal plane of a telescope. Light diverging from the slit is brought into a parallel beam by the collimating system, and then enters the dispersing element, which may be either a prism or a DIFFRACTION GRATING; this disperses the light into its constituent wavelengths (or colours). Finally, the imaging system focuses the spectrum of starlight onto the photographic plate (or the equivalent).

The spectrograph is usually mounted at the Cassegrain focus (◊CASSEGRAIN REFLECTOR), or with large telescopes, the COUDÉ FOCUS. The dispersion of the spectrum on the photographic plate (i.e. the extent to which spectral lines are spread out) is usually quoted in angstroms (Å) per millimetre; the higher the dispersion, the longer the exposure required to record a spectrum.

Spectroheliograph, spectrohelioscope. An instrument designed to allow astronomers to study the Sun in the light of one wavelength only (by direct vision in the case of the spectrohelioscope, and photographically in the case of the spectroheliograph). Basically, the instrument consists of a SPECTROSCOPE which is used to isolate one spectral line (e.g. an emission line of hydrogen or calcium), combined with some means of scanning the Sun's visible disc so as to build up a complete image of the

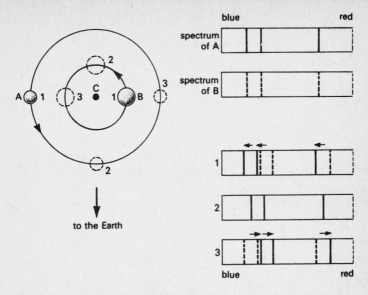

Figure 40. Spectroscopic binary. On the left, we see the orbits of two stars, A and B, round their centre of mass, C. Star B is more massive than star A, and hence lies closer to C. On the right (top), three identical spectral lines are shown in the spectra of A and B, with the wavelengths these lines would have if both A and B were stationary relative to the Earth. The combined spectrum of the two stars is shown below, illustrating the different appearance at positions 1, 2 and 3 in the orbits of the two stars. At position 2, the two stars are moving across the line of sight (i.e. neither approaching nor receding from the Earth), and the two sets of lines coincide. At position 1, A is approaching (its spectral lines are blue-shifted) and B is receding (its spectral lines are red-shifted), while at position 3 the situation is reversed. Star B, lying nearer the centre of mass, moves more slowly than star A; consequently the amount by which its spectral lines are shifted is less than the shift in A's spectral lines.

Sun. The instrument allows PROMINENCES, filaments and SOLAR FLARES to be studied.

Spectroscope. A device which allows the SPECTRUM of a light source to be studied visually. (◊SPECTROGRAPH.)

Spectroscopic binary. A BINARY in which the two component stars are too close together to be seen as individual objects, but the spectrum of their combined light reveals that two stars are present. As the two stars revolve round each other (see Figure 40), then at any instant, if one star is approaching us, the other will be receding from us. Now, radial motion of this kind causes displacement in the wavelengths of spectral lines ($\diamond$ DOPPLER EFFECT) in the spectra of these stars; the star which is approaching will exhibit blue-shifted lines, and the receding star will display red-shifted lines. As the motion of the stars proceeds their individual spectral lines will separate out in a periodic fashion, so revealing the presence of two stars. The orbital period of the two stars and their relative velocities may be deduced from such observations, and a study of their velocities allows the relative masses of the two stars to be determined; the values of the individual mass, however, can only be determined under restricted circumstances.

If one of the component stars is very much less luminous than the other, only the spectral lines of the brighter star will be seen; nevertheless, the periodic wavelength changes of these lines will reveal the presence of the invisible companion. Such stars are referred to as single-line binaries. If the orbital plane of the two stars coincides with the line of sight from the Earth to the binary, the two stars will alternately pass one in front of the other, giving rise to an ECLIPSING BINARY.

Spectroscopy. The study of the spectra ($\diamond$ SPECTRUM) of astronomical sources of radiation. Optical spectroscopy had its origins in the work of Fraunhofer ($\diamond$ FRAUNHOFER LINES) and Wollaston in the early part of the nineteenth century, although it was not until 1859 that there came any real explanation of the nature of spectra ($\diamond$ KIRCHHOFF'S LAWS OF SPECTROSCOPY). The contribution which spectroscopy has made and continues to make to our understanding of the universe can scarcely be overestimated. By means of spectroscopy it is possible to study the chemical compositions of stars and interstellar matter, to determine RADIAL VELOCITIES, rotational velocities, temperatures, magnetic fields, etc., and the advent of spectroscopy laid the foundations for the study of ASTROPHYSICS.

Optical spectra are studied by means of the SPECTROGRAPH; in recent decades the techniques of spectroscopy have extended virtually throughout the entire electromagnetic spectrum.

Spectrum (pl: spectra). In general terms, the distribution of intensity of electromagnetic radiation with wavelength; thus when we examine the spectrum of a star we are looking at a map of this brightness distribution. In the context of visible light, the visible spectrum is the band of colours produced when white light is passed through a glass prism which has the effect of spreading out light according to wavelength. From long to short wavelength the colours so obtained are red, orange, yellow, green, blue, indigo, violet, and these are the colours which make up the rainbow (although in practice not all of these colours may be discerned).

Such a spectrum is a *continuous spectrum*, or continuum (i.e. a continuous distribution of radiation over all wavelengths) and is emitted by a hot solid body or hot gas under high pressure (◊ BLACK-BODY); a continuum is also emitted by the FREE–FREE RADIATION and SYNCHROTRON RADIATION processes, but the form of the spectrum is different in each case.

A *line spectrum* is emitted by a gas under low pressure. If an electron in a high energy orbit (i.e. of large radius round the atomic nucleus; ◊ATOM) makes a downward transition to an orbit of lower energy, then the difference in energy between the two orbits, ΔE, is released as a quantum (or 'packet') of radiation having a particular wavelength, λ, and frequency, f. The relationship between ΔE, λ, and f is as follows:

$$\Delta E = hf = hc/\lambda,$$

where c is the velocity of light and h is Planck's constant.

Each possible transition results in its own characteristic *spectral line*; in the hydrogen atom, the simplest atom, there is a number of series of spectral lines due to the possible transitions (see Figure 41). For example, all the possible transitions down to the lowest energy level give rise to the LYMAN SERIES of emission lines which are characteristic of hydrogen, and hydrogen alone (◊◊ PASCHEN SERIES; BALMER SERIES). Heavier elements have more complex spectra, and the spectra of molecules are complicated by vibrational and rotational energy states.

Dark *absorption-line spectra* are produced when atoms and molecules absorb radiation (from a background source) at the same wavelengths at which emission takes place by the mechanism described above. For example, a dark line of wavelength, λ, is produced when electrons of a given element absorb energy ΔE and make *upward* transitions from lower to higher energy orbits.

Sphere of influence. That region around a planet within which its gravitational field exerts a greater influence than the field of the Sun or other celestial bodies.

Spherical aberration. The inability of a spherical lens or mirror to bring all rays of light to a focus in the same plane; this diminishes the quality of the image produced, and reduces the RESOLVING POWER of a telescope employing such lenses or mirrors.

Spicules. Flame-like projections reaching up from the base of the solar CHROMOSPHERE to heights of about 10000 km, large numbers of which make up the structure of this layer of the Sun's atmosphere. They appear to be surges of hot hydrogen gas propelled up from the surface and dissipating into the CORONA. Individual spicules last for only a few minutes.

Spiral galaxy. ◊GALAXIES, CLASSIFICATION OF.

Sputnik. Name, meaning 'satellite' (literally 'fellow traveller'), given to the earliest Soviet artificial satellites. Sputnik 1, the world's first artificial satellite, was launched on 4 October 1957 into an elliptical orbit of PERIGEE altitude 229 km and APOGEE altitude 947 km, inclination (to the equator) 65 degrees and period 96 minutes. It was spherical in shape and, with a diameter of 0·58 metres and a mass of 83·6 kg, was considerably larger and more massive than the satellites which the USA had planned to launch during the International Geophysical Year (◇IGY). The launching of Sputnik 1, which had not

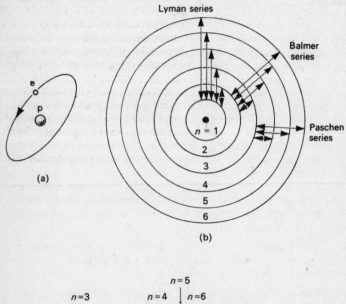

(a)

(b)

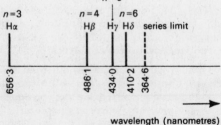

(c) Balmer series

previously been publicized, came as a considerable surprise to Western nations.

Transmitting a pulse of radio signal of 0·3 seconds duration every 0·6 seconds, its characteristic 'bleep, bleep' signal became the symbol of this first venture into space. Sputnik 1 eventually re-entered the atmosphere and burned up ninety-two days after its launching.

Sputnik 2, launched on 3 November 1957, was much more massive (just over 500 kg) and contained a separate pressurized compartment which housed the dog, Laika, the first animal to be placed in orbit. Sputnik 3, launched on 15 May 1958, was more massive again (1327 kg) and remained in orbit for 691 days.

Star. A self-luminous hot globe of gas such as the Sun. The majority of stars shine in the same way that the Sun does, by radiating away energy produced by nuclear reactions in their central regions (⊳ PROTON–PROTON REACTION; CARBON CYCLE).

The total number of stars visible to the unaided eye over the whole CELESTIAL SPHERE is about 6000, but an observer, on an average clear night, is not likely to see more than 2500. With optical aid, the number of visible stars increases rapidly with increasing aperture. The apparent brightnesses of stars (⊳ APPARENT MAGNITUDE) depends upon their distances, the amount of light they emit (LUMINOSITY) and the effects of INTERSTELLAR EXTINCTION.

The distance to the nearest star, PROXIMA CENTAURI, is some 4·2 light years, and the mean separation of stars in our GALAXY (2) is between three and four light years. Luminosities range from well over 10000 times to under one ten-thousandth that of the Sun; surface temperatures (⊳ EFFECTIVE TEMPERATURE) may exceed 30000 K or may be less than 2000 K but most lie between these limits (the Sun has an effective temperature of 5800 K). The majority of stars have masses

Figure 41. Spectral lines and the atom. (a) The hydrogen atom may be envisaged as consisting of a positively charged proton (the nucleus of the atom) around which revolves a negatively charged electron.

(b) The electron is allowed to move only in certain specified orbits denoted by $n = 1, 2, 3 \ldots$ etc., the lowest orbit, $n = 1$, being the ground state. An electron falling from a higher level to a lower level releases radiation of one particular wavelength; thus, the electron, in falling from level 3 to level 2, emits radiation of wavelength 656·3 nm (if the electron absorbs the same quantity of energy it moves up from 2 to 3). This particular transition between levels 3 and 2 produces H α lines of the Balmer series (c). The Balmer series consists of the spectral lines produced by transitions between level 2 and higher levels; the lines lie in the visible part of the spectrum.

Other series of lines include the Lyman series (ultra-violet) and Paschen series (infra-red).

209

in the range 10 to 0·1 solar masses, while radii lie between several hundred solar radii (for SUPERGIANTS) to about the size of the Earth (for WHITE DWARFS). Extremely compact bodies, known as NEUTRON STARS, may be only of the order of 10 km in radius. It follows that the densities of stars (if neutron stars are included) range from less than 10^{-7} times that of the Sun to 10^{15} times greater than the Sun's value.

Steady-state theory. A theory which suggested that the overall appearance of the universe is unchanging in space and time. According to this theory, the universe is infinite in space and time, and as galaxies move apart (and evolve), new galaxies form to take their places, so maintaining the same overall mean density of galaxies in space. This theory is not supported by current observations. (◊COSMOLOGY.)

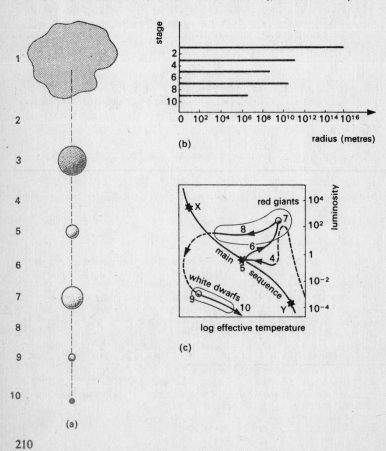

(b)

(c)

(a)

Stellar evolution. The ways in which stars proceed through their life cycles from 'birth' to 'death'. Although there are many aspects of stellar evolution which are poorly understood, there is general agreement on the broad outline given below (see Figure 42).

Stars are thought to originate from clouds of gas which are known to exist in our Galaxy (◊INTERSTELLAR MATTER). Regions in such clouds having higher than average density may begin to contract under gravitational forces, and as such a gas cloud contracts, its internal temperature increases, causing it to emit infra-red radiation, and then visible light. Such embryonic stars (protostars) have been detected in gas clouds by infra-red techniques. When the central temperature exceeds some ten million degrees kelvin, nuclear reactions produce large amounts of energy from the fusion of hydrogen into helium (◊PROTON–PROTON REACTION and CARBON CYCLE); this process is essentially similar to what happens in the hydrogen bomb.

When the production of energy in the central core is established, further contraction of the star is halted by the outward pressure of the hot gas in the star balancing the inward force of gravity. As long as the production of energy is constant, the star remains stable, emitting a constant amount of radiation. It is then known as a main-sequence star (◊HERTZSPRUNG–RUSSELL DIAGRAM) and spends most of its existence in this stable state. For example, the Sun has been on the main sequence for some 5000 million years and is expected to remain so for at least as long in the future.

The length of time for which a star remains on the main sequence is

---

Figure 42. Stellar evolution. The various stages in the evolution of a star similar in mass to the Sun are illustrated in (a). The radius of the star at various stages is depicted in (b); and the changing luminosity and temperature values are shown by the evolutionary track of the star on the Hertzsprung–Russell Diagram (c).

(1) The star begins as a cloud of interstellar material perhaps a light year in radius. (2) The cloud contracts until, after a few million years, it is about the size of the Earth's orbit and the young protostar (3) has a temperature of about 2000 K. Thereafter, for a short time, the luminosity increases to several hundred times the Sun's present value before dropping down prior to the final approach (4) to the main sequence. This process takes a few tens of millions of years. (5) The star remains on the main sequence for some ten thousand million years, then (6) moves away from the main sequence to become a red giant (7). After a few hundred million years the star evolves (8) to become a white dwarf (9), finally cooling down over thousands of millions of years to become a black dwarf.

The position of a star on the main sequence depends on its mass (mass–luminosity relationship). Thus in (c), the star X is ten times the Sun's mass, while star Y is one tenth of the Sun's mass.

limited; eventually the core becomes exhausted of hydrogen 'fuel'. The more massive the star, the sooner this happens, for the MASS–LUMINOSITY RELATION shows that the more massive the star, the faster it consumes fuel. For example, a star ten times as massive as the Sun might consume its fuel at a rate up to ten thousand times faster than the Sun does, and despite the fact that it has ten times as much fuel as the Sun, it will exhaust this supply within something like a thousandth of the Sun's main-sequence lifetime.

When the core is exhausted of hydrogen, it contracts (under the weight of the rest of the star) and the hydrogen-burning reactions spread outwards in shells surrounding the core. The luminosity of the star increases and so it expands until the internal pressure and gravitational forces are once again in balance; it becomes a large, luminous, cool star, a RED GIANT. When this happens to the Sun, it will increase in brightness by a factor of several hundred, certainly destroying life as we know it on Earth. Inside a red giant, further reactions go on (e.g. producing carbon from helium) and, in the most massive stars, a whole chain of elements up to iron may be produced by means of fusion.

A star remains a red giant for a short time compared to its main-sequence lifetime (possibly for a hundred million years in the case of the Sun), and eventually all sources of nuclear energy become exhausted. A solar-type star will then contract to form a hot, highly compact object known as a WHITE DWARF. Eventually, a white dwarf cools down to become a non-luminous solid body, sometimes called a black dwarf.

Theory shows that a star more than 1·4 times the mass of the Sun (1·2 solar masses according to recent theory) cannot become a white dwarf unless it sheds enough mass to bring itself below this limit (the Chandrasekhar limit). Such a star collapses to a much denser state to form a NEUTRON STAR possibly only some 10 km in radius; in practice the formation of a neutron star may be accompanied by a SUPERNOVA explosion.

The most massive stars of all may in the end collapse without limit, and no known force can prevent a star of final mass (after all fuel is exhausted) greater than two or three solar masses collapsing to a point of infinite density. At some stage in the collapse a BLACK HOLE will be formed and the collapsing star will vanish from view. Although stars can shed mass in a number of ways, it seems likely that stars whose initial masses are in the range 10 to 50 solar masses must stand a very good chance of suffering this fate.

Stellar magnitude. ⊳ABSOLUTE MAGNITUDE; APPARENT MAGNITUDE; BOLOMETRIC MAGNITUDE.

Stellar populations. The stars in the GALAXY (2) may be divided into two broad classes known as Population I and Population II. Stars of

Population I are, relatively speaking, quite rich in metals, being similar in composition to the Sun with about 2 per cent of their mass being made up of elements heavier than hydrogen and helium. The most conspicuous Population I stars are the hot, young and highly luminous O and B type stars (◊SPECTRAL CLASSIFICATION). Population I objects (including the Sun) are found in the disc of the Galaxy, which is also where the gas and dust clouds are located.

Stars of Population II are metal deficient, having, typically only about 10 per cent of the proportion of heavier elements that we find in the Sun (and in some cases appreciably less than this). They are found in globular clusters and the galactic halo and nucleus.

Stars of Population I are considered to be second (or later) generation stars formed out of interstellar material which had been enriched by heavy elements formed in SUPERNOVA explosions; Population II stars probably originated from material which had more nearly the original hydrogen and helium composition of the young Galaxy.

Stratopause. ◊STRATOSPHERE.

Stratosphere. The layer of the Earth's atmosphere which lies between the tropopause (mean altitude 12 km) and the stratopause (mean altitude 50 km). Within this layer, temperature increases with height from about 220 K to 270 K; at the top of the stratosphere, the atmospheric density is about one thousandth of that at ground level.

Sun. The nearest star and the centre of the SOLAR SYSTEM. The Sun is basically a self-luminous gaseous globe made up of some 71 per cent hydrogen, 27 per cent helium and about 2 per cent of all the other elements (figures in terms of relative masses). It is by far the most massive body in the Solar System, 333000 times the mass of the Earth, and 1047 times the mass of the largest planet, Jupiter.

The visible surface of the Sun is the PHOTOSPHERE (see Figure 43) (this is not a solid surface), the principal observable features of which are the SUNSPOTS, relatively dark, cooler patches, the study of which reveals the differential rotation, i.e. the equatorial regions of the Sun rotate in about twenty-five days, but the period increases at higher latitudes (e.g. twenty-eight days at 40° latitude). Above this lies a thin (less than 10000 km thick) region of more rarefied gas, the CHROMO-SPHERE, in the lower part of which are produced the dark lines in the solar SPECTRUM. Beyond this, and extending out to several solar radii, is the extremely rarefied CORONA, the outer atmosphere of the Sun, normally seen only during total solar eclipses. (◊SOLAR WIND.)

In the interior of the Sun is a central core, extending out to about one-tenth of the solar radius, where the temperature is estimated to be 15000000 K and the central pressure some $3\cdot4 \times 10^{16}$ N m^{-2}. In the core, under these conditions, energy is produced by nuclear fusion

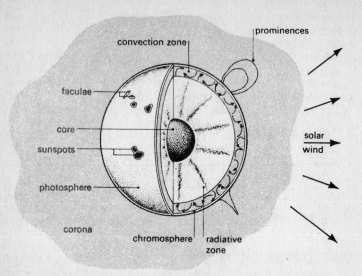

Figure 43. The Sun. The internal structure of the Sun is illustrated in the cross-section (core, radiative zone, convective zone). The visible surface is the photosphere on which are seen the dark sunspots and the bright faculae. Above this lies the chromosphere, and then the hot rarefied corona. The stream of atomic particles moving out through the corona into space is the solar wind.

reactions involving the conversion of hydrogen to helium (◊PROTON–PROTON REACTION). A small proportion of the mass involved in these reactions (about 0·7 per cent) is converted into energy, and in the case of the Sun, this mass-loss amounts to about 4 million tonnes per second. The steady production of energy maintains the Sun's near-constant radiation output, which in turn sustains life on Earth, and maintains the balance between internal pressure, which would cause the Sun to expand, and gravitation, which would cause the Sun to contract. The Sun is estimated to have sufficient hydrogen 'fuel' in its core to maintain itself in its present state for a further five or six thousand million years (◊STELLAR EVOLUTION; ◊SOLAR NEUTRINO PROBLEM). (See Plate 3.)

Solar data

		(Earth = 1)
Mass	$1·99 \times 10^{30}$ kg	333 000
Radius	696 000 km	109

Mean density	$1 \cdot 41 \times 10^3$ kg m^{-3}	0·255
Effective temperature (of photosphere)	5780 K	—
Spectral type	G2 V	—
Luminosity	$3 \cdot 83 \times 10^{26}$ watts	—
Apparent magnitude	$-26 \cdot 7$	—
Absolute magnitude	$+4 \cdot 83$	—
Mean distance from Earth	$1 \cdot 496 \times 10^8$ km	(1 astronomical unit)

Sunspot cycle.   ◊ SOLAR CYCLE.

Sunspots.   Relatively dark patches on the visible surface of the Sun (◊ PHOTOSPHERE and Figure 43). A larger spot will have a darker central region (the umbra) surrounded by a lighter outer region (the penumbra). Sunspots are regions which are cooler than the surrounding photosphere (the temperature of which is about 6000 K), typical umbra temperatures being about 4200 K, with associated penumbral temperatures of about 5600 K. Because of their lower temperatures, sunspots emit *less* radiation than the surrounding photosphere, and so appear dark by contrast. Diameters of individual spots range from 1000 to a few tens of thousands kilometres, but they are sometimes found in groups up to about 100 000 km across.

Sunspots are associated with strong magnetic fields (the field at the centre of a typical spot would be several thousand gauss) and, generally speaking, they tend to occur in pairs, each spot in the pair having opposite magnetic polarity (i.e. if one is a north magnetic pole, the other will be south). Large groups divide into two regions of opposite polarity (they are known as bipolar groups). There is, too, evidence of the flow of material outwards from sunspots.

There is no entirely adequate theory of the formation of sunspots, but there is little doubt that the surface magnetic field of the Sun is responsible in some way. The number of spots visible varies from year to year in a quite well-defined cycle of about eleven years' duration (◊ SOLAR CYCLE). (◊ BUTTERFLY DIAGRAM, Figure 7.) (See Plate 4.)

Supergiant.   A star of extremely high luminosity, and of greater radius than a giant of the same spectral class (◊ SPECTRAL CLASSIFICATION). A typical red supergiant would be 100 times as luminous as a typical RED GIANT, which, in turn, would be some ten thousand times as luminous as a main-sequence star of the same spectral class (◊ STELLAR EVOLUTION; HERTZSPRUNG–RUSSELL DIAGRAM and Figure 24).

Superior conjunction.   A planet is said to be at superior conjunction when it lies precisely on the opposite side of the Sun to the Earth (◊ PLANETARY CONFIGURATIONS, Figure 32).

Superior planet. A planet having a mean distance from the Sun greater than the Earth's distance. The superior planets are Mars, Jupiter, Saturn, Uranus, Neptune and Pluto. (◊PLANETARY CONFIGURATIONS, Figure 32.)

Supernova (pl: supernovae). A star which flares up rapidly in luminosity until, exceptionally, it may be as bright as an entire galaxy, after which it fades away; it is thought that a supernova represents a star which suffers a cataclysmic explosion and blows itself apart. The increase in luminosity may be by a factor of greater than one hundred million compared to the original luminosity of the star. There are two principal types of supernova, Type I (which may occur in stars of Population I or II) and Type II (which tends to occur among Population I stars); the former attain maximum brightnesses corresponding to an ABSOLUTE MAGNITUDE of -19, the latter reach absolute magnitude values of about -17 (i.e. Type II supernovae are fainter than Type I by a factor of about 6) but tend to fade more slowly. A Type I supernova at its peak is several thousand million times more luminous than the Sun, and if such an event were to occur within a distance of about one light year (and no star is as close as this), the supernova would appear brighter than the Sun in the sky.

The average frequency of Type I supernovae in galaxies such as our own is about one per century (Type II are about twice as frequent); the three most recent supernovae to be observed in our Galaxy occurred in the years 1054, 1573 and 1604 – in a sense, the next one is overdue. The supernova of 1054 was recorded by Chinese observers as a star which suddenly appeared (a 'guest star') in the constellation Taurus, became bright enough to be seen in daylight, then after a few months faded from view. Its position coincides with a turbulent, expanding cloud of gas, visible in telescopes, and known as the CRAB NEBULA; there is little doubt that this represents the remnant of the star which was seen to explode in 1054. A number of supernova remnants have been identified in the Galaxy. (◊STELLAR EVOLUTION.)

Precisely how supernovae are caused is uncertain, but it seems likely that they are caused by the collapse of massive stars resulting in the explosive heating of their outer layers, which are then hurled into space. Possibly as much as 90 per cent of a star's mass may be lost in this way; the collapsed central remnant of a supernova may be a NEUTRON STAR. It is worth pointing out, however, that the agreement between theory and observation regarding supernova explosions is not particularly good; some astronomers would go so far as to suggest that the observational supernova and 'theoretical supernova' have very little in common.

Surface gravity. The gravitational force experienced by a unit mass at the surface of a massive body such as a planet or a star. It is equal to the acceleration due to gravity ($\diamond g$) at the surface of that body. For a body of mass, m, and radius, r, the surface gravity is given by Gm/r^2 where G is the GRAVITATIONAL CONSTANT.

Surveyor. A series of US soft-landing lunar space probes, the first of which landed successfully on the Oceanus Procellarum (one of the lunar MARE regions) on 2 June 1966. Between 1966 and 1968, there were seven launchings, five of which achieved successful landings. These probes returned photographs from the surface and made analyses of surface material.

Synchronous orbit. $\diamond$ SYNCHRONOUS SATELLITE.

Synchronous satellite. Term applied to an artificial satellite which is in an orbit (synchronous orbit) such that it completes one revolution in a period of time exactly equal to the Earth's rotation period of 23 hours 56 minutes. Provided the orbit is circular (so that the satellite moves at a uniform rate) such a satellite will remain vertically above a fixed point on the Earth's surface (for the point and the satellite are moving round at the same angular rate). A synchronous orbit round the Earth has a radius (measured from the Earth's centre) of about 42000 km, corresponding to an altitude above the surface of just under 36000 km.

Such orbits are ideal for communication satellites, since the transmitters and receivers of the ground stations may be directed permanently to one spot in the sky, and the satellite is permanently above the horizon at these stations. There are many satellites established in such orbits (e.g. the INTELSAT series). Soviet communications satellites follow different, highly elliptical orbits of twelve-hour periods due to the difficulty of placing satellites in orbits parallel to the equator from launching sites at high northerly latitudes. The term 'synchronous' is also applied, as in this case, to satellites whose periods are simple fractions of a day.

Synchrotron radiation. Radiation emitted by ELECTRONS moving at very high speeds (approaching the speed of light) in magnetic fields. An electron follows a helical path around a magnetic field line ($\diamond$ MAGNETIC FIELD) and at relativistic (i.e. close to the speed of light) velocities emits radiation in a narrow cone in the direction of its motion. Synchrotron radiation has a characteristic SPECTRUM and generally exhibits a high degree of polarization ($\diamond$ POLARIZATION OF LIGHT). The synchrotron process is an important source of radiation from astronomical sources.

Synodic period. The time interval between two successive similar alignments of two celestial bodies. In the case of a planet, the synodic period may be taken to be the mean time interval between, say, two successive OPPOSITIONS or two successive CONJUNCTIONS. It is this period which determines the times at which particular planets will be visible in the night sky.

Syzygy. Term applied to the situation where the Earth, Sun and Moon are in line (i.e. at new moon and full moon). The word is rarely used in astronomy (though encountered in science fiction) but is a boon to compilers of crosswords and ardent Scrabble players.

T

T Tauri star. A star which shows some variability in its brightness, appears to be surrounded by clouds of material, and which lies above the main sequence in the HERTZSPRUNG–RUSSELL DIAGRAM (see Figure 24). Such stars are thought to be young objects still in the stage of initial contraction on to the main sequence. The variability in brightness is due at least in part to the surrounding material; and it may be that planetary formation is going on around such stars.

Tachyons. Hypothetical 'faster-than-light' particles; they remain a theoretical concept at present.

Tau Ceti. One of the nearest stars of a similar type to the Sun. It lies at a distance of 11·8 light years, is of spectral type G8 (◊ SPECTRAL CLASSIFICATION) and therefore slightly cooler than the Sun, and has ABSOLUTE MAGNITUDE +5·7 (its luminosity, therefore, is just under 20 per cent that of the Sun). Because of its general similarity to the Sun, it has been argued that it may be of a type suitable for having life-bearing planets in orbit round it. Consequently, it was one of the first stars to be examined in a programme attempting to detect artificial signals from extra-terrestrial technology (◊ OZMA PROJECT).

Telescope. An optical instrument designed to make distant objects appear closer. There are two principal types of optical telescope, the refractor (Figure 44a) and the reflector (Figure 44b). The former uses a lens (the objective, or object glass) to form an image of the object under study, while the latter uses a mirror (the primary mirror) for this purpose. The clear diameter of the objective (or primary mirror) is called the aperture of the instrument, and a telescope is usually described in terms of this; thus, for example, a telescope with a 1 metre aperture would be referred to as a '1 metre telescope'.

The size of the image produced depends directly on the focal length (i.e. the distance between the objective and the image) of the instrument. Magnification of this primary image may be achieved by means of an eyepiece, a lens of short focal length; the magnification, or magnifying power, M, of a telescope is calculated from:

$$M = \frac{\text{focal length of objective}}{\text{focal length of eyepiece}}.$$

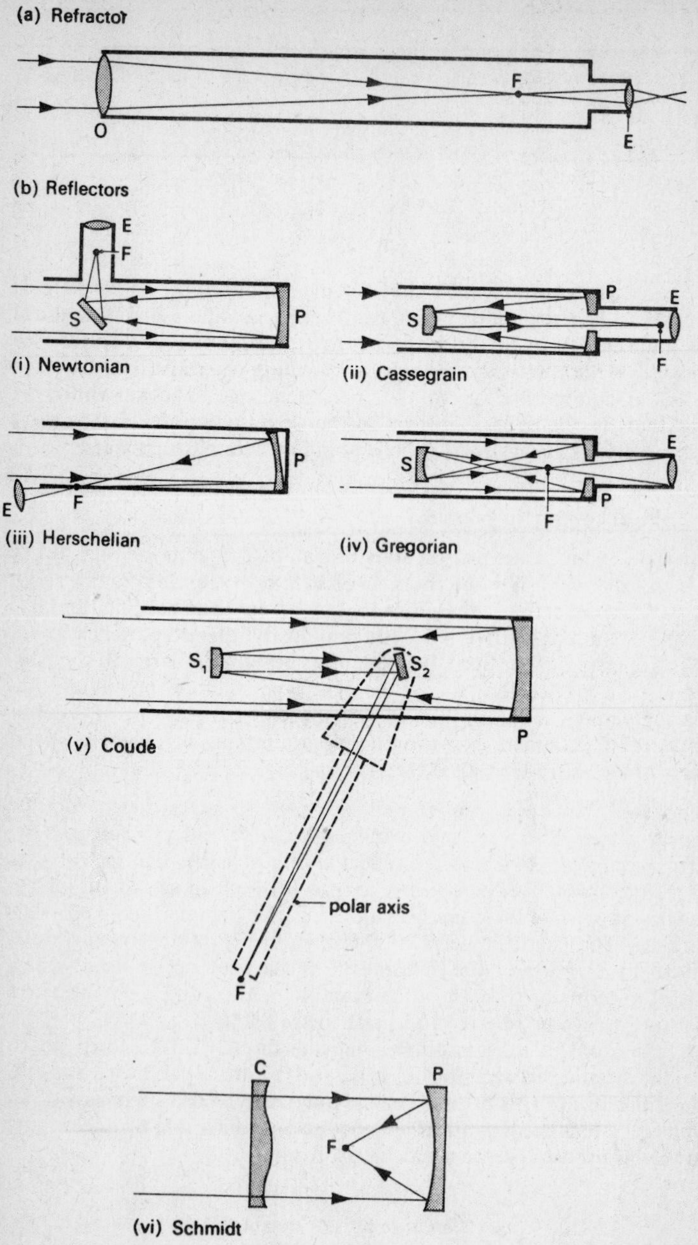

(a) Refractor
F
O
E
(b) Reflectors
E
F
S
P
(i) Newtonian
P
S
E
F
(ii) Cassegrain
P
E
F
(iii) Herschelian
E
S
P
F
(iv) Gregorian
S_1
S_2
P
(v) Coudé
polar axis
F
C
P
F
(vi) Schmidt

For example, a telescope of focal length 1 metre, with an eyepiece of 10 mm focal length, would produce a magnification of $1/0.01 = 100$.

For the astronomer, a telescope fulfils two main functions:

1. It collects more light than the unaided eye, so allowing fainter objects to be detected; this light-gathering power depends upon the area of the objective or primary mirror, i.e. it is proportional to the square of the aperture.

2. It reveals fine details which cannot be seen with the unaided eye; this RESOLVING POWER is directly proportional to the aperture.

Thus a 1 metre telescope will collect one hundred times as much light as a 0.1 metre telescope, and will reveal details ten times finer than the smaller instrument can show.

The invention of the refracting telescope is generally credited to the Dutch instrument maker, Hans Lippershey, in about 1608, although there is some uncertainty about this. Isaac Newton constructed the first reflecting telescope in 1671.

Figure 44. Telescopes. (a) In essence the refractor consists of the object glass, O, which collects light and brings it to a focus, F. The eyepiece, E, is placed beyond F to produce a magnified image.

(b) A selection of different types of reflector is illustrated here.

(i) Newtonian. Light is reflected from a concave paraboloid primary mirror, P, and the converging cone of light is intercepted by a small, flat, secondary mirror, S, set at 45° to the axis of the telescope. This reflects the focus, F, to the side of the tube, where the eyepiece, E, is located.

(ii) Cassegrain. Light from the primary, P, is intercepted by a convex secondary, S, and reflected through a hole in the centre of the primary to a focus, F.

(iii) Herschelian. Rarely encountered, this instrument utilizes a tilted primary, P, which reflects light directly to a focus, F, at the side of the tube.

(iv) Gregorian. Similar to the Cassegrain, but utilizes a concave secondary, S, to produce an erect image.

(v) Coudé. This may take a number of forms. In the example shown light is reflected from the primary, P, to a convex secondary, S_1, as in the Cassegrain. The converging cone of light is then reflected from a flat mirror, S_2, through an aperture in the telescope tube and thence down the hollow polar axis (◊ EQUATORIAL MOUNTING, Figure 20) to a fixed-focus position, F.

(vi) Schmidt. This employs a concave spherical mirror, P, to bring light to a focus, F. The spherical aberration of the primary mirror is corrected by the correcting plate, C, placed at the centre of curvature of P (i.e. at twice the focal length of the primary in front of the primary). The Schmidt is used for photographing large areas of sky.

The term 'telescope' is sometimes applied to instruments used for the detection of other types of electromagnetic radiation (for example, ◊RADIO TELESCOPE). Alternatively, the term flux collector may be used to describe such instruments. (See Plate 1.)

Terminator. The boundary between the sunlit and dark hemispheres of a planet or satellite, e.g. the terminator of the Moon represents those points on its surface at which the Sun is rising or setting. In the vicinity of the terminator, the long shadows cast by the low Sun throw features such as craters and mountains into sharp relief.

Terrestrial planets. Planets which are similar to the Earth in their general properties, i.e. they are compact, have relatively high mean densities (e.g. 5×10^3 kg m^{-3}), and are composed primarily of silicates and metals with little, if any, free hydrogen and helium.

Thermocouple. ◊INFRA-RED ASTRONOMY.

Thrust. The propulsive force generated by a rocket motor as a result of the ejection of exhaust gases (◊REACTION (1)). Under ideal (vacuum) conditions, thrust is equal to the product of the mass ejected per unit time multiplied by the EXHAUST VELOCITY of the ejected matter; it is expressed in units of kilogrammes (kg) weight (1 kg weight is the force experienced by a mass of 1 kg on the Earth's surface due to the gravitational attraction of the Earth). Alternatively, thrust may be expressed in terms of force, the newton being the SI unit of force.

If a rocket is to lift off the ground it must generate a thrust greater than its own weight.

Tidal theory, The. ◊SOLAR SYSTEM, ORIGIN OF.

Tide-raising force. ◊TIDES.

Tides. The tides in the Earth's oceans, i.e. the twice-daily rise and fall of the sea level, are due primarily to the gravitational attraction of the Moon. In essence, the ocean on the hemisphere of the Earth closer to the Moon is subject to a stronger gravitational attraction than is the centre of the Earth's globe (the force of gravity is inversely proportional to the square of distance), and is accelerated towards the Moon, so building up a hump (rather less than 1 metre in height) on the Moon-ward side. The ocean on the opposite side of the Earth is further from the Moon than is the Earth's centre; consequently it is subject to a weaker attraction and is 'left behind' as the Earth accelerates away from it. In this way a second hump of water is built up on the side away from the Moon.

As the Earth rotates on its axis, the tidal bulges move steadily west-wards, causing the sea level at a particular point on the Earth to rise and fall twice daily. The Sun exerts a similar, but smaller, effect; its tide-raising force (see below) is less than half that of the Moon. When the Sun and Moon are in line (at new moon and full moon) they act in unison to amplify the tidal bulges, giving large spring tides; when they are at right angles to each other (first and last quarter) the two effects tend to cancel, giving a small rise and fall, or neap tide. The height of the tide at any particular place on the coast is greatly influenced by local conditions (e.g. the shape of the shoreline) and by barometric pressure, winds, etc.

In general terms, the tide-raising force exerted by one body on another is the *difference* in gravitational attraction across the body. The value of the tide-raising force is proportional to the mass of the attracting body, and inversely proportional to the cube of its distance; thus, although the Sun is some 28000000 times more massive than the Moon, because it is also 400 times further away, and 400^3 is 64000000, it follows that the Sun's tide-raising force on the Earth is only 28/64 times that of the Moon – i.e. less than half ($\Diamond$ROCHE LIMIT).

Tidal forces are important in various astronomical phenomena.

Time dilation (or dilitation). According to the SPECIAL THEORY OF RELATIVITY, the rate at which time passes on an object moving at velocity, v, relative to a stationary observer is slower than the rate at which time passes for this stationary observer by a factor of $\sqrt{(1 - v^2/c^2)}$, where c is the velocity of light. The closer the moving object approaches the speed of light, the slower time passes; if it were possible for the object to travel at the speed of light, time would stand still relative to the stationary observer's time.

Thus the time which elapsed on the moving object during one hour of the stationary observer's time would be as follows:

Velocity of moving object	Time elapsed
0·5c	0·86 hours = 51·6 minutes
0·9c	0·44 hours = 26·4 minutes
0·99c	0·14 hours = 8·4 minutes
0·999c	0·04 hours = 2·4 minutes

There follows from this the famous 'Twins Paradox', namely that if one member of a pair of twins were to remain on Earth while the other travelled away and returned at a velocity close to that of light, the latter would find he had aged much less than his twin who had remained on Earth. For example, if the astronaut twin were to travel to a star 12·5 light years away and immediately return, travelling throughout at a constant speed of 0·999c (clearly we are neglecting acceleration, deceleration, and turn-round times) he would return to Earth after a period of twenty-five Earth-years. He, however, would have aged only by one year.

The time-dilation effect has been verified experimentally in a number of ways. For example, certain types of sub-atomic particles (muons) generated in the upper atmosphere by the arrival of COSMIC RAYS reach ground level, despite the fact that their normal lifetimes are too short to allow them to cover this distance before they decay; because they are travelling close to the speed of light, the time-dilation effect extends their lives sufficiently to let them reach ground level. Again, in 1974 an experiment was carried out with two identical clocks, one of which was kept stationary in a laboratory, and the other carried round the Earth in a jet aircraft. When the two clocks were compared, the time-dilation effect was confirmed.

Titan. ◊SATURN.

Titius–Bode law. ◊BODE'S LAW.

Topocentric coordinates. Coordinates measured from a point on the Earth's surface. The coordinates of astronomical bodies (◊CELESTIAL COORDINATES) are usually expressed in terms of geocentric positions (i.e. positions related to the centre of the Earth) and, as far as the positions of stars on the CELESTIAL SPHERE are concerned, there is no detectable difference in the two coordinate systems. However, in the case of the Moon and planets allowance must be made for the difference in position between the observer and the centre of the Earth (planetary parallax).

Trajectory. The path pursued by a moving body or particle. The term may be applied to the path followed by a ballistic missile or a space probe moving under the influence of gravity. It might equally be applied to the path followed by a ray of light.

Transfer orbit. The path pursued by a spacecraft in moving from one orbit to another, e.g. from the orbit of the Earth to the orbit of Mars. Generally speaking, such an orbit will be an ellipse which intersects the orbit of the target plane; if the spacecraft is to enter orbit round the target planet, or effect a landing, then the motors must be fired to achieve the correct trajectory. The transfer orbit requiring the minimum expenditure of energy is an ellipse which *just* touches the orbits of the Earth and the target planet (see Figure 45) and is known as the Hohmann

---

Figure 45. Transfer orbits. (a) The Hohmann transfer orbit takes the form of an ellipse which just touches the orbits of Earth, E, and target planet, T. A spacecraft launched when the Earth is at E_1 and the target planet at T_1 will reach the orbit of the target planet when it is at point T_2.

(b) Two high velocity transfer orbits. A is a highly eccentric ellipse and B a hyperbola. Such orbits require much more energy than the Hohmann orbit, but less time is required to reach the target planet.

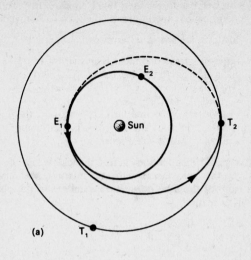

(a)

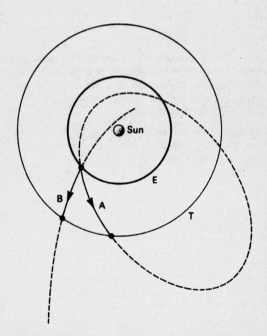

(b)

orbit; such an orbit involves long flight times. A fast transfer orbit, requiring much greater expenditure of fuel, would be hyperbolic.

Transit.   This term is used in a number of contexts:

(a) The passage of an astronomical body across an observer's MERI-DIAN. Clearly, as the Earth rotates, a star will cross the meridian twice in the course of a day; the transit at which the star reaches its maximum altitude above the horizon (*culmination*: for an observer in the northern hemisphere this occurs when the star passes between the north celestial pole and the south point of the horizon) is called upper transit; the other is called lower transit (see Figure 46).

(b) The passage of a smaller body across the visible disc of a larger one. For example, this may occur with the planets Mercury or Venus passing in front of the Sun, or with the satellites of the planet Jupiter in front of that planet.

(c) The passage of the shadow of a satellite across the surface of its planet is referred to as a shadow transit.

Triton.   ◊NEPTUNE.

Tropical year.   ◊YEAR.

Tropopause.   ◊STRATOSPHERE.

Troposphere.   The lowest layer of the Earth's atmosphere, extending from ground level to the tropopause, at a mean altitude of 12 km. At this altitude the mean temperature is about 220 K and the mean air density about one-quarter of that at sea level. It is in this layer that most weather phenomena occur.

True anomaly.   For a particle moving in a conic orbit (◊CONIC SECTION), the true anomaly is the angle between the point of closest approach to a focus, the focus, and the position of the particle. In the case of a planet moving round the Sun in an elliptical orbit, its true anomaly at any particular instant is the angle between its PERIHELION position, the Sun (which lies at one focus of the ellipse), and the position of the planet at that instant (see Figure 47).

21-centimetre radiation.   Microwave radiation of 21·1 cm wavelength (1420 MHz frequency) is emitted by clouds of neutral hydrogen gas. That such radiation should be emitted was predicted in 1944 by H. C. van de Hulst, and was first discovered six years later. Study of this radiation has allowed astronomers to map the distribution of hydrogen gas in the Galaxy.

Tycho Brahe.   ◊TYCHONIC SYSTEM.

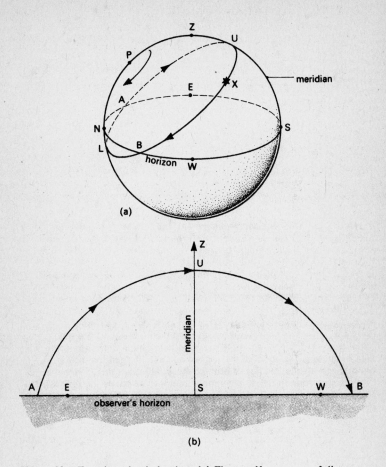

Figure 46. Transit and culmination. (a) The star X appears to follow
the path shown due to the apparent daily rotation of the celestial sphere.
The star crosses the observer's meridian at two points, and is said to
be at upper transit, U, when it crosses between P (the north celestial
pole) and S (the south point of the horizon), and lower transit, L, when
it crosses the northern part of the meridian. (This applies to observers
in the northern hemisphere; the situation is reversed in the southern
hemisphere.) At upper transit the star is at its maximum altitude above
the horizon and is said to be at culmination. At lower transit the altitude
of the star is minimum.

(b) The observer's view of the motion of the star.

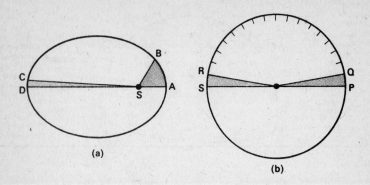

Figure 47. True and mean anomaly. (a) The true anomaly, v, of a planet located at B in its elliptical orbit round the Sun is equal to the angle ASB; i.e. it is the angle between the major axis of the orbit and the radius vector of the planet, SB, measured at the Sun, S. It is taken to be zero when the planet is at perihelion, A. The planet moves more slowly when further from the Sun, but by Kepler's second law (◊KEPLER'S LAWS), if the time taken to travel from C to D equals the time taken to travel from A to B, then the shaded areas are equal.

(b) In a circular orbit, the radius is constant, and the velocity is constant. Thus, the time taken to travel from R to S equals the time taken from P to Q and, again, the shaded areas are equal. If the total area of circle (b) is equal to the area of ellipse (a), then the orbital periods and areal velocities of both orbits will be the same. Since the motion is uniform in (b), it is a simple matter to calculate the time taken for the planet to travel from one point to another in its orbit; the non-uniform motion of the planet on the elliptical orbit makes this a difficult calculation. In order to make this calculation for an elliptical orbit, a mean anomaly, M, is defined which is the position reached on a hypothetical circle (having the same area as the ellipse) by an imaginary body which has been travelling for the same time interval as the real planet. The values of mean anomaly corresponding to the true anomaly of the planet at its initial and final positions may be computed, and this allows the time of travel of the planet to be obtained.

Tychonic system. The world system proposed by the Danish astronomer Tycho Brahe (1546–1601). Unable to accept the Copernican doctrine (◊COPERNICAN SYSTEM) that the Earth moves round the Sun, he put forward the view, later disproved by Kepler (◊KEPLER'S LAWS), that the planets move round the Sun, but the Sun and Moon move round the Earth.

U

UFO – Unidentified Flying Object. An object seen, or apparently seen, in the sky and whose nature cannot be determined by the observer. By far the majority of sightings can be explained in terms of known phenomena with which the individual observer was unfamiliar (e.g. the planet Venus, high altitude balloons, artificial satellites, etc.), but there remains a residue of sightings which cannot adequately be explained, either because of an insufficiency of reliable data or, possibly, because a phenomenon which is not yet understood has genuinely been observed.

The most popular explanation (and certainly the most glamorous one) is that such unexplained sightings are due to extra-terrestrial spacecraft, or FLYING SAUCERS, to use a popular term. While the possibility of the Earth's being visited by alien spacecraft is one which cannot wholly be excluded (◊LIFE IN THE UNIVERSE), the nature and frequency of such sightings makes this 'explanation' a most improbable one.

Ultra-violet radiation. ◊ELECTROMAGNETIC SPECTRUM.

Umbra. The dark central region of a shadow. To an observer located in the umbra, the light source responsible for casting the shadow is wholly invisible. Thus an observer standing within the umbra of the Moon's shadow would experience a total eclipse of the Sun (◊ECLIPSE, Figure 15).

The term is also applied to the darker central part of a SUNSPOT.

Universal time. ◊MEAN TIME.

Universe. The sum of everything which exists and of which we can be aware; the entirety of space. There is a semantic difficulty in talking about the universe; on the one hand, we define it to be 'everything', but it may be (a) that our universe is finite, yet unbounded; (b) that the accessible universe is only a small part of a much larger entity, most of which we cannot observe; or (c) that there exist other universes of which we are not 'aware'.

Universe, Origin of. It is not certain that the universe had an origin, in the sense of being created at one point at one time. The BIG-BANG THEORY suggests that the universe as we know it originated in a hot dense fireball between ten and twenty thousand million years ago, and the evidence at the moment tends to favour the general features of this theory. The STEADY-STATE THEORY, although now widely rejected in its original form, suggested that the universe had no beginning and might continue to exist forever. The OSCILLATING UNIVERSE THEORY suggests the possibility of the universe expanding and contracting periodically, so that a 'Big-Bang' occurs at regular intervals. If this is so, then it may be argued that the last 'Big-Bang' was not truly the origin of the universe. (⟡COSMOLOGY and Figure 13.)

Upper transit. ⟡TRANSIT.

Uranus. The seventh planet in order of distance from the Sun, Uranus is one of the four giant or JOVIAN PLANETS. It was discovered by William Herschel on 13 March 1781, and was the first planet to be discovered with the aid of the telescope (the six planets closer to the Sun can all be seen without telescopic aid).

At a mean distance from the Sun of 19·2 astronomical units, it has an orbital period of just over eighty-four years. It looks, in many ways, rather like a scaled-down version of JUPITER; its equatorial radius of about 24 500 km is little over one-third that of Jupiter but is still almost four times that of the Earth. Due to its rapid rotation, the planet bulges at the equator to the extent that the equatorial radius exceeds the polar radius by a factor of 1·06. Telescopically, little detail may be seen, apart from ill-defined cloud belts at the top of its atmosphere, these containing a large proportion of methane. The mean density is a little higher than that of Jupiter, and it may be that although hydrogen is a major component, Uranus may possess a fairly substantial rocky core.

A peculiar feature is the inclination of the axis of rotation; this is inclined to the perpendicular to the orbital plane by 98° (the Earth's axis is inclined by 23½°), so that the poles lie almost in this plane. Uranus has five satellites, all of which are small (radii ranging from about 120 km to some 500 km), all moving in near-circular orbits parallel to its equator.

A Mariner-type space probe is scheduled to be launched in 1979 for a close fly-by mission, reaching Uranus by about 1985.

Uranus data

		(Earth = 1)
Mean distance from Sun	2 870 000 000 km (approx.)	19·2
Orbital eccentricity	0·047	—
Orbital inclination	0° 46′ 23″	—
Sidereal orbital period	84·01 years	84·01

Axial rotation period	23h (approx.)	0·96
Mass	$8·7 \times 10^{25}$ kg	14·54
Radius (equatorial)	24 500 km	3·84
Mean density	$1·6 \times 10^3$ kg m^{-3}	0·29
Surface gravity	11·3 m s^{-2}	1·15

V

Van Allen Belts. Radiation belts, i.e. regions of charged atomic particles, which exist round the Earth and whose existence was first demonstrated by the US physicist James Van Allen as a result of an experiment carried on the US satellite Explorer 1 in 1958. There are two Van Allen Belts, the inner belt, centred at a radius (measured from the Earth's centre) of about 1·6 Earth radii, and the outer belt, centred on a radius of about 3·7 Earth radii; the latter was discovered by the US probe Pioneer 3 in December 1958.

They are doughnut-shaped zones formed by the lines of force of the Earth's magnetic field, and within which charged particles (e.g. electrons and protons) become trapped. A proportion of the particles, particularly those in the outer belt, originate from the Sun (◇SOLAR WIND); others come from the interaction with the Earth's atmosphere of COSMIC RAYS. 'Leakage' of these particles into the upper atmosphere from those regions in the belts close to the north and south magnetic poles give rise to the phenomenon of the AURORA.

Variable stars. Stars whose brightness varies. In terms of their visual appearance, we can recognize three principal groups, regular (or periodic) variables, the brightness of which varies in a regular cyclic way; irregular variables, which display no obvious pattern in their variations, and semi-regular variables which show some degree of periodicity, but their behaviour in successive cycles need not be closely similar.

Fundamentally, there are two different classes of variable stars, intrinsic variables and extrinsic variables. The former are stars in which the light output varies because of some process acting in the star itself, while the variation in the latter is caused by some external agency. For example, ECLIPSING BINARIES are extrinsic variables, because the apparent brightness variation which we see is due to the eclipsing of one star by the other.

The regular variables have periods ranging between a few hours and 600 or 700 days (those with periods longer than 100 days are termed LONG-PERIOD VARIABLES). The majority of these stars are giants or supergiants, and the evidence suggests that these stars are physically pulsating (expanding and contracting in a period equal to the period of variation). The best known of the regulars are the CEPHEID VARIABLES. The semi-regular variables seem to be similar in nature, examples being the red giants, Betelgeuse and Antares. The irregular variables are not well understood.

Variables which may be partly intrinsic and partly extrinsic are the T TAURI STARS; these are young, pre-main-sequence (⟡HERTZ-SPRUNG–RUSSELL DIAGRAM) objects surrounded by clouds of material.

In a different category again are the cataclysmic variables such as NOVAE (stars which flare up dramatically and then fade back to their original state) and SUPERNOVAE (stars which apparently blow themselves apart). (⟡FLARE STARS.)

Variable stars in a constellation are denoted as follows: by the roman capital letters R, S, . . ., Z, and after these are exhausted, by two letters, RR to RZ, SS to SZ, etc., to ZZ, e.g. RV Tauri, SS Cygni, etc. Alternatively, they may be denoted by the letter V, followed by a number, e.g. V^{346}.

Variation of mass. ⟡ SPECIAL THEORY OF RELATIVITY.

Velocity. Rate of change of position. Velocity has both magnitude (speed) and direction. It is expressed in terms of units of length per unit time, e.g. metres per second (denoted m s^{-1}), kilometres per second, etc.

Velocity of light. The velocity of light in a vacuum (a constant, denoted by c) is currently estimated to be $2 \cdot 9979246 \times 10^{8}$ metres per second. In round figures, this is very close to 300000 km s^{-1}.

Venera. Series of Soviet Venus probes, the first of which, Venera 1, was launched on 12 February 1961 and, although radio contact was lost after fifteen days, it is believed to have passed within 100000 km of the planet. The first real success was achieved with Venera 4 which, in June 1967, transmitted information during its descent through the atmosphere until failing at an altitude of about 26 km. Veneras 7 and 8 (of 1970 and 1972) transmitted directly from the surface while Veneras 9 and 10 achieved soft-landings in 1975 and returned the first photographs of the surface rocks (⟡VENUS); Veneras 9 and 10 also included orbiting probes.

Venus. The second planet in order of distance from the Sun. At INFERIOR CONJUNCTION it can approach to within forty million kilometres of the Earth, closer than any other planet. It is quite closely similar in size and mass to the Earth, but until recently very little definite information was known about it. This situation was due to a number of factors, notably (a) when the planet is at its closest, the un-illuminated hemisphere is turned towards the Earth, so that it cannot be studied; (b) the planet is completely shrouded in a dense, cloudy atmosphere. Thus, such factors as surface temperature, atmospheric composition, axial inclination and rotation period were not known until the fly-by missions of some MARINER SERIES space probes, and the series of landings achieved by the Soviet VENERA series. The first successful fly-by was Mariner 2 in 1962, and the first landing mission to transmit successfully from the surface was Venera 7 in 1970.

It is now well established that the mean surface temperature is about 475°C, that the atmosphere is composed largely of carbon dioxide (over 97 per cent), that the atmospheric pressure at ground level is about 100 Earth-atmospheres, and that the clouds, which reach altitudes of some 60 km, contain quantities of sulphuric acid. The axial rotation period has been shown to be 243 days retrograde ($\Diamond$RETROGRADE MOTION (3)), a period which is longer than the orbital period (i.e. the sidereal 'day' is longer than the 'year'). However, the upper cloud layers appear to rotate around the planet in a period of about four days. Investigations by Veneras 8 onwards indicate the existence of surface rocks akin to terrestrial granite, and photographs taken from the surface by Veneras 9 and 10 show little evidence of erosion, indicating that these rocks may be of fairly recent origin.

The very high temperature is considered to be due to the GREENHOUSE EFFECT, the carbon dioxide atmosphere acting as a 'blanket' to retain heat and maintain a fairly uniform temperature over the entire planet (i.e. 'day' and 'night' temperatures are not significantly different). (See Plate 7.)

Venus data

		(Earth = 1)
Mean distance from Sun	108 200 000 km	0·72
Orbital eccentricity	0·0068	—
Orbital inclination	3° 23′ 40″	—
Sidereal orbital period	224·7 days	0·62
Mean synodic period	583·9 days	—
Axial rotation period	243 days (retrograde)	243
Mass	$4·87 \times 10^{24}$ kg	0·82
Radius	6070 km	0·95
Mean density	$5·2 \times 10^3$ kg m^{-3}	0·94
Surface gravity	8·6 m s^{-2}	0·87

Vernal equinox. The point on the CELESTIAL SPHERE defined by the intersection of the ECLIPTIC and the CELESTIAL EQUATOR at which the Sun moves from south to north of the celestial equator (see Figure 9b). It is the point on the celestial sphere reached by the Sun on or about 21 March each year; at this time, the Sun is vertically above the terrestrial equator, and day and night have equal length at all points on the Earth's surface.

The vernal equinox provides a reference point for the equatorial and ecliptic systems of CELESTIAL COORDINATES.

Viking. Name given to two US spaceprobes designed to investigate the planet Mars, both of which achieved successful landings on that planet in the summer of 1976. Each spacecraft consisted of two principal components, an orbiter (having a mass of some 2300 kg) and a lander (a three-legged structure with a mass of some 600 kg). Viking 1 was launched on 20 August 1975, entered orbit round Mars on 19 June 1976, and achieved a landing on 20 July 1976 in a relatively flat region known as Chryse Planitia (Martian latitude 22·5°N, longitude 48°W). By a curious chance the landing was precisely seven years after the first manned Moon landing (◊APOLLO PROJECT). Viking 2, launched on 9 September 1975, landed on 3 September 1976 in a region known as Utopia (48°N, 226°W, about 6500 kilometres north-east of Viking 1).

The orbiters' principal investigations are imaging (detailed study of the Martian surface), atmospheric water vapour mapping and thermal mapping (plotting temperature variations over the planet). The landers have eight principal experiments: landing-site imaging, biology, molecular analysis, inorganic chemical analysis, meteorology, seismology, physical properties and magnetic properties. It is hoped that the Viking spacecraft will continue to function for a full Martian year (i.e. to about the middle of 1978).

Results to date have been spectacular. The surface at each landing site is rock-strewn and covered with reddish dust which seems to be similar to limonite, a material encountered on Earth; the basic composition of the surface material is similar to terrestrial rocks. The sky is basically pink due to suspended dust particles; the wind speed measured during the first few weeks ranged up to 40 kilometres per hour, but winds more than ten times faster than this are to be expected occasionally. Water vapour has been detected, and the polar caps shown to be made of water ice. For the first time, nitrogen, argon and oxygen have been detected in the atmosphere. (See Plates 10, 11 and 12.)

One of the principal lander objectives was to search for evidence of living material. To date, the results have been inconclusive and confusing. Some of the biological experiments have given results which *could* be interpreted as evidence of the presence of living material in soil samples, but chemical analyses of these samples do not support this view.

The Viking missions have proved to be to be an outstanding success (◊MARS).

Voskhod. Series of two Soviet manned spacecraft, capable of carrying up to three cosmonauts, which followed the VOSTOK series. It incorporated an AIRLOCK and had a mass of about 5·3 tonnes. On the

Voskhod 2 mission, launched on 18 March 1965, Alexei Leonov made an EVA (or 'spacewalk') for $12\frac{1}{2}$ minutes; this was the first time such a manoeuvre had been attempted.

Vostok. Series of Soviet manned spacecraft, the first of which, Vostok 1, carried the first man into space, Yuri Gagarin, on 12 April 1961. Gagarin's flight lasted 1 hour 48 minutes, during which time he completed one full orbit of the Earth, reaching a maximum altitude of 327 km. The Vostok series consisted of six missions, the last of which, Vostok 6, carried the first woman in space, Valentina Tereshkova; launched on 16 June 1963, she completed forty-eight orbits.

The Vostok spacecraft had a mass of 4·7 tonnes, and contained a spherical re-entry module with accommodation for one cosmonaut. The name 'Vostok' means, literally, 'east'.

Vulcan. A hypothetical planet which at one time was supposed to move in an orbit closer in to the Sun than Mercury. Its existence was proposed in the nineteenth century by the French mathematician, U. Leverrier, and it was supposedly observed by an amateur astronomer, Lescarbault, in 1859. Recent observations have eliminated the possibility of such a planet.

W

Wavelength. The distance between two successive crests of a wave motion. The term is applied to ELECTROMAGNETIC RADIATION which is regarded as a wave motion; for example, blue light has a wavelength of about 440 nanometres, red light about 700 nanometres; X-rays have wavelengths of the order of 10^{-10} metres, radio waves of the order of metres.

Weight. The force experienced by a body resting on, for example, the surface of a planet. A person standing on the Earth's surface experiences weight because the surface on which he is standing resists the effect of the force of gravity which otherwise would accelerate that person towards the centre of the Earth; i.e. there is a REACTION (1) up through his feet equal and opposite to the gravitational attraction exerted upon him by the Earth. The weight of a body depends upon the gravitational force to which it is subjected; on the surface of a planet it is equal to the mass of the body times the SURFACE GRAVITY. For example, a body which weighed 100 kg on the surface of the Earth would have the following weights on the surfaces of the bodies listed below:

the Moon   16 kg
Mars   38 kg
Jupiter   264 kg
the Sun   2790 kg
a white dwarf   30000000 kg

It is important to note that an identical feeling of apparent weight is experienced by a person located in an accelerating object, e.g. an astronaut in an accelerating spacecraft. (◊GRAVITATION; *g*; WEIGHTLESSNESS; INERTIA.)

Weightlessness. The sensation experienced by a body falling freely under the influence of gravity, i.e. experiencing no resistance to his acceleration. An astronaut in a spacecraft which is coasting in a gravitational field experiences no sensation of weight as both he and his surroundings are 'falling' at the same rate. (◊WEIGHT; ◊◊FREE FALL, Figure 21.)

White dwarf. A compact and highly dense star of high surface temperature (hence 'white' in appearance) but low LUMINOSITY. A typical white dwarf would have a mass comparable to the Sun, but a radius comparable to that of the Earth (i.e. 0·01 solar radii). Consequently, the mean density of such objects lies between 10^8 and 10^9 kg m^{-3}, i.e. between 100 000 and 1 000 000 times that of water. A thimbleful of such material would weigh several tonnes here on Earth.

The first white dwarf to be identified was the faint companion of the star SIRIUS; it has a mass almost exactly equal to that of the Sun, a radius of about one-fortieth that of the Sun, and an ABSOLUTE MAGNITUDE of 11·3 (i.e. it is about 1/440 of the Sun's luminosity). The effective temperature is about 7000 K. White dwarfs are typically about 10 000 times less luminous than main-sequence stars of the same spectral class (◊SPECTRAL CLASSIFICATION; HERTZSPRUNG–RUSSELL DIAGRAM).

They represent stars in their final evolutionary stages (◊STELLAR EVOLUTION and Figure 42) when nuclear fuel has been exhausted and the stellar material has been packed to very high densities by gravitational forces. The electrons in such a star have established themselves in a rigid structure which resists further gravitational contraction; such material is said to be degenerate. White dwarfs shine by radiating away their internal reservoirs of heat, so that over long periods of time they cool down and fade away.

The Sun is likely to become a white dwarf in about six thousand million years' time.

Wien displacement law. According to this law, the wavelength at which a BLACK BODY emits its maximum quantity of radiation is inversely proportional to its absolute temperature. This law may be used to give the approximate wavelength, λ_{max}, at which a star of EFFECTIVE TEMPERATURE T_e has its peak emission; expressing wavelength in nanometres (nm),

$$\lambda_{max} = 2·89 \times 10^6 / T_e,$$

where T_e is expressed in degrees kelvin.

Winter solstice. The point on the ECLIPTIC reached by the Sun on or about 22 December each year. The Sun is then at its greatest southerly DECLINATION of $-23·5$ degrees and is then vertically overhead at the Tropic of Capricorn. In the northern hemisphere it is then midwinter and at midday the Sun attains its minimum possible value of noon altitude.

X

X-ray astronomy. That branch of astronomy which studies X-radiation from astronomical sources. As the Earth's atmosphere is opaque to such short-wave radiation, these studies must be made from high-altitude rockets or artificial satellites; consequently, the development of X-ray astronomy has taken place only in recent years, the earliest rocket experiment being carried out in 1962. Among the satellites which have made major contributions to the subject are UHURU (otherwise known as Explorer 42), which surveyed much of the sky and catalogued some 125 sources, and Ariel 5 (UK-5), a British satellite launched by NASA in 1974.

Cosmic X-rays may be produced in a number of ways; for example,

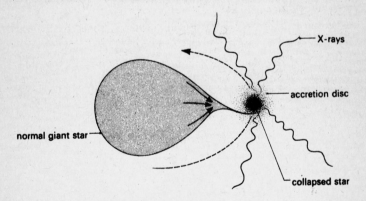

Figure 48. X-ray binary. Among the most exciting of X-ray sources are the X-ray binaries. These may take a number of forms; one possibility is illustrated here. A normal star is a member of a binary system containing a collapsed star (a white dwarf, neutron star or, possibly, a black hole). As the normal star expands (in the giant phase of evolution) material flows from it towards the collapsed star, giving rise to an extremely hot disc of material (known as an accretion disc) round the collapsed star. This disc is a source of X-rays. It has been argued that the object Cygnus X–1 is an X-ray binary containing a black hole.

by the synchrotron process ($\diamondsuit$SYNCHROTRON RADIATION), or by thermal emission from very hot gas (say at a temperature of the order of 100 million degrees kelvin). Among the sources so far identified are the Sun (e.g. X-rays from SOLAR FLARES), the CRAB NEBULA, some close binary systems (X-ray binaries; see Figure 48) involving neutron stars or white dwarfs, extragalactic objects, such as QUASARS and, possibly, intergalactic material, and systems possibly involving BLACK HOLES ($\diamondsuit$CYGNUS X-1).

This is a rapidly developing and important branch of astronomy which owes its existence almost entirely to the development of space technology.

X-rays. Term applied to very short wavelength ELECTROMAGNETIC RADIATION. The wavelength range extends approximately from a few tens of nanometres (i.e. a few times 10^{-8} metres) to about 0·01 nanometres (10^{-11} metres). In the literature of X-ray astronomy it is usual to describe cosmic X-rays in terms of the energies associated with X-ray photons; these energies being expressed in terms of ELECTRON VOLTS, where 1 keV (one thousand electron volts) corresponds to a frequency of $2·42 \times 10^{17}$ Hz, i.e. to a wavelength of 1·24 nanometres. Thus, 0·01 nm corresponds to an energy of some 80 keV, while 10 nm corresponds to 0·8 keV. Most astronomical X-ray observations have been made in the range 1–10 keV.

Y

Year. The period of the Earth's revolution round the Sun, or of the apparent motion of the Sun on the ECLIPTIC. It may be defined in a number of ways, each of which leads to a slightly different value:

Sidereal year: the time interval during which the Sun apparently completes one revolution of the CELESTIAL SPHERE relative to the stars (which, for this purpose, are regarded as being fixed in space); this is equal to the revolution period of the Earth round the Sun as measured relative to the stars, and is equivalent to 365·2564 mean solar days.

Tropical year: the time interval between two successive passages of the Sun through the VERNAL EQUINOX. Its length is 365·2422 mean solar days, about twenty minutes shorter than the sidereal year; the difference arises because of the effects of PRECESSION. As this definition of the year is related to the recurrence of the seasons, the term 'year', if unqualified, is generally taken to mean 'tropical year'.

Anomalistic year: the interval between two successive passages of the Earth through the perihelion of its orbit which, because of a slow change in the position of perihelion, is not quite the same as the sidereal year. Its length is 365·1596 mean solar days.

Gregorian calendar year: this is the value of the year adopted for calendar purposes, and is equal to 365·2425 mean solar days. For practical purposes it can be taken as equal to the tropical year (the difference amounts to 0·0003 mean solar days).

Z

Zenith. The point on the CELESTIAL SPHERE which is vertically above an observer on the Earth's surface (see Figure 9b). It is 90° distant from any point on the horizon.

Zero gravity. A term sometimes used to describe the state of WEIGHT-LESSNESS or FREE FALL. However, it is important to note that this does not imply that there is no gravity acting: a person in a freely falling lift will experience no weight, but both he and the lift are falling in the Earth's gravitational field.

Zodiac. A circular band on the CELESTIAL SPHERE, centred on the ECLIPTIC and extending in width to about 9° on either side (see Figure 49). Within this band the motion of the visible planets, the Sun and the Moon take place. It is divided into twelve zones, each 30° long, called the signs of the Zodiac, and the Sun passes through one of these 'signs' each month. The signs of the Zodiac are named after the constellations which corresponded to these zones in the time of the Greek astronomer Hipparchus in the second century B.C. and are named eastwards (i.e. in an anticlockwise direction) from the VERNAL EQUINOX which at that time lay in the constellation Aries (hence its alternative title of the 'First Point in Aries'). In order from the vernal equinox, the signs are: Aries, Taurus, Gemini, Cancer, Leo, Virgo, Libra, Scorpius, Sagittarius, Capricornus, Aquarius and Pisces. Due to the phenomenon of PRECESSION, the signs no longer coincide with the constellations of these names, and the vernal equinox is presently located in the constellation Pisces.

The term 'zodiac' means, literally, 'circle of animals' since all but one (Libra) of the constellations represent living creatures. The Zodiac was (and still is) regarded as of great significance to ASTROLOGY.

Zodiacal light. A faint glow visible under ideal conditions in the sky in the vicinity of the point at which the Sun has set. It is due to the reflection of sunlight from dust in the plane of the ECLIPTIC.

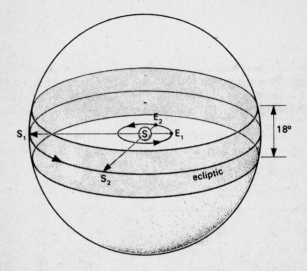

Figure 49.   Ecliptic and Zodiac. As the Earth moves round the Sun,
from E_1 to E_2, so, projected against the celestial sphere, the Sun, S,
appears to move from S_1 to S_2. In the course of a year the Sun appears
to trace out a complete circle, the ecliptic. The Zodiac is the band round
the celestial sphere extending 9° either side of the ecliptic, within which
the planets are normally to be found. The constellations which lie within
this band are the zodiacal constellations. For the purposes of astrology,
the Zodiac is divided into twelve equal areas, the signs of the Zodiac.

The Greek Alphabet

Greek letters are frequently encountered in a number of contexts. For example, the brighter stars in a constellation are denoted by Greek letters in order of descending brightness; again, the principal spectral lines are labelled by Greek letters.

Name	letter	capital	Name	letter	capital
Alpha	α	A	Nu	ν	N
Beta	β	B	Xi	ξ	Ξ
Gamma	γ	Γ	Omicron	o	O
Delta	δ	Δ	Pi	π	Π
Epsilon	ε	E	Rho	ρ	P
Zeta	ζ	Z	Sigma	σ	Σ
Eta	η	H	Tau	τ	T
Theta	θ	Θ	Upsilon	υ	Y
Iota	ι	I	Phi	φ	Φ
Kappa	κ	K	Chi	χ	X
Lambda	λ	Λ	Psi	ψ	Ψ
Mu	μ	M	Omega	ω	Ω

Guide to Further Reading

The number of astronomy books, journals and review articles is so large that the following list of suggested further reading can be no more than an imperfect personal selection. There are many excellent introductory texts treating the subject as a whole, and I have included only a few of these which I happen to like; another author would probably produce a quite different list. The pace of development in astronomy is such that general texts and even specialized books become dated in many aspects quite quickly. For that reason I have attempted to include a good selection of recent review articles.

General astronomy

B. E. Clotfelter, *The Universe and its Structure*, McGraw-Hill, 1976.
   A clear introduction emphasizing physical principles and placing more emphasis on the overall structure of the universe than is usual in such books.
R. Jastrow and M. H. Thompson, *Astronomy, Fundamentals and Frontiers*, John Wiley, 1972.
   A highly readable textbook which reverses the conventional order of topics and works inwards from the universe to the Earth and planets.
D. H. Menzel, F. Whipple and G. de Vaucouleurs, *Survey of the Universe*, Prentice-Hall, 1971.
   Although dated in some respects this book represents a good comprehensive survey of the subject.
P. Moore, *Concise Atlas of the Universe*, Mitchell Beazley, 1974.
   Highly illustrated reference book.

The Sun and Solar System

G. Abetti, *The Sun*, Faber & Faber, 1963.
   Although dated, this represents a good survey of the observed (visual) properties of the Sun.
J. N. Bahcall and R. Davis Jr, 'Solar neutrinos: a scientific puzzle', *Science*, vol. 191, 23 January 1976, pp. 264–7.
   Review of the theory and observations relating to the flux of neu-

trinos from the Sun; the results may lead to a modification of theories of how the Sun works.

D. Gough, 'The shivering Sun opens its heart', *New Scientist*, vol. 70, 10 June 1976, pp. 590–92.
Brief introduction to the observations of solar oscillations.

W. K. Hartmann, *Moons and Planets*, Bogden & Quigley, 1972.
Thorough yet readable introduction to the scientific study of planets and their satellites.

J. S. Lewis, 'The chemistry of the Solar System', in O. Gingerich (ed.), *New Frontiers in Astronomy*, W. H. Freeman, 1975, chapter 5.
Discusses the chemical composition of the system in the light of space-probe results and relates this to the origin of the system.

P. Moore, *Guide to the Moon*, Lutterworth, 1976.
New and up-to-date edition of this celebrated introduction, aimed at the amateur observer.

B. C. Murray, 'Mars from Mariner 9', in O. Gingerich (ed.), *New Frontiers in Astronomy*, W. H. Freeman, 1975, chapter 2.
Survey of pre-Viking knowledge of Mars.

M. M. Nieto, *The Titius–Bode Law and the Origin of the Solar System*, Pergamon, 1972.
Detailed, partly mathematical, study of theories of the origin of the Solar System.

J. M. Pasachoff, 'The solar corona', in O. Gingerich (ed.), *New Frontiers in Astronomy*, W. H. Freeman, 1975, chapter 6.
Includes recent X-ray observations.

Scientific American, vol. 233, no. 3, September 1975, Scientific American Inc.
A special edition devoted entirely to recent Solar System results.

P. Stubbs (ed.), *New Science in the Solar System*, IPC Publications, 1974.
A reasonably up-to-date review of the state of knowledge concerning the members of the Solar System in the light of space-probe and satellite results.

S. R. Taylor, *Lunar Science – A Post Apollo View*, Pergamon, 1975.
Survey of Apollo results, technical in parts (much emphasis on chemical composition of lunar rocks) but readable none the less.

F. L. Whipple, 'The nature of comets', in O. Gingerich (ed.), *New Frontiers in Astronomy*, W. H. Freeman, 1975, chapter 3.
Review article by one of the originators of the 'dirty-ice' model of comets.

Stellar astronomy

B. J. Bok, 'The birth of stars', in O. Gingerich (ed.), *New Frontiers in Astronomy*, W. H. Freeman, 1975, chapter 11.

Discussion of observations of the clouds in which young stars are forming.

A. J. Meadows, *Stellar Evolution*, Pergamon, 1967.
Dated in some aspects but a very readable introduction to the general outline of the way in which stars are thought to evolve.

D. H. Menzel, F. Whipple and G. de Vaucouleurs, *Survey of the Universe*, Prentice-Hall, 1971.

P. Moore, *Guide to the Stars*, Lutterworth Press, 1974.
A good general introduction for the layman and the amateur observer.

R. J. Tayler, *The Stars: Their Structure and Evolution*, Wykeham Publications, 1970.
More advanced mathematical treatment of models of stars.

Interstellar matter and the Milky Way

L. H. Aller, *Atoms, Stars and Nebulae*, Harvard University Press, 1971.
Good introduction.

B. J. Bok and P. Bok, *The Milky Way* (fourth revised edition), Harvard University Press, 1974.
Clear, detailed and beautifully illustrated.

D. H. Menzel, F. Whipple and G. de Vaucouleurs, *Survey of the Universe*, Prentice-Hall, 1971.

R. H. Sanders and G. T. Wrixon, 'The center of the Galaxy', in O. Gingerich (ed.), *New Frontiers in Astronomy*, W. H. Freeman, 1975, chapter 14.
Discusses observations indicative of past violent event in the galactic nucleus.

B. E. Turner, 'Interstellar molecules', in O. Gingerich (ed.), *New Frontiers in Astronomy*, W. H. Freeman, 1975, chapter 15.
Review of the twenty-six interstellar molecules known in early 1973.

Galaxies

S. Mitton, *Exploring the Galaxies*, Faber & Faber, 1976.
A new and up-to-date survey of galaxies and related objects.

I. Nicolson, 'Galaxies, peculiar galaxies and quasars', in P. Moore (ed.), *1972 Yearbook of Astronomy*, Sidgwick & Jackson, 1971.
Brief introduction to the relationships between these objects.

M. J. Rees and J. Silk, 'The origin of galaxies', in O. Gingerich (ed.), *New Frontiers in Astronomy*, W. H. Freeman, 1975, chapter 19.

H. Shapley (revised by P. Hodge), *Galaxies*, Harvard University Press, 1974.
The classic introduction to galaxies.

The universe and cosmology

J. R. Gott, J. E. Gunn, D. N. Schramm and Beatrice M. Tinsley, 'Will the universe expand forever?', *Scientific American*, vol. 234, March 1976, pp. 62–79.

Good survey of the state of theory and observation, suggesting that the evidence favours an open, expanding universe.

F. Hoyle, *Astronomy and Cosmology*, W. H. Freeman, 1975.

A textbook on astronomy but with a strong emphasis on cosmology. The emphasis throughout is on basic physical principles, and the author develops his personal view of cosmology in a thought-provoking manner.

L. John (ed.), *Cosmology Now*, BBC Publications, 1973.

A fine collection of articles by noted cosmologists on various aspects of the subject. It requires little previous knowledge.

W. J. Kaufmann, *Relativity and Cosmology*, Harper & Row, 1973; revised edition 1977.

A clear exposition in simplified terms (intended for non-scientists) of general relativity and its role in the field of cosmology. Fun to read.

M. Schmidt and F. Belloc, 'The evolution of quasars', in O. Gingerich (ed.), *New Frontiers in Astronomy*, W. H. Freeman, 1975, chapter 30.

Discussion of these enigmatic objects (one of the authors was instrumental in their initial discovery), their energy sources and their relationship to other objects.

D. W. Sciama, *Modern Cosmology*, Cambridge University Press, 1971.

A more advanced text intended for specialist students, but nevertheless very readable, clear and concise.

A. Webster, 'The cosmic background radiation', in O. Gingerich (ed.), *New Frontiers in Astronomy*, W. H. Freeman, 1975, chapter 29.

A clear survey.

Life in the universe

I. Ridpath, *Worlds Beyond*, Wildwood House, 1975.

A well-illustrated and entertaining introductory book.

C. Sagan (ed.), *Communication with Extra-Terrestrial Intelligence (CETI)*, MIT Press, 1973.

Report on a conference on this topic. Although much of the book is devoted to the subject matter suggested by the title, there are, too, useful general chapters on life and where it may occur.

Instruments and observing techniques

B. V. Barlow, *The Astronomical Telescope*, Wykeham Publications, 1974.

A lucid account of optical telescopes.

D. S. Evans, *Observation in Modern Astronomy*, English Universities Press, 1968.
More advanced, detailed discussion of observational techniques with particular reference to optical astronomy.

P. Moore, *The Amateur Astronomer*, Lutterworth Press, 1974.
Still an outstanding introduction to observing for amateurs.

Specialized aspects of astronomy

D. A. Allen, *Infra-red – the New Astronomy*, Keith Reid Ltd, 1975.
Clear and well-written survey of the development and scope of infra-red astronomy.

H. Gursky and E. P. J. van den Heuvel, 'X-ray emitting double stars', in O. Gingerich (ed.), *New Frontiers in Astronomy*, W. H. Freeman, 1975, chapter 23.

G. Neugebauer and E. E. Becklin, 'The brightest I-R sources', in O. Gingerich (ed.), *New Frontiers in Astronomy*, W. H. Freeman, 1975, chapter 16.
Deals with the very young and very old stars revealed by infra-red techniques.

F. G. Smith, *Radio Astronomy*, Penguin, 1974.
A clear introduction to radio astronomy.

G. L. Verschur, *The Invisible Universe*, English Universities Press, 1974.
Very readable introduction to radio astronomy for the non-specialist.

History of astronomy

A. Pannekoek, *A History of Astronomy*, Allen & Unwin, 1961.
A comprehensive text.

C. A. Ronan, *Discovering the Universe*, Heinemann Educational, 1972.
Very readable introduction to history of astronomy which treats the development of astronomy subject by subject rather than taking an overall chronological approach.

Star atlas

A. P. Norton, *Norton's Star Atlas*, Gall & Inglis, 1973.
Sixteenth edition of this invaluable atlas for student and amateur.

Miscellaneous

O. Gingerich (ed.), *New Frontiers in Astronomy*, W. H. Freeman, 1975.
An outstanding collection of review articles on a wide range of astronomical topics (some of these are itemized in the preceding sections).

P. Moore and I. Nicolson, *Black Holes in Space*, Ocean Books; W. W. Norton, 1974.

Simple introduction to these objects.

R. C. Parkinson, 'Planetary spacecraft for the 1980s', *Spaceflight*, vol. 17, no. 10, 1975, pp. 346–51.

A useful guide to proposed missions.

M. Rees, 'Black holes', *Observatory*, vol. 94, no. 1001, August 1974.

A clear review article.

F. G. Smith, 'Pulsars', *Reports on Progress in Physics*, vol. 35, no. 4.

Comprehensive discussion of the state of knowledge on these objects.

K. S. Thorne, 'The search for black holes', in O. Gingerich (ed.), *New Frontiers in Astronomy*, W. H. Freeman, 1975, chapter 25.

Particularly good description of observational aspects of black holes.

T. C. Van Flandern, 'Is gravity getting weaker?', *Scientific American*, vol. 234, February 1976, pp. 44–52.

Investigates the evidence which may support the idea that the gravitational constant decreases with time.

Periodicals

Apart from the technical journals, a most useful monthly magazine is: *Sky and Telescope*, Sky Publishing Corporation, 19 Bay State Road, Cambridge, Mass., 02138, USA.

Articles of an astronomical nature appear from time to time in *New Scientist*, *Nature*, *Science* and *Scientific American*.

Developments in space exploration are covered by *Spaceflight*, published by the British Interplanetary Society.